51 /23   HIS/SCI   £4.50

D1644905

Co DUBLIN.
29- 3 -75

VICTORIAN DOCTOR

A WILDE (K) NIGHT IN IRELAND'S EYE.

"To see is to believe."

VICTORIAN DOCTOR

Being the Life of

SIR WILLIAM WILDE

by

T. G. WILSON

M.B., Litt.D., F.R.C.S.I., M.R.I.A.

*With 61 Illustrations by the Author
and a Half-tone Frontispiece*

EP PUBLISHING LIMITED
1974

Reprinted 1974 by EP Publishing Limited
East Ardsley, Wakefield
Yorkshire, England

Published with the kind permission
of the copyright holder
First published Methuen & Co. Ltd., London, 1942

ISBN 0 7158 1037 5

Please address all enquiries to EP Publishing Limited
(address as above)

Printed in Great Britain by
REDWOOD BURN LIMITED
Trowbridge & Esher

To MARY and LUCINDA

FOREWORD

THIS IS the story of a man who, like his son, had many faults. Like his son also his achievement was great—in fact I am not sure that when the final judgement is made, he will not be pronounced the greater man of the two.

Whatever the judgement of posterity, there can be no doubt that his is already a big enough figure to stand alone. For this reason, I have written this biography entirely as a life of Sir William Wilde. Here I am interested in Oscar only as his father's son.

Sir William Wilde reached maturity early, and his decline had begun even before his tragic social eclipse in middle life. For this reason, and because of the rich interest of the period, I have given somewhat more detail of the earlier part of his career than is usual in works of this type. The eccentricities of his later years are already well known: what has not yet been properly recognized is the very high quality of his scientific achievement, particularly in the field of aural surgery.

Although Wilde spoke Irish fluently from the days of his boyhood, he had no deep knowledge of the written language. In consequence, he often wrote Irish words phonetically, or, as it would appear at times, in whatever way the spirit moved him. I, unfortunately, know even less of the language than Sir William, and to correct his orthography is a task far beyond my ability. Perhaps I should have asked some authority to do this for me. Instead of doing so I have taken the easier path of following Sir William exactly, trusting that the purists will forgive me in their pleasure at identifying and correcting his mistakes.

If Sir William's shade were to visit this twentieth century, it must be admitted that he would find his once great reputation sadly tarnished. There are, however, three bodies who would receive him with affection and respect. I, therefore, hope that my colleagues on the staff of Dr. Steevens' Hospital, my fellow-members of the Royal Irish Academy, and my brother Medico-Phils, will find this book worthy of its subject.

I wish to take this opportunity of thanking some of those

who have helped me in writing this book. They include Dr. T. P. C. Kirkpatrick, who has placed his rich store of knowledge freely at my disposal; Mr. Becher Somerville-Large, who has given me great assistance with the parts dealing with ophthalmological history; and Mr. Howard Kilbride-Jones, who has read the archæological sections. Professor J. Brontë Gatenby has given me generous help with the Natural History, and Mr. L. E. Steele has come to my aid in the chapters dealing with Egypt and Palestine. Dr. Douglas Guthrie of Edinburgh has given me permission to use material from his article, *The Renaissance of Otology, The Journal of Laryngology*, Vol. LII, No. 3, March, 1937. Mr. Justice Gavan Duffy and the members of his family have allowed me to draw from *Young Ireland, The Life of Thomas Davis*, and other writings by their father, Sir Charles Gavan Duffy. The executors of the late W. B. Yeats have very kindly given me permission to quote the poem on p. 315. Mr. Horace Wyndham has allowed me to use material from the article *Sir William and Lady Wilde* in his book *Victorian Sensations*. Messrs. Sands & Co. (Publishers), Ltd., have authorized me to quote a passage from *Pitcher in Paradise* by A. M. Binstead; and Messrs. Constable & Co., Ltd., to use a passage from *Oscar Wilde* by Frank Harris, to whose literary executors my apologies are due, if I have failed, in war conditions, to discover their addresses. I am also indebted to Mr. George Bernard Shaw for permission to quote two passages from his writings. Mr. William Doolin, F.R.C.S.I., M.R.I.A., and Dr. Brian Pringle have corrected the proofs. Dr. F. S. Bourke, Dr. Robert Collis, Dr. Dudley Forde, Professor W. R. Fearon, Mr. Frank Fitzgibbon, K.C., Professor Eleanor Knott, Mr. Owen Murphy, Mr. G. S. Phillpotts, and my brother Dr. C. H. Wilson have also helped me with material and suggestions. Dr. Euphan Maxwell and Mr. Henry Stokes, P.R.C.S.I., have given me permission to reproduce illustrations. To the many kindnesses shown me by Mr. W. F. Forrester I have to add that of composing an admirable index. Finally I wish to thank my secretary, Miss Alice Brew, who has carried out much valuable research in addition to her other duties, and my wife, who has corrected the proofs and helped me with the work in many other ways.

T. G. W.

Dublin,
April 1942

CONTENTS

PART VI. SUCCESS

PART VII. CATASTROPHE

PART VIII. THE ELDERLY ECCENTRIC

FRONTISPIECE

A WILDE (K)NIGHT IN IRELAND'S EYE, *from a coloured lithograph by Spex*

VICTORIAN DOCTOR

HELL OR CONNAUGHT

I

POSTERITY HAS not done justice to Sir William Wilde. He is known principally as the father of a brilliant son. Apart from this he is looked upon as a provincial doctor of mediocre attainment; as a fusty old antiquary with a penchant for chasing girls, who accumulated an enormous brood of illegitimate children. In the following pages I have tried to show that this is less than the truth.

II

He came from Connaught, the Irish province which is the most westerly part of the land-mass of Europe and Asia. It is a land of fairy-legend and romance, which has been the nursery of many famous writers, from Goldsmith to Oscar Wilde, Synge, Moore and Yeats. Rich pastures alternate with brown bogland dotted with lakes, and interspersed with occasional fields of startling viridian. To the westward cobalt mountains and seas of ultramarine bound the scene, whose beauty is enhanced by the soft opalescent light which is peculiar to Ireland. A summer sunset in Connemara, when the sun drops into the western ocean in a glory of light and colour, is an event of indescribable loveliness.

It is a glorious country indeed, but a hard one from which to wrest a living. Wilde's father knew this well, for he was a doctor in his native county of Roscommon. In those days there was but one road leading from north to south in the county, and working conditions for a doctor must have been very difficult. But regularly qualified medical men were as scarce as the roads themselves, and Thomas Wilde soon had an extensive connexion. His practice ranged all over the countryside and included rich and poor, peasant, priest and landlord alike.

Thomas Wilde practised all his long life, and did his rounds on horseback until the end. He must have been worth seeing, when at nearly eighty years of age he cantered along on his spanking chestnut, encased in his voluminous, many-caped riding-coat, broad-brimmed leather hat, buckskin smalls, top-boots, overalls, and spatter-dashes, with a red culgee coming up to the middle of his nose. 'Oh, it was a great sight to see that man strip in the hall of a cold night afore he went up to the ladies. No representative of Hamlet's gravedigger . . . ever threw off the same amount of covering and no doctor ever will again, we are sure.'

The Wilde family had been settled in Connaught for about a hundred years. The first of the line in Ireland was Ralph Wilde of Walsingham, near Durham, who, attracted by the prosperity of Georgian Dublin, crossed the Irish Sea and became a builder in that city. Two of his sons settled in Ireland and one of them, also named Ralph, sought his fortunes in Connaught. He became agent to Lord Mount Sandford at Castlerea, and married Margaret O'Flyn, of Caher, in the same country. This lady came of a very ancient Irish family which gave its name to the district in Roscommon known as O'Flyn's county. Three sons came of this union, one of whom was Thomas Wilde; he, as we have seen, became a doctor. Another son, Ralph, entered the Church and was widely known for his learning. Amongst other distinctions he won the Berkeley Gold Medal for Greek in Trinity College, Dublin, a prize later to be awarded to his grand-nephew, Oscar. The third son, William, went to Jamaica.

Dr. Wilde married a Miss Emily Fynne, or Finn, daughter of John Fynne of Ballymagibbon, near Cong, Co. Mayo. By doing so he became connected with some of the most distinguished families in Connaught, amongst them the Surridges, noted for their scholarship, and the Ouseleys. Sir Ralph Ouseley, Bart., was British Ambassador to Persia and a great Orientalist. His brother, Sir William, was Lord Wellesley's secretary in India. Sir Ralph Ouseley won distinction and a General's command in the Peninsular War.

The division between genius and madness is very narrow. The Fynnes were undoubtedly very unstable mentally, and there can be no doubt that much of the later peculiarities of the Wilde family, and perhaps much of their genius, can be traced to the Fynne strain in their blood. John Fynne was an enthusiastic member of the sect of 'Dippers'. It is said that he used to bribe impecunious peasants to allow him to baptize them in a spring near his house.

> 'If you were in Ballymagibbon
> Convenient to Cross,
> It's there you would see them
> Like water-rats creepin',
> When they were baptized
> By the Tyrant, John Fynne.'

The Fynnes were important people in Connaught, and when young Thomas Wilde married Emily Fynne he was looked upon as her social inferior. As a result a fable grew up which is still believed by some in the west, where people have long memories. It is to the effect that Thomas Wilde was really the son of a hedge schoolmaster. John Fynne took notice of him, saw that he was a promising boy, and had him educated to be a doctor. In return young Wilde changed his religion and married Fynne's daughter. He also adopted the name of Wilde because of the similarity of the sound of the word Fynne to that of the Irish word *Fiadhain* which means 'wild'.

Like his father, Dr. Thomas Wilde had three sons, of whom the future Sir William Wilde was considerably the youngest. He was born in the village of Kilkeevin, near Castlerea, in the year 1815. From his mother he derived a great deal more native Irish blood than the majority of the 'Anglo-Irish' possess, and to this mixture of blood may perhaps be attributed his love for his land and people, as well as much of his genius. Little record remains of his schooldays at the Royal School, Banagher, and at the Diocesan School, Elphin, but he is said to have spent more of his time exploring cahirs and duns, attending cockfights, or fishing with his friend, Paddy Walsh, than at his studies.

III

Paddy Walsh was a great character who could have existed only in Ireland. He stood five foot nothing on one leg, and five foot six on the other. Instead of the usual knee-breeches and long stockings he wore corduroy trousers, surmounted by a double-caped greatcoat, the skirts rolled up into a twisted rope and tucked up into the small of his back, under which his fiddle was thrust. He had a wizened sunburnt face, freckled like a turkey's egg, devoid of whiskers, eyebrows or beard, but topped by a plentiful head of tow-like wool. He wore an old glazed and battered hat, generally encircled by casting lines and flies.

Paddy was a great fiddler, particularly at a rousing tune, and on his arrival at a wake he was hailed as Strauss might have

been at the *Goldenen Biern* in Vienna, for nobody knew the ritual of that festival better than Paudeen Brannagh. His social virtues were many. He could sing the 'Black-stripper' or 'Nell O'Flaherty's Drake' with anybody, or else make himself useful by helping the women to lay out the corpse. He could show them how to lay the lid athwart the coffin to form a cross, and how to cover it with saucers containing pipes, tobacco and snuff for the use of the company. He was adept at cutting the white paper gloves which were to hang on the hoops of the garland to be placed on the middle of the grave, and in dressing the peeled sally wands carried in the funeral processions of the young. Like St. Patrick's Aunt, he 'understud distillin'', but he was too cautious to make poteen himself. But whenever anything went wrong for the ordinary manufacturer, if the wash ran through the still-head, or ran through the worm, Paddy could always provide the remedy. At the more mundane pursuits of shoeing horses, heeping a churn, or even tilling the land he could shine at a pinch. In short, Paddy was a man of many parts.

His sporting accomplishments also were great—he was as good a shot as was in the Barony of Athlone, and he could feed, clip, and spur a cock with any man that ever stood in the pit of an Easter Monday. But it was as an angler that Paddy reached his greatest heights of artistry, and he found young Wilde a devoted disciple. Many a Hare's Ear and Fiery Brown he taught his young friend to tie, and many a trout they took between them out of the waters of the Suck. Although he could throw a Black-and-Orange under the nose of a trout five-and-thirty yards away, with his light and whippy rod springing from the very 'wheel', Paddy was not too particular in his methods of killing fish. If, on a bright calm day, they would not rise to the fly, he would make a snare with a switch and a lock of hair from a cow's tail, and soon an unsuspecting trout would be neatly lifted out of its native element. Or he would plunge up to his middle in the stream and 'tickle' the trout under a stone. In the Mayfly season they would use the cross line with a rod on either bank, dapping the natural fly suspended from droppers five feet long, with murderous effect. But to his credit be it said that Paddy would go any distance to destroy a net or inform on its owner.

Another of Wilde's instructors in sport was one who typified many of the 'gentry' of the west at that period. 'With all your faults, Dick Blake, I cannot but remember how you taught me to ride, keeping my "hands low down on the saddle"; what skilful directions for shooting, and training setters and pointers, you gave me; and with what pride you used to see me shoot the rising trout from off the bridge of Cross . . . years ago.'

The Rev. Patrick Prendergast, the last Lord Abbot of Cong, was also a great friend of Wilde's. When the few remaining canons were driven from this monastery they were harboured

by Wilde's mother's people, the Fynnes of Ballymagibbon,
and upon one of their farms Father Prendergast lived until
in 1829, at the age of eighty-eight, he died and was buried
in the Abbey. He was a fine, courteous, white-haired old
man and it is probable that from him Wilde first derived his
interest in the relics of ancient Ireland and in the Irish language.
Father Prendergast had in his possession the wonderful Cross
of Cong, reputed to be one of the finest specimens of enamelled
and jewelled metal work of its age in the western world. Except
at Christmas and Easter, when it was placed upon the altar of
Cong Chapel, the Cross was casually kept by Father Prendergast
in a corner cupboard in his sitting-room. Although a good
scholar, Father Prendergast was very careless of these historic
memorials of his country. A valuable collection of Irish MSS.
was transmitted to him with the Cross and other treasures.
One day when he left home a tailor who was working in his
house laid his hands on the vellums, and cut several into strips
for his 'measures'.

He also possessed the shrine of St. Patrick's tooth, a beautifully
jewelled and decorated reticule of wood, traditionally said to
have been constructed to hold one of the saint's teeth. In later
life, it was said, St. Patrick naturally began to lose some of his
teeth, and as they dropped out they were preserved by his
friends and disciples, who gave names to churches to commemorate the event; as for instance, Kilfeakle, 'the church of
the tooth,' near Tipperary. Father Prendergast came into
possession of the shrine in a somewhat irregular manner. A
man named Reilly made a living by going about with it, 'performing cures on man and beast'. Far and near the population
and the flocks were 'the better of the blessed tooth', and ladies
and ewes held it in especial repute. One day Reilly met the
Abbot and showed him the *Fiachal*. 'Whose is this?' said the
priest. 'It belonged', said Reilly, 'to the Abbots of Cong.'
'Then,' said Father Prendergast, 'as I am the last of the
Augustinian canons of that place, I'll keep it.' And so, to the
amazement, and doubtless displeasure, of its erstwhile custodian,
he rode off with it. The Cross of Cong and the *Fiachal Phadrig*
are now both in the collection of the Royal Irish Academy in
the National Museum.

Another of the Abbot's relics was the *Foil-a-ree* or King's
Blood. This was a bit of discoloured ribbon, said to have

been dipped in the blood of Charles Stuart at the time of his decapitation at Whitehall, which was believed to possess the royal faculty of curing the King's Evil. Hundreds came from all parts to be touched by Father Prendergast—in all probability the last instance of the exercise of this rite in the British Isles.

Wilde had another elderly friend, whose religious tenets did not agree very well with those of the good Abbot. This was Gideon Ouseley, a brother of General Ouseley, and a man whose talents and inclinations were very different from those of the rest of his family. He was a famous Methodist preacher, the author of *Old Christianity*, and was called the John Wesley of Ireland. His sermons were delivered in the Irish language at fairs and markets, often at considerable personal risk, and were long remembered by the people of Roscommon. Years later, Oscar Wilde retailed many of his father's stories about this personage. He was greatly taken by the sonority of the name and it is said that he recommended a friend of his to write a book with the title *Gideon Ouseley*. Such a title, he said, could not fail to attract the public. In more recent times Oliver Gogarty seems to have felt its spell, for he calls himself 'Gideon Ouseley' in some of his books.

IV

During the Napoleonic wars agricultural Ireland was comparatively prosperous, and there was trust and confidence between all classes. Wilde, who was a fluent Irish speaker, mixed freely with his fellow-countrymen, and delighted in the picturesque and sometimes turbulent life of the peasantry. He attended many of the patterns, now almost extinct, which were then a feature of the countryside. As his faith was not that of the majority, he probably omitted the more serious part of the day's ceremonies, but instead repaired early to the neighbouring field where tents and 'standings' were erected. Here dancing, courting, games and drinking prevailed until the close of the day. These functions were often marred by faction fights, in which the more unruly elements delighted. The origin of the feuds was in most cases lost in antiquity, and the members of opposing factions lived peacefully side by side except when they met together for a fight. On these occasions one man would 'wheel' for his party, walking up and down flourishing his blackthorn, and shouting his battle-cry, until a member of the other faction took up his challenge. Instantly hundreds of sticks were up, and soon hundreds of heads were broken.

This was Wilde's first introduction to medical practice. He assisted his father to dress 'many dozens' of injuries received in these fights. Occasionally a wound would prove fatal, a wake would follow, and next day a pitiful, picturesque funeral procession would wind its way over undulating pastures or bleak bogland to the graveyard. The red cloaks and white caps of the women, the bright yellow waistcoats, frieze tail-coats and corduroy breeches of the men, would lend colour to the lonely landscape, while the wild 'keening' of the women heightened the effect of macabre.

After the downfall of Napoleon the high prices for agricultural products prevalent in war-time dropped, and a period of economic distress followed. The slump was aggravated by the fall in the price of wheat, with a consequent return to pasture, and unemployment was common amongst the rapidly increasing peasant population. The partial failure of the potato crop in 1817 and again in 1822 made matters worse. Agrarian discontent became rife, and manifested itself particularly by a constant growling and smouldering resistance to the collection of rents and tithes, a resistance which absorbed the lawless energies of the peasants previously expended in faction fights. Hence arose the Hearts-of-Steel, the Caravets and Shanavests, the Croppies, White-Boys, Right-Boys; the Peep-o'-day Boys, Ribbonmen, and the Molly Maguires. The peasants were stirred up and banded themselves in secret societies, with signs and passwords, by which the initiated might be recognized at fairs and markets. A grip of the hand or a nudge of the elbow, the way in which a man hitched up the tails of his coat, or the waistband of his breeches; or the manner in which he lifted his glass, or knocked his quart-pot on the public-house table; any of these actions might be used as signs of recognition. The village schoolmaster wrote out and copied the regulations, and oaths were administered. The people assembled at dead of night on lonesome roads or on some neighbouring hill, and some renegade pensioner drilled, marched and counter-marched them. Faction fights ceased at the fairs, and instead men drank and conversed in low tones at the back of tents and in the upper rooms of public-houses.

Soon Ribbonism came dramatically into the open. Decorations and processions characterized the Connaught disturbances of 1823 and 1825. The men wore white shirts outside their clothes, and were invariably adorned with ribbons of many colours tied to their arms and hats, which incidentally made them excellent marks for any soldiers with whom they might come in contact. There was a frolicsome spirit of adventure and enterprise for the young men in meeting thus attired, armed with an old flint lock or rusty halbert and marching by moon-light to the sound of fiddle or bagpipes. Many of them thought no more of doing so than they had of their childhood's mummery as 'Wran-boys' or 'May-boys'. The more determined, how-ever, had more serious ends in view. Pounds were pulled down, cattle were barbarously mutilated. Reprisals against gaugers and tithe-proctors and attacks on police barracks were frequent and often tragic occurrences.

In opposition to this state of affairs were the magistrates and the military, aided by the usual spies and informers. The military were comparatively immobile in the large towns, and of little use. The magistrates' first act was to prevent all merry-makings and amusements. Tents and 'standings' were pulled down, public-houses cleared, and all assemblies dispersed, foot-ball and hurling were interdicted, but the ire of the authorities was particularly directed against the 'cakes' and country dances. Acting 'upon information received' the magistrate and his mounted posse, each man dressed in long blue surtouts and buckskin breeches and carrying a heavy cavalry sword as his only weapon, repaired to the locality where a dance was being held. They broke up the assembly, spilt the good whiskey, trampled on the fiddle, and incarcerated the owner of the house in the nearest 'black hole' or guardroom. The only amusements left to the people were wakes and funerals, and it is no wonder that a number of these were held around a very healthy corpse.

The country gentlemen from whom the magistrates were chosen could be quite as lawless as the Ribbonites themselves, and it is to the credit of a harassed government that they were sometimes punished almost as severely. Thomas Martin, J.P., M.P., of Ballynahinch, Co. Galway, was imprisoned for many months for leading his clan against the 'ferocious O'Flaherties' at the famous 'Battle of the Bog' at Oughterard. About the same time a gentleman of Roscommon abducted a drove of pigs from a neighbouring magistrate with whom he happened to be dining, for which crime he was transported for life to a penal colony, where he died many years later.

In time the Ribbonmen became more daring. Large bodies of insurgents approached the towns during the hours of darkness, pulled down pound-gates, attacked the houses of the magistrates, and assaulted the process-servers. Disruption and lawlessness were prevalent everywhere, and now in the midst of the turmoil a new force appeared—the 'Peelers'. A terrible punishment was meted out to the rebels, and the old jail of Roscommon became a focus of horror for the inhabitants of the town.

The jail is a high, gloomy building of mediæval appearance, standing in the market-place in the middle of the town. A small doorway in the third story, a simple iron beam and pulley above, and the hinged horizontal lapboard below, with its sliding bolt, formed the essentials of the longest hangman's drop in Ireland. No masked mystery-man, no decrepit ruffianly pensioner, officiated upon this gallows high. A woman—a dark-eyed, swarthy, and not uncomely woman—was the executioner. 'Lady Betty' she was called, and for many a year her memory was invoked to bring slumber to wakeful children in Connaught.

This woman was reputed to be a native of Kerry. She had been convicted for murdering her son, and sentenced to death in company with the usual dockful of sheepstealers, shoplifters and White-Boys. No executioner was at hand, and the Sheriff and his deputy being men of refinement, education and humanity, could not possibly be expected to fulfil the duty for which they were being paid. In this emergency, the only person who could be found to perform the office was Lady Betty. She officiated as hangwoman, unmasked and undisguised for a great many years afterwards. She also flogged publicly in the streets. A curious sidelight on her character is given by the fact that she was in the habit of drawing charcoal portraits of her victims upon the walls of her apartment—an authentic Grand Guignol touch.

Before daybreak on a certain Monday following an attack upon the police barracks of Ballintober, a squad of labourers guarded by police were seen in the middle of the market-square erecting two tall scaffold poles about six or eight feet apart from each other. A cart emerged from the back entrance to the jail, and from it a body was taken and hoisted to a position midway between the top of the poles. The corpse was suspended by the hands, the breast exposed to show the wounds by which the unfortunate creature had died. On the dangling head a hat was jammed—a pathetic relic bedizened with ribbons —with a placard pinned upon it on which the word 'RIBBON-MAN' was written. When the day broke the inhabitants of Roscommon had this spectacle before their eyes, placed there

by order of the Governor of the district. Rain soon came down in torrents. Every spout and eve-course gave forth a cascade, and the dirty streets ran seas of mud. Around the gibbet stood a guard of military and police, and on the kerbstone sat two huddled female figures, whose muffled sobs occasionally changed to wild cries of grief, 'keening' as only Irish peasant women can.

Towards evening the rain cleared off, and was succeeded by a smart frost during the night. The sun rose large and ruddy the following morning, lit up the old castles, cabins, abbeys and jails, and evoked a reeking steam from all the dunghills in the dirty lanes of Roscommon. Hundreds of peasantry were seen approaching the town from all directions. Magistrates and country gentlemen, armed to the teeth, with the frost hanging in white spray upon their hair and whiskers, arrived in gigs and tax-carts. The rumour of a great spectacle had gone abroad. The town was thronged; every window was occupied, and many climbed to the house-tops. There was none of the customary light-hearted spirit amongst the people, but sullen anger and fierce determination for savage revenge was depicted on every face.

That beautiful regiment of dragoons, the 'Green Horse', with their bright helmets and flourishing horse-tails, paraded the town, and parties of foot-soldiers and police took up their positions. At noon the body was taken down, placed in a sitting position in a cart, with arms extended and tied to pikes. Around it were arrayed the pikes, guns and scythes captured from the rebels on various occasions, and on some of these were placed Ribbonmen's hats picked up on 'fields of battle.' This spectacle, followed by three horse-drawn carts, formed a procession which moved slowly through the streets. At the tail-board of each cart was bound a man, naked to the waist, who had been sentenced to be flogged three times through the towns of Roscommon, Strokestown and Castlerea.

The military lined the streets; the procession moved slowly on to 'flogging pace'. The rear was brought up by a cavalcade of magistrates, in the centre of which was an open chariot wherein sat the Major of the 'Peelers' who directed the proceedings. By his side lolled a large unwieldy person, 'with bloated face and slavering lip—the ruler of Connaught—the great gauger-maker of the West—*the* Right Honourable'.

Well might Wilde say later—'if this was not Connaught, it was Hell'.

v

Medicine and politics, however, do not mix, and Wilde, true to his future trade, had a detached interest in humanity which allowed him to see the faults on both sides. If we think of him sitting at the feet of the good Abbot Prendergast, or leaning over Paddy Walsh's chair as that worthy made his flies from silk, hair and feather, we shall form a truer picture of his boyhood. Or we may think of him fishing the evening rise in the still, calm hours of twilight, when the bats circled and wheeled over his head, the corncrake commenced its nightly serenade, and the only discordant note was the night-jar's shriek, as it flapped its feathery wings in noiseless flight along the hedgerows. We may see him wandering along the river's banks, watching the enormous cannibal trout plunge through the deep pools in search of prey, or listening to the almost inaudible 'plop' of the heavy evening fish as they sucked the spent gnat from the surface. Halcyon days were these, if occasionally marred by scenes of horror; days of comparative prosperity for the countryside, to be remembered sorrowfully in the dreadful famine time which was to come.

It was decided that Wilde should follow his father's profession. Consequently in the year 1832 a dark, ferrety-looking young man, below the average size, with retreating chin and a bright roving eye, took his place in the coach for Dublin.

CHAPTER I   STEEVENS'

I

WHEN WILDE came up to Dublin in 1832 he was a short, slender young man, with a pale, oval face framed in black hair worn long in the style of the period, for all the world like that of the girl of the present day. His forehead was lofty, but narrow, his pale eyes were somewhat prominent, but shrewd and considering. The nose was long, straight and well-shaped. So far this face was ordinary enough, but its lower half at least redeemed it from the commonplace. The mouth was wide, with sensuous lips, the upper protruding somewhat, the lower upthrust and full. Beneath, the chin was long and receding. Altogether, a face which reflected the more voluptuous side of its owner's nature, but gave little indication of his brilliant intellect and still less of his determination of character.

1837

Old Dr. Wilde had decided that surgery rather than medicine was his son's bent, and he had therefore apprenticed him to the celebrated Abraham Colles at Dr. Steevens' Hospital, where he was to learn the practical side of his work. For the more academic part he attended the Park Street School in what is now Lincoln Place. Had he been more interested in medicine he would, in all probability, have gone to Trinity, where his two brothers had graduated in Arts some years before, but the teaching of the School of Physic was then unsuited for those who wished to become surgeons.

Steevens' Hospital, where Wilde was to live for the greater part of the next four years, lies on the western outskirts of Dublin, on the southern bank of the Liffey. It is still in the first rank of Dublin hospitals, and its surgical unit is particularly active. In those days it reigned supreme in the domain of surgery, as the Meath did in that of medicine. It is a sombre two-story building of Jacobean type, with a large central quadrangle surrounded by a colonnade on the ground floor. Although it is the oldest of the Dublin hospitals, in structure it is still practically the same as when it was built. The Irish Hospital Sweepstakes, which have built new hospitals and rebuilt others, have so far done very little for its living inmates, although they have provided it with a very elegant new mortuary.

Steevens' is a hospital with many interesting historical associations, not the least of which is the curious legend about Madam Grissel Steevens, the sister of the founder, who is still popularly supposed to have had a pig's face. Wilde remembered when, as a boy, he paid a penny to see a peep-show in which the chief attraction was a representation of Madam Steevens feeding out of a silver trough; and when he came to Steevens' he found that credulous visitors were shown a trough from which she was supposed to have eaten. The fame of the 'Pig-faced Lady' was not, however, confined to Dublin or Ireland. George Morland engraved a picture of an Irish lady with a similar affliction 'fed out of a Silver Hog Trough and called to her Meals by Pig—Pig—Pig', and 'Madam Stevens, the Pig-faced Lady' was one of the chief side-shows of the Hyde Park Fair, held in the year of Queen Victoria's accession. In this case 'Madam Stevens' was really a fine brown bear, whose face and paws were kept closely shaved so as to show the white skin beneath the fur. When the showman asked her questions, replies in the form of grunts were elicited by carefully concealed small boys who prodded the unfortunate animal with sticks. Needless to say, the real Madam Steevens, who died at the age of ninety-three in the hospital for which she gave up her fortune, had no facial deformity. The myth probably arose because she was usually veiled when she went amongst the poor.

Jonathan Swift was one of the hospital's original trustees, and later an active governor. It is no exaggeration to say that his influence has been felt throughout its history. Stella also contributed largely to the funds, and one of the female wards is now 'Stella's Ward'. Immediately to the south of Steevens' is St. Patrick's Hospital, founded by Swift 'for lunaticks and idiots'.

> 'He gave what little wealth he had
> To build a house for fools, and mad;
> And showed by one satiric touch
> No nation needed it so much.'

II

Wilde now found himself one of about thirty pupils resident in Steevens', of whom about one-third were apprentices of Colles or his fellow assistant surgeon, Wilmot, while the remainder were indentured to the Resident Surgeon. These young men were of all degrees of seniority, from the entered apprentice to the man going up for his degree; they lived anywhere and everywhere, in pupils' rooms and in holes and corners, as best they could be stowed away. In addition to them were about the same number of non-resident pupils, all

studying surgery in spite of the fact that the hospital possessed
a very active physician in the person of Sir Henry Marsh.

On the whole they were an idle lot, as medical students are
apt to be, but they learned much by experience. Wilde tells
us that the accident bell rang on an average once every two
hours, and then the whole class, idle and industrious apprentices
alike, rushed to the reception room. There they saw, in 'all
their original freshness', fractures, cut throats, burns, head
injuries, poisonings, lacerated wounds, crushed limbs, and all
the routine of casualty practice. The Resident Surgeon or the
clinical clerk did what was necessary—picked up a bleeding
vessel, administered a stimulant, or gave an antidote, and then
one of the 'young gentlemen' was given charge of the case.
This was an excellent practical supplement to the precepts of
their masters and the lectures they received outside the hospital.

The mental and moral upbringing of these young men was
mostly in the capable hands of the Resident Surgeon. His
position was very different from that of the present-day house
surgeon, for instead of his being in a subservient position, he
was perhaps the most important man on the staff. In the
hundred years which had passed since the hospital had been
founded only five men had held the post. The Resident
Surgeons lived, married and kept their families in the hospital,
nor did their appointment debar them from private practice
outside the hospital.

When Wilde was in residence in Steevens' the Resident
Surgeon was James William Cusack, an angular saturnine man
of great force of character, a brilliant surgeon and lecturer, who
after Colles was accepted as the greatest surgeon of his time
in Ireland. He had already been President of the Royal College
of Surgeons in Ireland, and could command what fee he liked.
At Steevens' he reigned supreme over a heterogeneous collection
of patients, students, nurses and hospital officials.

The nurses in Steevens' were no better than elsewhere, and
very different from the trim and efficient young ladies who
nowadays minister to the patients. This state of affairs was
changed when the Sisters of St. Vincent's Hospital showed the
way of reform to Florence Nightingale, but at this period
nurses were dowdy, illiterate, and often drunken sluts. The small
rooms they occupied off the wards were regarded as their
private property, and man and wife, or mother and daughter

often served the hospital together. Many families were housed under the hospital's roof, from those of the Resident Surgeon and Chaplain down to the nurses and porters. The social status of the nurses may be assessed by the fact that a nurse was assigned to look after each apprentice's room.

At the beginning of the nineteenth century the curriculum of the medical student was very much more lax than it is to-day. To qualify as a surgeon a man had only to complete his indenture as an apprentice, and pass the examination of the Royal College of Surgeons, for compulsory courses of lectures were unknown. How or where the students acquired their knowledge was left to themselves to decide. In consequence, many private medical schools sprang up in Dublin, as in London, each with its dissecting-room, laboratory and museum. There are records of over thirty of these schools in Dublin between 1800 and 1860.

Steevens' later had its own flourishing medical school, but at this time most of its apprentices were pupils at the famous Park Street School, which was situated near the back gate of Trinity College, and this was the institution Wilde chose to attend. His choice was probably influenced by the fact that most of its young and energetic staff were connected with Steevens' Hospital. An exception was the illustrious Robert James Graves, who with his contemporaries, William Stokes and Abraham Colles, were the greatest lights of the Dublin school of medicine, at this time at its full flowering.

It was a strange new world in which young Wilde now found himself, and very different to that which he had left beyond the Shannon. No doctor ever forgets the impressions of his first days in his medical school. The change from boyhood's restrictions to the comparative freedom of the university, the new faces, the dissecting-room with its poor dried-up relics of mortality, the strange sights and the pungent smells, all produce an unforgettable atmosphere. To Wilde the change was greater than this, for in addition to his work at Park Street he was plunged straight into the turmoil of hospital practice.

The natural result of this happy-go-lucky educational system was that Wilde and his fellow-students became a tough, Bohemian crowd, much given to orgies of porter, and in some cases to friendships with the more enterprising of the ladies of the town. The dissecting-room was a sort of club wherein Dickensian students, Bob Sawyers and Joe Muffs, moved and laughed and sang in a haze of tobacco smoke. Dissecting the cadaver in those days was not only unpleasant, but often extremely dangerous, for the bodies were often partly decomposed, and the students were sometimes affected by the fœtid vapours which arose when the body was opened. A finger prick with the dissecting knife might prove a catastrophe. Sir Henry Marsh originally intended to become a surgeon, but lost the index finger of his right hand as the result of a dissecting wound. Colles was fully alive to the dangers of dissecting, and insisted that every wound should be immediately cauterized and plunged in a cup of oil of turpentine with which every dissecting table was furnished.

Whatever the quality of the bodies dissected, their numbers were never short, for the Dublin resurrectionist had reduced his trade to a fine art. Not only was he able to supply the needs of the Dublin schools, but also to conduct a flourishing export trade, mostly to Scotland *via* the North of Ireland. Most of the bodies came from the famous 'Bully's Acre' in the grounds of the Royal Hospital at Kilmainham, about half a mile from Steevens'. The common people brought their dead to this place, and as they were too poor to employ night watchmen, the graves were often robbed of their grisly contents, usually with perfect impunity. The caretaker of the graveyard was in league with the resurrectionists, and usually gave them the 'all clear' by showing a lighted candle in his window, before they entered the burial ground. The work was done with the greatest expedition and skill. The head of the coffin was exposed with shovels and picks, the top broken open with a pick-axe, and the body dragged forth by means of a rope round the neck. Once on the surface the body was stripped stark naked, and the grave clothes stuffed back into the coffin, for it was a more serious offence in law to steal the shroud than to make off with the corpse it contained. The bodies were usually carried off in a covered cart, but woe betide the 'fisherman' found conveying his prize to the dissecting-room. An inquisitive watchman was usually amenable to a bribe, but if a crowd collected the consequences were apt to be very unpleasant for the practitioner, who was lucky if he escaped with a 'ducking' in the Liffey. Two members at least of the fraternity lost their lives—one was kicked to death by the mob, and the other died after receiving the benefits of a wire cat-o'-nine-tails.

At the beginning of the nineteenth century bodies were easily procured in Dublin at a guinea each. As the number of medical students increased through the efforts of Graves, Stokes and Colles the demand for bodies became more insistent and the resurrectionists formed a ring to demand higher prices for them. Soon six or eight guineas was paid for a body for dissection, and more money was obtained for what might be called the 'by-products'—the teeth and hair. Macartney, the famous Professor of Anatomy in Trinity, wrote a letter to the papers in which he said: 'I do not think that the upper and middle class have understood the effects of their own conduct when they take part in impeding the process of dissection, nor does it seem wise to discountenance the practice by which many of them are supplied with artificial teeth and hair. Very many of the upper ranks carry in their mouths teeth which have been buried in the Hospital Fields.'

Resurrectionists were, as might be expected, a depraved, vicious caste, although not devoid of courage. The more adventurous students were, however, thrilled by their exploits, and the necessity of getting subjects had long overcome any moral scruples in the mind of the profession. In consequence, many bodies were brought to Steevens' and elsewhere for which no tax was paid to the body-snatchers. A favourite plan of the students consisted in putting an old suit of clothes on the corpse, and, with a student supporting it on either side, to make it stagger along like a drunken man. A ghoulish trick, but what a thrill for the actors! Wilde may have taken part in some of these forays, but the passing of the Anatomy Act towards the end of his first year at Steevens' put an end to the practice.

CHAPTER II THREE
TEACHERS

I

IN BINDING his son to Colles, Dr. Wilde had chosen well, for Colles was one of the greatest surgeons of his time. The purely medical side of the young man's education was in the hands of two equally illustrious physicians. The names of Robert James Graves, William Stokes and Abraham Colles are still the greatest in the history of Irish Medicine.

The physicians of the eighteenth century, 'the golden age of quackery,' were pompous, periwigged creatures whose ignorance was as extreme as their vanity. Bleeding, blistering, and violent purgation were their principal methods of treatment; feminine chastity and love-sickness were diagnosed by the inspection of a glass of urine in the sunlight. Some doctors were scholarly enough, others were mere charlatans, but most of them were utterly devoid of scientific conceptions. Soon all this was to change, for with the beginning of the nineteenth century medicine began to emerge from the mists of superstitious ignorance which had enshrouded it since primitive ages. Colles, Graves and Stokes take high place amongst the pioneers of modern medicine, and Wilde was fortunate enough to be caught up in the advancing wave.

When he began his medical career, operations were usually limited to amputations, the removal of stones from the bladder, and the tying of arteries for aneurysm. The unhappy patients were bound down with ropes, and the operation was accompanied by screams of terror unless the unfortunate patient fainted. Wilde was lucky in his generation, for he was to see most of the horrors of the operating-theatre removed by the discovery of anæsthesia.

During the earlier part of his career, however, the only soporifics known were alcohol and opium. If muscular relaxation was needed to facilitate the reduction of fractures or dislocations, an effort might be made to make the patient faint. He might be placed in a hot bath, and when well flushed removed from it, bled thoroughly, and given tartar emetic to make him vomit. If these measures did not produce the required degree of faintness, the procedure was repeated. Wilde was familiar with another ingenious method which was practised by Colles at Steevens' Hospital. This was the injection of an enema of tobacco smoke into the rectum by means of a long silver tube connected with a large bellows—a proceeding which was sometimes attended with disastrous results, but which was nevertheless continued until the introduction of ether anæsthesia in 1846.

In those days speed in surgery was essential, and he who

could amputate a limb or remove a stone from the bladder in quicker time than his contemporaries was accounted the better operator. The surgeon amputated a thigh by cutting and sawing with his right hand while compressing the main artery with his left. His speed was so great that if the spectator sneezed or turned his head he missed seeing the operation—it was over. Operating theatres were small, stinking amphitheatres, often crowded to the roof with students. The filth was indescribable. The surgeon came direct to the theatre from the post-mortem room, and neither changed his clothes nor washed his hands. He was proud of his old operating coat, the incrustations of blood and pus upon which testified to his experience.

These were the conditions under which Colles worked; but in spite of them he reached great heights in both anatomy and surgery. In anatomy every medical student knows Colles' fascia and Colles' ligament. In 1814, he described the fracture of the forearm above the wrist which has ever since been known as Colles' fracture. His account was written before he had an opportunity of verifying his observations by dissection, but his description of the appropriate treatment was so clear that little has been added to it since, although the fracture is so common as to be every house-surgeon's bugbear.

As a surgeon, Colles was bold and skilful, qualities which he transmitted in no small degree to his pupil. He was the first surgeon in Ireland to tie the subclavian artery. When we remember that this artery lies at a considerable depth behind the collar-bone, amongst most important structures, the lung and large nerves, arteries and veins, we realize that it was no small feat to tie it without an anæsthetic of any sort. Colles could do it only because his knowledge of anatomy was minute and extensive. His description of the first occasion he performed this operation is intensely dramatic. The reader cannot fail to visualize the scene—the small theatre with its wooden operating table and benches, the assistant surgeons, youngish gentlemen in black, with high collars and cravats, revolving around the masterly central figure of the surgeon, and assisting him by restraining the patient, or holding forceps and ligatures —the row of awe-struck pupils and apprentices beyond. The patient grows faint, and is raised up to a sitting position to give relief, drinks 'very largely' of whey, while the great surgeon goes on calmly dissecting down on the artery, at first with the knife, then with his forefinger and finger-nail, for a knife would be too dangerous in the deeper parts of the wound. The ligature is passed, and the noose tightened. The patient complains of an oppression at his heart—his face grows pale, and every one present fears his instant death. Many of the onlookers now leave the room, not wishing to see him die before their eyes. But Colles continues, and fearlessly completes the operation, and the patient is returned to his bed more than an hour after he left it. Colles performed this operation three times. It was a great feat of surgery, but in each case he was defeated by a factor which science had not yet learned how to deal with. On each occasion the patient died of sepsis, several days after the operation.

Wilde soon proved to be one of his master's most useful pupils. Colles at this time carried out a number of experiments on the growth of bone and the union of fractures, and in these researches he was materially assisted by Wilde. Colles, who ever gave honour where honour was due, gave his pupil public acknowledgement in one of his professorial lectures in the Royal College of Surgeons—a great feather in the young man's cap.

Colles must have been an inspiring teacher and one calculated to instil the highest principles in those under him. A large number of his beds were set aside for the treatment of syphilis. Accommodation for the venereal cases in Steevens' was provided on the top corridor, which had previously been used for the overflow of wounded Peninsular heroes from the Royal Hospital. These wards filled a very important function in the Dublin medical school. They provided the only clinical material for teaching students the diagnosis and treatment of this important group of diseases, since apprentices and students were strictly forbidden to enter the wards of the Lock Hospital. There was, and still is, a plentiful supply of patients for the venereal wards in Steevens', and it was from the experience gained therein that Colles was able to write his famous book, *Practical Observations on the Venereal Disease and on the Use of Mercury.*

This monumental work was published in 1837, in the last year of Wilde's apprenticeship, and Wilde, if he did not help in its preparation, must at least have been familiar with many of the cases described therein. Many of them are human documents of the most poignant nature. To medical men the most interesting chapter in Colles' book is that in which he describes the congenital syphilis of infants. He describes the symptoms admirably. He admits freely that he is unable in many cases to explain how the infection is transmitted to the child, or why parents, who appear to have been cured of the disease, produce syphilitic children. With his usual frankness he records the facts as he had met them, and he does not make any attempt to make them fit in with his views of the disease. It is in this chapter that he makes the statement which has ever since been known as 'Colles' Law'. As this law is sometimes misquoted, it may be given in his own words: 'One fact well deserving our attention is this: that a child born of a mother without any obvious venereal symptoms, and which, without being exposed to any infection subsequent to its birth, shows this disease when a few weeks old, this child will infect the most healthy nurse, whether she suckle it or merely handle and dress it: and yet this child is never known to infect its own mother, even though she suckle it while it has venereal ulcers on the lips and tongue.' The reason the mother does not appear to be infected is, of course, that she already has the disease, although in her it is quiescent.

II

Wilde, being a surgical apprentice, was mostly occupied in the surgical wards; nevertheless he found much to interest him in the twenty-five beds devoted to medical cases. These were nominally under the charge of John Crampton, but actually most of the medical work of the hospital was in the hands of Crampton's cousin, Henry Marsh.

Marsh was a man of distinguished ancestry and connexions. His early ambition was to become a surgeon, so that he could take part in the Peninsular campaign, but, as we have seen, he lost his right forefinger as a result of a dissecting wound, and turned to medicine in consequence. He was rapidly successful, both in practice and as a lecturer, and soon enjoyed a reputation equal to those of Graves and Stokes. That this reputation has not lasted is solely due to the fact that his original writings were few. He did, however, write a number of short articles for the medical journals—notably on inflammation of the epiglottis, and on a disease of children which he, for the first time, called 'spasm of the glottis'. He was one of the founders of the Park Street School, and Professor of Physic at the Royal College of Surgeons. This latter appointment he relinquished during Wilde's first year in Steevens'.

Marsh's clinical lectures during each winter session were one of the highlights of medical teaching in Dublin, and Wilde became an eager and attentive listener. The professor spoke forcefully and was felicitous in description. His class was large and sedulously attended, and nobody was more attentive than Wilde. From his beginnings he realized that a good doctor, be he physician or surgeon, must be thoroughly grounded in all the branches of his profession, and to this end he gave all the energy at his command. Marsh soon became aware of the young man whose practical ability and rapid assimilation of knowledge made him outstanding in the class, and they became fast friends.

Wilde also attended Graves' lectures at Park Street, the *Clinical Lectures* which, when published later, were to set the seal on their author's reputation. Graves was handsome, dark and debonair, of joyous, generous disposition, and full of energy, mental and physical. He was the type of man to whom adventures seem to come naturally and inevitably. After qualifying

in arts and medicine in Trinity College, Dublin, he had travelled in the customary manner on the Continent, visiting Berlin, Göttingen, Vienna, Copenhagen, France and Italy. In Austria he was thrown into prison for ten days, as a spy, for it was said no Englishman could speak German as well as he did. Travelling in the Alps, his diligence was boarded by a man who looked like a ship's mate ashore. From time to time this man took from his pocket a note-book across which his hand moved with great rapidity. Graves at first thought his companion was insane, but he changed his opinion when he found that what he had taken for the scribblings of madness were in reality notes of passing cloud-forms, drawn with the surety of genius. The artist was J. M. W. Turner, and Graves was privileged to see the first Swiss sketchbook in the making. The two travelled together for several months before either discovered the other's name. Graves has recorded that Turner would outline a scene, sit doing nothing for perhaps several days, then suddenly exclaim: 'There it is!' and work feverishly until he had put down the effect he wished.

After passing through Italy, Graves embarked for Sicily at Genoa, he and a Spaniard being the only passengers on the brig. They encountered a terrific north-easterly gale, and the ill-found and worse-manned vessel was soon in difficulties. The sails were blown away, the pumps choked, and the crew determined to abandon ship, leaving the passengers to their fate. The terrified Spaniard communicated this cheerful news to Graves, who was lying sea-sick in his bunk. He ran on deck and stove in the only boat with an axe. 'Let us all be drowned together,' said he, 'it is a pity to part good company.' He then mended the suckers of the pumps with leather from his own boots, and virtually took command of the ship.

He returned to Dublin in 1821, was appointed Physician to the Meath Hospital, and helped to found the Park Street School in the same year. He threw his great energies into teaching. He condemned whole-heartedly the Edinburgh method in which the teacher interrogated the patient in a loud voice, the clerk repeated the patient's answer, and the crowd of students around the bed, most of whom could not see the patient, made notes of the questions and replies. Instead, he taught students to examine patients for themselves, and to discuss with him the diagnosis, pathology and treatment of each case. This is real bedside teaching as it is understood to-day, and to Graves belongs the honour of having introduced it into the British Isles. William Stokes joined in the reformation five years later, and it is no exaggeration to say that these two men were the founders of British clinical teaching, and that they made the Dublin School of Medicine famous all over the world.

Graves' reputation does not rest upon his teaching alone. His *Clinical Lectures* were published in 1843, and rapidly spread his fame all over Europe. It was translated into French by Trousseau, who entreated his pupils to consider it their breviary, declaring that of all the books published in his time there was none more useful. He himself had read and re-read it incessantly, he knew it almost by heart, but he could not refrain from reading a book which never left his study. There was certainly much that was novel and true in its pages, and the claim that many thousands of the sick owed their lives to it is probably justified. In style the book is easy, and the matter is never dull. It included the description of the case of a young lady who suffered from exophthalmic goitre. It is a single case, simply recorded. On the strength of it Trousseau suggested that exophthalmic goitre be called Graves' disease, and Graves' disease it is to this day.

Wilde and Graves were mutually attracted, and their association, which began in Wilde's student days, soon ripened into an affectionate intimacy, which only ended by the senior man's death.

III

Another of Wilde's teachers was William Stokes, Graves'

William Stokes, F.R.S., D.C.L.

famous younger associate. Stokes, who was some ten years older than Wilde, had many interests in common with him. The rôles of teacher and pupil were soon forgotten, and an intimacy developed which lasted for Wilde's lifetime.

In the scientific circles of Dublin the name of Stokes signifies a dynasty rather than simply a family. Since Gabriel Stokes left Shropshire in 1680 the family has been brilliantly represented in Ireland, as happily it still is, in the person of the President of the Royal College of Surgeons in Ireland. Amongst its members who went farther afield were Sir George Gabriel Stokes,

Professor of Mathematics at Cambridge, and President of the Royal Society, and that wonderful endearing personality, Adrian Stokes, Professor of Bacteriology in Trinity College, Dublin, and later of Pathology at Guy's Hospital. His death in Africa from yellow fever, the disease in which he was conducting brilliantly fruitful research, was a major loss to science.

William Stokes spent his childhood at Ballinteer, in the foothills of the Dublin mountains. He loved the out-of-door life, and spent much time reading the newly published Waverley Novels, in which he delighted for the rest of his life. He studied medicine at the Meath Hospital, and at Glasgow and later at Edinburgh, where he graduated M.D. in 1825. He returned to Dublin and in the following year was elected physician to the Meath Hospital in his father's place, having as his senior colleague the illustrious Graves. His son, Sir William Stokes, said: 'For years they worked together in the Meath Hospital, assisting one another in their clinical researches, and in the initiating and carrying out of a system of clinical instruction, till then unknown in this country, which eventually acquired a world-wide fame for the Dublin School of Medicine. Never did any disagreement arise between them.'

Stokes' teaching soon became famous. He took immense care with his lectures. The night before his first address was given he stayed up until three working at it. From sheer exhaustion he was then driven to bed, but was up again by six o'clock. The lecture was a great success; others equally successful followed, and Stokes was generally congratulated, and recognized as a great clinician.

His capacity for work was tremendous. 'I rise early, write till breakfast, then go to the dispensary, where I sit in judgement on disease for an hour; then to the hospital where I go round the wards attended by a crowd of pupils; from the hospital I return home, write again till two, then go round and visit my patients through various parts of the town attended by a pupil.'

While Stokes was still a school-boy, a young French physician named Lænnec performed an experiment which revolutionized the practice of internal medicine. A girl came to see him, suffering from heart-disease. Normally he would have listened to her heart by placing his ear directly on her bosom; but he shrank from this procedure because of her youth. He may also have suspected that he might not hear much in this way, for the young lady was rather stout. Instead, he had a brilliant idea. Rolling up a quire of paper, he applied one end to the patient's chest, the other to his own ear. Immediately he heard the heart sounds clearly and distinctly; for his roll of paper was the first stethoscope.

Stokes became interested in the instrument and ever after took the greatest interest in diseases of the heart and lungs. To him belongs the honour of being the first man to publish an account of the stethoscope in English, which he did at the age of twenty-one. To the modern medical man, however, he is probably better known through 'Cheyne-Stokes respiration' and the Stokes-Adam's syndrome.

Stokes, like Graves, took his place naturally amongst the brilliant intellectual aristocracy of the time. Both were eventually recipients of many honours, including the F.R.S. But as Acland says in his Memoir: 'Stokes is to be thought of above all else as the physician of the poor. "My patients have one great defect—instead of giving money, they too often, unfortunate beings, have to solicit it from their medical attendant; and who, with the heart of a man, would refuse to relieve their sufferings when he has a shilling in his pocket? A poor woman whom I attended for long, and who ultimately recovered, said: 'Oh, doctor, you have given me a good stomach, but I have nothing to put into it.' "'

Stokes was keenly alive to the beauties of art and nature, but there was another facet to his character which attracted Wilde to him. Like all his family, he was keenly interested in the antiquities of his native land. He was not as great an archaeologist as Wilde proved to be; for all his energies were devoted to his profession. Nevertheless, it was he who was chosen to write the life of George Petrie; and he educated his daughter, Margaret, to become one of the leading authorities on Irish ecclesiastical architecture. He became President of the Royal Irish Academy, an honour not lightly bestowed.

CHAPTER III

APPRENTICE
SURGEON

I

AMONGST WILDE'S fellow-students in Steevens' was Charles Lever, who like his contemporary, Keats, was later to desert medicine to achieve lasting fame in literature. He was not perhaps a very industrious pupil, for he did not take kindly to discipline, but his spirits were as ebullient as champagne, and he found an outlet for his energy in many practical jokes. He wrote ballads, and when in Trinity often stole out at night like Goldsmith of old to try their effect on the citizens. These were the palmy days of ballad singing in Dublin, the days of

Zozimus and Rhoudlum. Lever sometimes disguised himself as these famous characters, and on one occasion at least was detected and only rescued from the wrath of the mob by his fellow-students from the hospital.

His most famous exploit in Steevens' was when he succeeded

in impersonating Cusack to his class. Wilde ever after took great pleasure in telling the story. Cusack, who was eccentric like many other great men, was in the habit of lecturing his class from his bed in the early hours of the morning. What his wife did on these occasions we do not know, but it is not always comfortable to be the wife of a great man, and doubtless she was expelled from her couch before the class arrived. One grey dawn Lever arrived first at the bedroom and found a notice to say that his chief had been called out on a case, and would not take the class that morning. Lever tore down the notice, hopped into the bed, put on Cusack's red silk night-cap, and pulled the blankets round him. The great bell boomed, feet were heard on the stairs, and gradually the room filled with eight shivering students, more than half asleep. Lever took the roll. 'Where's Lever?' 'Absent, sir.' 'I'm sorry for that. Lever is a man of great capacity, if he were only to apply himself. What's the subject, O'Reilly?'

O'Reilly: 'Cancer, sir.'

(Here a snore came from the bed, and the 'professor' woke up again with a start.)

Lever (surprised): 'Cancer, O'Reilly?'

O'Reilly: 'What about it, sir?'

Lever: 'What about it yourself?'

O'Reilly: 'Cancer, sir, is a malignant disease.'

Lever: 'You're a stupid ass, O'Reilly.'

(O'Reilly, although described as 'an uncultivated, red-haired County Meath boor', was the best student in the class.)

Keane: 'Cancer, sir, affects the lower lip of males.'

Lever: 'What more? What colour is it?'

Keane (who had a lisp): 'Wed, sir.'

(Here Lever belched vigorously, in imitation of Cusack, who expressed disgust in this way.)

Keane (in alarm): 'Yellow, sir.'

(Another eructation from the bed.)

Keane (prompted): 'Blue, sir.'

At this stage Lever burst out laughing, and had to run for his life.

Although an idle student, Lever was deservedly popular, and could get away with almost anything. Cusack was famous for his shabby clothing; on one occasion he got a new suit of a bright brown colour. Lever scrutinized the garments with a stare which Cusack mistook for admiration. 'What do you think of them?' he asked. 'Oh,' said Lever, 'Cullinan told me you had fallen into a keg of brown paint, but I'm glad to see he was mistaken.' Cusack, who never liked Lever, was definitely not pleased.

II

Wilde's student career soon suffered a rude, though temporary, interruption. In the year 1832 the all-absorbing topic of the day amongst all classes in Dublin was the swift approach of

that dreadful scourge, Asiatic cholera. This disease, which still occurs sporadically in India, fortunately is not now seen in Europe. In the early nineteenth century, however, the rapid development of steamboat communication and the complete ignorance of elementary sanitation which prevailed helped the disease to overflow from its Asiatic focus along the trade routes to Europe and America. It reached Sunderland in 1831. As early as 1826 Graves had lectured on the disease, being warned of its approach by Dr. Brinkley, Lord Bishop of Cloyne, an acute observer who also foretold the failure of the potato crop and the subsequent famine.

Wilde was present at Marsh's last course of lectures as Professor of Physic in the Royal College of Surgeons, and later described the excitement which pervaded the city when it was announced that cholera was to be the subject of the lectures. On each evening, long before the advertised hour, crowds of pupils from every class and medical school in Dublin besieged the doors for admission. The public was also admitted, as was usual in those days. Clergymen, barristers and judges thronged the theatre, and long before the Professor took the chair, every avenue to the doors was blocked by masses of disappointed would-be listeners. Well might the citizens be terrified, for the typhus epidemic of 1826 had shown how ineffective were the measures in vogue for the treatment of acute fevers.

Early in March the disease appeared in Belfast. Later in the same month William Stokes and a colleague named Rumley were sent for to investigate a sudden and mysterious death which had occurred at Kingstown, then a small seaside village (whose name had recently been changed from Dunleary in honour of the visit of George IV, but is now once more Dun Laoghaire). The two physicians pronounced the cause of death to have been cholera—Asiatic cholera in its worst form. Outside the house in which the body lay was an anxious crowd, patiently awaiting their decision. The announcement was at first received with silent dismay, then a burst of frenzied illogical indignation was directed against the doctors. A furious mob of men, women and children hurled stones, mud, brickbats at them from all sides. They escaped injury almost by a miracle; the carriage was battered and broken by the missiles thrown at them, and only by whip and spur did their postilion out-distance their pursuers. Within a few days their diagnosis was confirmed by the general outbreak of the disease in Ireland. In two years over fifty thousand people had died of it.

On the whole the people of Dublin faced the cholera with courage and fortitude, and none of the riots which occurred elsewhere were seen in the city. Nevertheless, a number of the better classes migrated from the city, leaving the poorer people, who were more liable to the disease, to fend for them-selves. As usual, the doctors fought in the front line. Wilde was only seventeen at the time, and his relatives were naturally alarmed for his safety. Much against his will he was haled back to Connaught, to take refuge from the disease. So far from escaping it, however, he walked straight into the danger, and with typical hardihood, defied it, and escaped unharmed. While staying with the Fynnes at Ballymagibbon, near Cong, the 'young docthor' was sent for from Kilmaine, where he found his patient to be a pedlar stricken with the cholera. He was already dead on Wilde's arrival and the owner of the lodging-house where he died had caught the disease. The villagers were panic-stricken, and would not enter the house or help in any way. Wilde took up his abode with the patient, saw him through the cholera, but had the disappointment of seeing him subsequently sink from exhaustion. The villagers were persuaded to supply a coffin, but there their services ended. Wilde, single-handed, placed his late patient in the rude shell, and then managed to enlist the services of a drunken pensioner to assist in the burial. Together they put the coffin on a donkey-cart, conveyed it to the burial ground, dug the grave, and buried the coffin in quicklime. When the corpse was disposed of, Wilde's duty to the living remained to be done. With his own hands he consigned all the *lares* and *penates* of the deserted house to the flames, and then fumigated it with sulphur fumes and—tobacco smoke!

On this occasion Wilde behaved heroically. By his prompt and efficient action he seems to have stamped out the disease in Kilmaine, for no further cases appeared in the village. It was no small feat for a youth of seventeen. His exploit received the attention it deserved, for Graves gave a full account of it in one of his lectures.

On another occasion he saved a child's life by opening its windpipe with a pair of scissors. The child had bolted a piece of potato which had 'gone the wrong way', and instead of passing down the gullet had become impacted in the larynx or upper part of the windpipe. Wilde happened to be passing by at the time, and his emergency operation was performed before the whole village community of Ballymagibbon on their way to church, for it was a Sunday. This was also a remarkable feat for a medical student to perform, although as the late Professor Gordon was wont to remark, he had the consoling knowledge that the worst thing which could happen was that the patient should die. In this case, however, the operation was attended by happy results.

The ravages of cholera in the remainder of the west of Ireland were truly dreadful. A number of young doctors, amongst them Lever, recently qualified, were sent to Connaught where many thousands of patients passed through their hands. Sheds were erected in Kilrush and Kilkee to serve as temporary hospitals. Decanters of brandy were placed on the tables to stimulate the doctors in their work, and in the hope of preventing them from catching the disease. The patients were bled by lancet, leech, and cup, even when the blood was 'as thick as treacle' and could barely move in their veins, and blisters were applied to the backs of their necks. Until the wisdom of Graves substituted opium for calomel, purgatives were fully administered. Death often took place in a couple of hours. In the last stages the patients were given inhalations of 'laughing-gas'—a curious precursor of its use in anæsthesia.

Bodies were burned with appalling haste. Dr. Hogan on visiting the cholera hospital at Limerick saw a huge pile of corpses waiting for coffins. Looking curiously at the mass of bodies, he saw one whose colour differed from the others. He pulled the victim out, and examined him with care, to find life was still present. The patient was placed in a bed, restoratives applied, and at length he was restored to consciousness.

It must not be thought that all the people of Ireland behaved like the good people of Kilmaine. On the contrary, the widespread affliction called up a humanity greater than itself, and commonplace people did glorious deeds of generosity and kindness for their stricken fellows.

III

The epidemic over, more normal times returned, and the medical student's life took up its even way. Operations and lectures began again, and Wilde and his fellow-students resumed their daily walk to Park Street. The matron, Miss Thompson, and Mrs. Cusack held dances in the hospital, which Wilde and Lever, now for a time once more in Dublin, attended. Lever, being a 'promised man', paid his attentions mostly to his hostesses, who could appreciate his wit. Wilde, we suspect, favoured the younger and handsomer ladies, and was not averse to the flighty ones. On other occasions supper-parties were held in the students' rooms, or in the club-room, when the table was decorated with skulls and other relics of mortality, while whist was played and much punch consumed. At intervals the Students' Medical Club met at Mr. Fannin's, No. 41, Grafton Street, where Wilde was a constant and fluent speaker.

He remained resident in Steevens' for four years, after which he went to the Rotunda Hospital to study midwifery. Before leaving Steevens' he wrote his first medical work—a treatise on spina bifida, a congenital malformation of the spinal canal. He read this paper to the Medical Philosophical Society in 1836. It attracted considerable attention, and was very favourably received by those of his seniors who were present. One of his friends, passing out of the room, said to him: 'You needn't trouble yourself going in for the examination now—that paper has settled the matter for you.'

Midwifery attracted Wilde considerably, and as usual he threw all his energies into the subject. At the annual prize examination, he was successful against the pick of the Irish and many English students. This was a noteworthy effort, for he had overtaxed his strength by hard work, and just before the examination he contracted 'fever'—probably typhus. In spite of his condition, and not heeding the authorities who endeavoured to dissuade him, he went through the examination and answered brilliantly. Immediately after the examination he collapsed, and within a few days his condition was considered hopeless. In his extremity Graves was sent for. He prescribed a glass of strong ale, to be taken every hour. The apparently dying student revived, and the following morning Graves found him sleeping comfortably.

The case affords a glimpse of Graves' unorthodox methods, for stimulants were then regarded as anathema in fevers. Graves, who always took the common-sense view, asked that 'He fed fevers' should be his epitaph.

On the eve of St. Patrick's Day, 1837, Wilde became a Licentiate of the Royal College of Surgeons. Immediately afterwards he was appointed resident clinical clerk and curator of the museum of Steevens' Hospital, for his seniors wisely decided not to let such a promising young man out of their sight. He might so easily have got lost in his father's practice in Roscommon.

Wilde retained the post of curator of the Steevens' museum for some months, while he slowly recovered from the illness which had so nearly cost him his life. He was far from well and suffering much from asthma. The fact that he suffered from this ailment gives us an important key to his character, for it is a disease which is accompanied by a temperament peculiarly its own. Asthma shares with migraine the distinction of being very definitely a disease of intellectuals. The allergic subject is usually a person of considerable artistic capabilities, whose finer qualities are above those of more common clay, but he can be at times moody, irritable and irrational.

Wilde was at this time but twenty-two, of an eager excitable disposition, and with the world before him. His talents had drawn the admiration of his masters, who had attended him in his illness with the greatest care and sympathy. When Sir Henry Marsh and Dr. Graves required a doctor to attend a patient on a health-seeking cruise to the Holy Land, Wilde was their natural selection for the post. He could be confidently recommended, and the trip would do him good.

We can imagine with what excitement he heard the proposal, with what joy he found himself accepted, and with what thrilling care he made his preparations. It was indeed a wonderful opportunity for a young man. The Napoleonic wars were long past, European travel was the vogue, and he had read many accounts of strange scenes in foreign lands. Now he was to see those scenes for himself.

CHAPTER IV
MADEIRA AND TENERIFFE

I

WE FIND him, therefore, on the 24th September of 1837, sailing down the Solent in the s.y. *Crusader*, R.Y.S., whose owner was his patient, Mr. Robert Meiklam. Who this gentleman was, or what his ailment, we do not know. There were a half-dozen of the name living in Glasgow about this time, to whom he may have been related. We may surmise that his disease was consumption. He obtained some relief by the trip, but we do not know whether it was permanent or not. In 1841 Wilde expressed the hope that 'you may long continue to enjoy that health which our voyage was so much the means of restoring'. On the other hand, the *Crusader* was sold three or four years after the travellers' return.

The *Crusader* was a fine ship of a hundred and thirty tons, small enough to our eyes, but an able vessel in every way. Rigged as a topsail schooner, with long raking bowsprit and clipper bow, every line showed beauty and graceful power. Her sea-going qualities were soon to be tested, for the winter of 1837–8 was bad everywhere, and she encountered many gales during her voyage. Wilde suffered considerably, for he was a bad sailor. Nevertheless, he was amply rewarded, for he drew dividends from his experiences for the rest of his life. He kept a full diary of the voyage, and his scientific knowledge was already sufficient to give importance to his observations. The record of his travels which he published in book form on his return was one of the most popular works of the time, and he also gathered material for a number of important scientific papers.

The *Crusader* wandered slowly down the western coast-line of Europe, putting in at Corunna to repair the ravages sustained in the Bay of Biscay, and incidentally giving the travellers an opportunity to visit the battlefield, in which Wilde was greatly interested. He reconstructed Wolfe's retirement for his companions, and drew an analogy between the action and the retreat of Xenophon, about which he later corresponded with Sir Charles Napier. At Lisbon they were entertained by Wilde's kinsman, grandiloquently described as 'Major-General Sir R. Ouseley', whose rank and title were, however, a little meretricious. He had been lent, as a major, by the English army to the Portuguese, who made him a Major-General and a Knight of the Tower and Sword.

From Portugal they sailed to Madeira, dropping anchor on the 24th October in the roadstead before Funchal. Wilde was completely captured by the beauty of Madeira, with its lime and orange groves, coffee plantations, wide-spreading bananas, and thousands of rare exotic plants. Here they spent many happy lazy days in the sunshine, wandering in shady glades roofed by the scarlet hibiscus or the snowy bells of the tulip tree. Wilde found endless pleasure in the beauty of the scene, roaming under coral trees, beneath wide-spreading plane trees and great willows, bending over the rivulets which cascaded from the hills. He rode through fruitful vineyards and between hedges of geraniums, fuchsias, and heliotropes, where myriads of insects with golden wings supped nectar from the flowers and added the low music of their wings to the melody of the woodland sounds. The fish market in particular attracted him. The glowing metallic lustre of the fish, and the unusual varieties offered for sale interested him so much that he brought home a number of specimens. He preserved them by a method of his own invention, which he claimed to keep the form and colour of the fish better than any process previously described.

Although Wilde's asthma troubled him considerably at Madeira, he was much impressed by the possibilities of the Canaries as a resort for invalids, particularly for those suffering from lung ailments. He thought many went there too late, as, indeed, was likely in those far-off days before the advent of bacteriology and X-rays, when the early diagnosis of consumption was most often a matter of conjecture. He wrote in his diary: 'Many—too many, seduced by a false and characteristic fatuity, hurry hither but to expend their latest sigh. Too many, and those the loveliest and fairest, voyage to this distant spot, to lay them down to rest beneath the cypress shade.

'Still, even that spot has its beauties, saddening though they be; for, here would I die, and be laid even in the simple cemetery of Funchal; and though no kindly hand should strew my grave with flowers, it would be garlanded by the fuchsia and the orange blossoms. Although no artificial incense was scattered o'er my tomb, the heliotrope and the myrtle would shed the fragrance of their perfume around me; and when night had wrapped her mantle o'er the scene, and no unhallowed sound disturbed the cathedral stillness of the hour, I should have those mystic lamps that light a world, hung in the vault of my sepulchre, to smile upon the sod that covered me.'

II

After some days spent wallowing refreshingly in orgies of sentiment such as this, Wilde rejoined the ship and they set sail once more, bound this time for Teneriffe. After nightfall on the second day they glided into Santa Cruz Bay, through a fleet of fishing boats, in each of which a fire of Canary pine was lit in order to attract the fish. Around the fire sat the fishermen, their furrowed faces grimed by smoke, clothed in long scarlet capes and jackets, looking like so many tempest-brewing spirits of the deep, as they sprang to view on the crests of the mountainous waves, and as quickly sank out of sight in the gulfs below.

On 5th December they anchored in the Bay of Gibraltar. With his first view of the Rock, Wilde was 'more astonished than pleased'. Tier after tier of guns pointed from endless batteries above the water's edge. Above these was the town of Gibraltar crowned by the old gateway and tower. Beyond this were a few consumptive-looking gardens, and then the brown blistered surface of the bare rock.

Closer acquaintance did not remove this impression. He liked the kaleidoscopic scenes of the streets, which he likened to a 'fancy-ball', but he always disliked the military caste, and poked ponderous fun at them whenever possible. The stiff erect figure of the English soldier, buttoned to the throat and with his neck stuck into a high regimental stock, he thought compared ill with the stately, athletic Moors.

Gibraltar, he thought, was 'no place for invalids'. Nor, one imagines, for anybody else, as far as he was concerned.

The weather was now becoming much colder, and it was

imperative for Robert Meiklam's sake to push on to warmer climates. Consequently, the *Crusader* commenced her voyage up the Mediterranean, intending to make Algiers the first port of call. They met the prevailing easterly winds, but made Algiers at dusk on the fourth day. Here they had to endure a five-days' quarantine, lying alongside all the dirty craft in harbour, with a Maltese guardian quartered on them to prevent communication with their neighbours, and they were lucky enough to escape the horrors of fumigation.

At Algiers the weather was still intemperate, and the *Crusader* carried on as soon as possible to Malta and Egypt.

THEY LANDED at Alexandria, but before proceeding to Cairo, Wilde, who was now the acknowledged leader of the party, took his friends to examine Cleopatra's Needle and Pompey's pillar, both of which were still in the country of their origin. It was not until many years later that these obelisks reached London and Paris, although Mahomet Ali had already generously presented them to the British Government. 'They are ours by right of conquest and presentation,' said Wilde.

The journey from Alexandria to Cairo took no less than five days, travelling along the Mahmoudie canal and later the Nile. The *kanghia* they travelled in was indescribably filthy and verminous, but no worse than any other available. The usual practice amongst Europeans was to sink their boat,for several days before embarking, in order to get rid of the livestock which infested it, but this was impossible for the 'Crusaders', who could not spare the time. The cabin was about the size of a dog kennel, and could barely hold four passengers. The waters of the canal were almost of the consistency of porridge, and flavoured with the essences of divers carcasses of buffaloes, camels and donkeys. This water was of considerable value as manure to the surrounding land, but unhappily the tourists had to use it for other purposes, as they had totally forgotten to bring a supply of pure water.

The nights were dreadful. The squeaking rats under their heads, the flight of cockroaches in their faces, the attacks of bugs and fleas, not to mention 'the loathsome crawling of other and more disgusting vermin', made sleep impossible. On reaching Atfe, however, they procured a cleaner *kanghia* to proceed up the Nile, and Wilde found interest and amusement on the banks by shooting wildfowl, and observing the countryside, of which nothing could be seen from the boat because of the height of the bank.

They found the English hotel in Cairo so full that they had to put up at the French hotel, which happily they found was kept by an Englishman. 'The accommodation was tolerable, though not so good as we should have had at the English.' They visited the arms factory, and saw muskets and brass cannons being made. They went to see the citadel, the scene of the massacre of the Mamelukes, and braved the scowls of the pious Moslems in the mosque of the Sultan Hassan, where the sole survivor had found sanctuary.

At this time Egypt was under the control of Mahomet Ali, a self-made ruler whose methods are strongly reminiscent of those of our present-day dictators. His predecessors in office had been the Mamelukes, a ruling caste of Sultans descended from the body-guard of Turkish slaves which had first been formed in Egypt by the successors of Saladin. These men had usurped authority in Egypt, and although at the end of the eighteenth century Turkey still retained a Pasha in Egypt, he was more the prisoner of the Mamelukes than the Sultan's Viceroy. As might be expected under such rule, the country was in a degraded condition. All the Arabic traditions of science and art were lost, and there was no commerce. Intestine dissension, extortion, slavery and murder were rife. Then Egypt became the theatre of war between England and France. When, in 1803, the armies were withdrawn, the Mamelukes and Albanians formed an alliance against the Turks.

It was then that Mahomet Ali saw his opportunity. He was an Albanian soldier of obscure origin, who by sheer lack of scruple, coupled with quick-witted energy, had forced his way to the front. He conceived the bold idea of regularizing and solidifying the government by the introduction of the science and commerce of Europe, just as Kemal Pasha did in Turkey a hundred years later.

Mahomet Ali had tremendous difficulties to deal with. His modern ideas were anathema to the Moslem faith, and he had the poorest of human material to work on. Nevertheless, his buoyant energy triumphed, and he became the despot of a country in whose markets he had once been sold as a slave.

In his rise to power, Mahomet Ali was as ruthless as any modern dictator. The Mamelukes proved to be the last of many obstacles in his path. He invited them all to a festival in the citadel. They arrived five hundred strong, and poured into a long narrow passage, one end of which led into the palace of the Pasha, the other into the precincts of the mosque of Sultan

Hassan. When the whole procession had crowded into this narrow pass, both gates were closed. Troops arose from behind both lateral walls, and poured down a devastating fire which, in a few moments, annihilated the dynasty of six hundred years. What a scene it was, with those five hundred bodies arrayed in gorgeous trappings lying amongst the still quivering bodies of their gaily caparisoned horses! One of the Mamelukes alone survived, a Bey, who, amidst the shower of lead, forced his horse to climb a narrow staircase leading to the ramparts. Fighting his way through the soldiers on the wall, he leaped in despair over the parapet, and although his horse was dashed to death in the fall, he himself escaped unhurt, and found refuge in the neighbouring mosque.

However savage the act, its result was immediately beneficial. The tide of science and learning, which had ebbed to expose a degenerate country, flowed once more. Mahomet Ali built and endowed colleges of law, physic, divinity, and literature, in which he clothed and maintained youths who had at first to be dragged from their native hovels by conscription officers. He erected dockyards, factories and arsenals. He kept in the closest contact with the various departments of his state, and every office was held by his immediate appointment. Wilde, who avowedly admired him, thought him to be 'perhaps . . . a governor better acquainted with all the different details of his Kingdom than any other ruler in existence'. But even Wilde admitted that the country was lamentably over-taxed. Mahomet Ali was a cruel ruffian, and left the country bankrupt when he died, but he did raise Egypt from the slough of despair.

In his person and surroundings Mahomet Ali exercised the frugal moderation we are familiar with in his modern prototypes. 'His household exceeds little that of a European noble, and his children are instructed in polite literature and accomplishments by an English lady of the Methodist connection.'

From the moment he landed at Alexandria Wilde was struck by the number of blind people he met with. Fully half the population had but one good eye, and of the remainder those who were not groping their way in total darkness were usually blear-eyed from disease. The ravages of the disease we know as trachoma caused by far the greatest number of cases. The wholesale methods of conscription adopted by Mahomet Ali accounted for a few, for a number of the young men deliberately put out one of their eyes to avoid military service. Others sacrificed an index finger to a similar end. That an eye should be regarded as the equivalent of a finger in such a land of darkness seems truly astounding, but the fact remains, and similar cases occur to this day. Perhaps it is simply an example of the contempt bred by familiarity.

Trachoma is a disease of great antiquity. It is said that Saul of Tarsus was a sufferer until he was cured by Ananias at Damascus. St. Francis of Assisi contracted it during the Crusades and died almost totally blind. Egyptian records go back much farther, for a papyrus of about the eighteenth dynasty describes the symptoms accurately. Epilation forceps have been found in tombs of the New Empire, as well as pots containing oxides of copper and zinc, and sulphates of lead and antimony. These pigments were used in the treatment of conjunctivitis, as well as for darkening the edges of the lids, just as kohl, which is really the same substance, is used to-day. Hippocrates, Herophilus and Euclid all studied the disease. In Nero's time the great Celsus studied it exactly. No fewer than sixty Arabian oculists of note existed between the eighth and fourteenth centuries. After this, with the decay of learning in the East, little more work was done on the disease, until Mahomet Ali took up the task.

Although the home of trachoma is in the Eastern Mediterranean where it is known as Egyptian ophthalmia, its distribution is wide-spread all over the globe from America to Polynesia, from South Africa to Siberia. Trachoma is a rare disease in Great Britain, but it is very common in southern Ireland. It is said that more than half the people of the world have, or have had, trachoma.

The disease is undoubtedly infectious, but the causative microbe has not as yet been discovered. It flourishes in conditions of dirt and overcrowding, and consequently is a disease of the poorer classes, few cases being seen in cleanly people, except amongst doctors and nurses who are much exposed to infection in their treatment of cases. The climate of Egypt seems to favour its spread no less than the dirty habits of the people. The amazing way in which Orientals will allow flies to settle in black masses over the eyes of their children, to feed on the purulent secretions caused by the disease, must be seen to be believed.

The manifestations of trachoma are, first, red granular in-flammation of the corners of the eyes and the under-surfaces of the lids. The granules coalesce, break down and form a scar tissue which in time grows over the pupil, obscuring the sight. All scar tissues contract slowly, and the scars along the edges of the lids by their contraction pull the eyelashes slowly inwards, so that they eventually turn into the eye itself. This is a most troublesome condition. For its cure an Alexandrian oculist of the seventh century, Paul of Aegina, described an operation which was performed amongst the fellahin until quite recently. This operation aimed at turning out the lashes ┌y removing an oval piece of skin from the upper lid. This was done by enclosing a fold of skin between two sticks tightly bound together at their ends. The enclosed skin, deprived of its blood supply, became gangrenous, and dropped off, together with the sticks, after a couple of days. The scar produced by the resulting wound turned the upper lid outwards and upwards by its contraction—occasionally.

The treatment of the condition, apart from preventive measures, consists mainly in squeezing out or scraping the granules, and the application of caustics. Little advance has been made since Wilde's time. It was he who actually first practised the expression of the granules. He squeezed them by means of a pair of none too clean finger-nails instead of a carefully sterilized forceps, but the therapeutic principle of expression remains the same.

Wilde, who was probably familiar with trachoma in Ireland, was greatly interested in what he saw of the disease in Egypt, and it is possible that this is what determined him to specialize in diseases of the eye. Mahomet Ali had constructed a large military hospital and medical school at the army depot, and had placed it under the charge of a young French physician. The name of Antoine Clot, known in Egypt as Clot Bey, with that of his German assistant, Pruner, is familiar to all students of ophthalmology. To this institution Wilde went his way, armed with a letter of introduction.

What he saw impressed him greatly—a noble building in the form of a square, each side about three hundred feet long, in the midst of a most charmingly tree-planted park. The hospital could accommodate about twelve hundred patients, of whom more than half were suffering from diseases of the eye. Wilde studied the trachoma cases closely for several days. His observations on the etiology of the disease show some confusion between cause and effect, which may perhaps be excused even in such an acute observer when we consider his youth and inexperience. For instance, he considers the accompanying trichiasis is a cause, not an effect. But he pours scorn on the theory held amongst Europeans at the time, that the disease was caused by 'suppressed perspiration'. 'Why should not the inhabitants of other warm countries be subject to a similar disease, where the heat is much greater?' He is nearer the truth when he ascribes it to contagion, the effect of sand drifts and hot winds, and extreme dirtiness. 'Little idea can be formed of this without seeing it; the eye, or face, is seldom washed; the natural discharge is allowed to accumulate, and often a number of flies will be found collected in the corners, to remove which would be considered unlucky. I have invariably remarked, that in the Moslim ablutions before prayer, although they wash the arms to the elbows, the feet, back of the neck, crown of the head, and behind the ears, they always avoid washing the eyes. I do not think that blackening the edge of the eyelids at all contributes towards ophthalmia, and females, even allowing for their comparative numbers, and the circumstances in which they are placed, are much less liable to it than men.'

Dr. Pruner transferred Wilde to the care of Dr. Sicher, the Professor of Anatomy, who proceeded to show him the medical schools. In the dissecting-room he found plenty of subjects. The provision of bodies for dissection was one of the greatest difficulties Mahomet Ali had had to face in the organization of his medical school, for the religious prejudices of the people in some cases prohibited even the touching of a dead body. Clot Bey had been murderously attacked on one occasion when performing a post-mortem. Mahomet Ali solved the problem in typical fashion. He referred it to the priesthood, who at first obstinately set their faces against it, declaring it utterly incompatible with the religion of the Prophet of Mecca. Ali answered, however, that it was his royal wish and pleasure that dissection should be legalized, and stated that if the priests did not speedily do his will, they themselves should form the first material for anatomical research. This ultimatum was effective, and all difficulties were rapidly smoothed away.

Wilde found no less than three hundred conscripted medical students, all clothed, fed, educated and paid by Mahomet Ali. The professors were all European, and the standard of education was good.

The background of the Cairo streets entranced him—in particular the processions formed by whole harems proceeding to the bath, the ladies close veiled, mounted cross-legged on donkeys, and attended by their guardian eunuchs. Wealthy Turks mounted on richly caparisoned horses cantered along the streets, attended by grooms and pipe-bearers, sometimes with their wives and children on donkeys bringing up the rear. He attended a public ball, and wondered at the number and diversity of costumes worn by the men in the native service. The ladies interested him more, whether they were French, native, Jewish, Copt or Syrian. 'The general effect of their costume was pleasing, though strange; the wide trowsers, tied tightly round the ancles, made their beautiful little feet look still smaller; the loose, flowing robe of pink or white, and the short under-garment, were very becoming. The bosom, however, is much more exposed than in England; indeed it is generally stripped in front as low down as the waist, which is worn immediately under the armpits.'

These ladies, however, were inert creatures, 'intended more for the ottoman than the dance'. The room was overcrowded and hot, and Wilde found the music of Pandean pipes, harpsicord, guitars and mandolins disagreeably loud and discordant. He took refuge in a neighbouring room, only to find a dense crowd surrounding a faro table.

CHAPTER VI TOMBS AND PYRAMIDS

I

LEAVING THESE doubtful pleasures to his companions, Wilde procured three donkeys and two guides, and sallied forth to explore the tombs and pyramids of Sakara and Dashur.

The science of Egyptology was at this time in its infancy. It is, perhaps, curious that the beginnings of our present knowledge of Egypt's past arose out of Napoleon's military adventures. Fired, like Alexander, with the ambition to found a great Eastern empire, he sent his army to Egypt. He appreciated the value of scholarship, and with his troops he sent a number of scientists to examine and record all they could of the temples and buildings they found there. The result was the compilation of a fine work of scholarship, the *Description de L'Égypte*, in twenty-five volumes of text and twenty of plates. This may be regarded as the foundation stone of the archaeological study of Egypt. Many of the facts compiled were not then understood, but there they were stated for future brains to unravel and explain. Wilde, with the youthful hot-blooded prejudice which characterized him at this time, decried the books, because of their French origin. He would not have done so a few years later.

The defeat of Napoleon's armies for a time called a halt in the work of investigation, and when the country was once more in a settled condition it was recommenced in a most haphazard way. There was no central Bureau of Control, as now. Any private individual could loot a tomb for his own amusement, or in the hope of personal gain. It is not surprising that incalculable damage was done to the ancient records and relics. Belzoni, for instance, forced an entry into a royal tomb by the barbarous use of a battering-ram made of the trunks of palm-trees. To-day the stones would be removed one by one with the utmost care, lest anything inside might be damaged.

The natives were quick to take their cue, and when they learned of the commercial value of the relics, the rifling of tombs became a general practice. This was the state of affairs when Wilde visited Egypt, for Lepsius, the first really scientific investigator since the French, did not visit the country until 1842.

Wilde's account of his explorations in those early days is extraordinarily interesting. He and his guides and donkeys were ferried across the Nile, and found themselves on the edge of the Libyan desert, looking towards Abusir, with the pyramids of Giza on their right. They climbed a wall of rock which ran parallel with the fertile land along the Valley of the Nile. 'Were I to offer an opinion of my own I should say that this rock once formed the enclosure of a vast city that extended all along the plain, between the pyramids and the river; and should any wealthy or enterprising traveller attempt to clear away some of the sand that now covers its face, at one or two points, I am strongly inclined to think, judging from what I saw at Sakara, that many tombs and excavations would be discovered, as it is more than conjecture that the catacombs extend the whole length of the pyramids.' This conjecture as to the extent of the 'catacombs' or more correctly, the cemeteries, has since been proved correct, or nearly so, by exploration.

The natural history of the Nile Valley did not escape his eye. Eagles, swallows, martins and kestrels flew overhead. The kestrels and swallows, at war in most countries, here were on the best of terms, possibly because the kestrel's prey was not birds, but a large sand-hopper, with remarkably brilliant crimson legs. This insect's protective colouring was so perfect that not even the eye of a hawk could spot it when on the ground. The kestrel, however, marked unerringly the place where it landed from its hop. When the insect again took flight, its red legs and underbody rendered it very conspicuous, and the kestrel took it on the wing. Wilde shot one of these birds, and full of curiosity, dissected it. He found that, instead of the usual membranous stomach of birds of prey, theirs had become a perfect gizzard, with a detached lining cuticle stained a bright red by the colouring matter of the sand-hopper. He also found the pratingole, a specimen of which he procured later and brought home with him.

Another animal which drew his attention was the scarabæus,

or sacred beetle, as they ran about in all directions in the warm sunshine, rolling the balls of clay and camel-dung in which they had deposited their eggs. He watched them rolling these globes over the sands all day long, the male pushing from below with the horny projections on his head, the female mounted in front and pulling the ball down with her fore feet. Others stood on their heads and pushed with their hind feet! When the day became suddenly clouded they left their charge and waddled off to their holes, but with the first gleam of returning sunshine out they came again, and resumed the work with renewed vigour. Wilde concluded that the purpose of the game was to ensure that the sun should act equally on all sides of the eggs—'it may, however, be but for the purpose of drying the surface.' Wilde closely observed the habits and customs of these insects, so famed in the story of Egypt, which take such a conspicuous part in the symbolism and mythology of her people. This was before the discovery of the Rosetta Stone, and the hieroglyphs could not yet be read, although Young and Champollion had explained the system a few years before. Wilde said 'the more I consider the habits and manners of animals, the more am I convinced that it was an accurate observation of their natural history and instinct that arrested the attention of the ancients, and on which was formed much of their hieroglyphic system.' 'Scarabaei, in every shape and attitude, and of all sizes, are figured on the Egyptian monuments, are used in the hieroglyphics, and models of them are generally found on the breasts of mummies; besides many of a smaller size form part of the necklaces worn by such. In these two latter positions they may have been used as amulets. Others are carved in different stones and gems, as signets having the names of the Ptolemies, etc., cut in hieroglyphics on the face.' This is an example of Wilde's acute observation and accurate powers of deduction, for his remarks on the use of the scarabæus beetle as an amulet and as a signet are quite correct.

The expedition passed the pyramids of Abusir, but were unable to spare time to examine them closely. Wilde thought them less carefully constructed than those of Giza or Sakara, and in this again he was quite right, for they show signs of jerry-building on the part of their constructors. The ground he rode over presented an extraordinary spectacle, strewn as it was for miles with the sackings of the tombs. The whole plain was covered with heaps of rubbish like molehills, which had been thrown out from the cemeteries by the Arabs. Human bones, animal remains, quantities of linen from the wrappings of mummies, broken crockery and mummy-cases formed a litter underfoot. The state of affairs found by Wilde furnishes an almost complete answer to those who question the morality of organized scientific excavation in Egypt, even if this entails the removal of ancient human remains for the sake of safety. If Egyptology had not been officially controlled in later years there is little doubt that many of Egypt's treasures would long ago have been completely destroyed.

On arriving in the afternoon at Sakara, they found a tomb which had been desecrated the day before by a Frenchman. This man's guides were still on the spot, having been deserted by their employer, who had decamped with what loot he considered valuable. The mummy-case and the remains of its late occupant were strewed around in fragments. The case had been one of great beauty and perfection, obviously belonging to a person of rank. The head, chest and arms of the mummy were lying in a corner of the funeral chamber, stripped of their coverings. Wilde found the mummy to be that of a male dwarf about twenty-five years of age. The arms interested him so much that they were added to his collection of trophies, and eventually brought home. When he published the description of his travels he described them in an appendix to the first volume, as an instance of a 'most remarkable deformity', which he could not understand. He also gave a woodcut which makes the cause of the deformity quite clear. It shows a typical bone from a sufferer from achondroplasia, a disease of great antiquity which is one of the commonest causes of dwarfism. In the second edition of his book this appendix has disappeared. It is very surprising that Wilde missed the diagnosis, but after all he had only been studying medicine for six or seven years, and probably had never seen an achondroplasic skeleton before. One imagines he must have seen at least one or two of these dwarfs in everyday life, unmistakable with their short arms and legs, disproportionately long bodies and small stern faces under a prominent gibbous brow. We need not wonder at the care with which this old Egyptian was interred, but rather deplore the rude disturbance of his sleep, for achondroplasic dwarfs are usually pleasant, intelligent little people, respected by all who know them.

As it was getting late in the evening Wilde determined to spend the night in this tomb amongst the ferocious-looking Bedouins who ordinarily slept there. As there were still several hours of daylight he decided to visit the neighbouring stepped pyramid of Sakara before retiring. This pyramid was seldom entered in those days. Its aperture was like a fox's earth, and nearly choked with sand and stones. Wilde was struck by the roof of the principal chamber, which is not made of large blocks of stones laid transversely as in the case of the other pyramids, but in a similar manner to the Bronze Age tumulus of New-grange, in Ireland, where the arch is made of large stones laid flat, each one projecting beyond that underneath, until finally the whole is crowned by one large stone laid transversely. There is this difference, that in the stepped pyramid wooden beams are used, whereas Newgrange is roofed by stone flags. The floor of the chamber was covered with dirt and stones which some vandal had left after trying to excavate its eastern side, but a large sarcophagus of polished granite remained untouched in a corner. From this chamber a low narrow gallery led to three smaller apartments, the doorways of which were decorated with flowers and other ornaments, and the walls were covered with hieroglyphs. These chambers, which Wilde erroneously considered to be contemporary with the large central one, were of exceedingly elegant design, but choked by stones and rubbish, having had their walls and roof pulled down in several places in the search for treasure, 'the Arabs say by the French some time ago'. Wilde concluded that this pyramid was older than those of Giza, and in this he was quite correct, for it belongs to the third dynasty, whereas those of Giza belong to the fourth. It was hazardous enough to explore it, as was testified by his torn clothes and bruised skin on returning to the light of day.

It was now evening, and the first day of this memorable adventure was nearly over. Wilde retraced his steps to the tomb of Bergami, and arranged his pallet in a corner, with the lid of a mummy-case for his pillow. The under part of the coffin was made into a corn trough for the donkeys. He was greatly annoyed by the natives—wild, savage creatures, each with a trifling bit of crockeryware or a small blue figure, crying:

'Antique, antique, baksheesh, baksheesh, Inglese, a baksheesh.'
'Odious word! How it yet echoes in my hearing!' He
turned them out by force—they crept back in augmented
numbers. He walked out himself, only to feel the hot breath
of some wily Arab in his ear, murmuring—'baksheesh!'
Even mention of the magic name of Mahomet Ali merely
made them bow their heads.

At last he shook them off, and mounted a neighbouring
hillock to survey the scene. This was the site of the once
great city of Memphis, formerly crowded with buildings and
noisy with the voices of its people. Here the Pharaohs reigned,
here Joseph ruled, and here Herodotus was initiated into the
mysteries of Egypt. These rocks and caves once echoed
anguished cries when the first-born of Egypt were smitten
by the Angel of Death.

He re-entered the cave, and finding it impossible to dispossess
the Arabs—whom in truth he admitted to have a better claim
to the place than he had—made the best of it, and lit a fire
with the decayed contents of some mummy-pots. The fire
burned with a bright flame which illuminated the whole cavern,
and fell full on the forms of the Arabs scattered through its
gloomy recesses—some stretched in sleep, some in the act
of prayer to Allah, and others squatted around the fire. The
aromatic smell of the fire, the dark sunburnt faces of the Arabs,
formed an atmosphere of the most eerie description. Wilde
amused himself by thinning some hieroglyphic tablets left by
the Frenchman, until he was ready for sleep, while the Bedouins
entertained him with wild songs and Eastern tales. The fire
flickered and faded to a glimmer, and pipes were put away,
but he found sleep a long time coming. Bodily exhaustion
eventually triumphed over an excited brain, and Wilde knew
no more until morning when he awoke strong and refreshed.

II

Wilde rose early, for he had determined to visit the ibis
mummy-pits the following morning, before proceeding on
his way to the pyramids of Giza where he had arranged to
meet the Meiklams. When, however, he arrived at the mummy-
pits he found to his great chagrin that he had forgotten to bring
any lights with him. Nothing daunted, he decided that if he

could not *see* his way, he would *feel* it, and bring home some of the embalmed ibises at all costs.

An arch cut out of the rock led into a small chamber or shrine. In the midst of the floor of this shrine a square shaft descended to the sepulchre of the sacred birds. Holes cut in the sides of this shaft enabled Wilde and his guide to descend thirty feet to a low, narrow vault, which was the ante-chamber to a series of chambers extending for acres on all sides.

All was utter blackness. The guide took Wilde by the hand and led him along amongst broken pots and sharp stones and rubbish which sank under him at every step. Coming to a narrow part of the gallery, they both lay down flat and wriggled through, Wilde holding his companion's feet. They scrambled through to comparative freedom, half suffocated by sand and scratched by broken vessels. This groping continued for many windings, and Wilde, almost exhausted by heat and exertion, felt that he was being led through some enchanted mausoleum.

At length they arrived at a place where they could stand upright. Creeping over a vast pile of pots, and sinking into the dust of thousands of animals, they came at last to urns which were still undisturbed, and piled in upright rows with the larger end upwards. With immense labour they succeeded in conveying to the surface six of these, which Wilde eventually brought back to Ireland. He was so exhausted that he had to be carried the last few yards to the open air, where he remained insensible for some minutes, in all probability overcome by foul air as much as by physical exertion. It was no mean feat to explore the mummy-pits in complete darkness, and one which called for tremendous courage, but it would have been even more dangerous had they used naked lights to show the way. The mummies being bituminous, are highly inflammable, and many lives have been lost by explosion of the gases. Wilde apparently did not know this, although he was alive to the danger of being suffocated in the foul atmosphere of the vaults.

On recovering his senses, Wilde's enthusiasm allowed him but a short rest before starting the long trek to Giza. Here he found his friends had spread their picnic table in the façade of one of the rock-tombs, at the foot of the pyramid of Cheops (Khufu), which they had just ascended. Several foreigners from Cairo had accompanied them, and in their various cos-

tumes, and by the diversity of their tongues, formed as motley
a group as ever visited the sepulchres of Egypt's ancient kings,
which had been the scene of priestly mystery long before the
countries they came from were ever heard of. If Wilde thought
his company incongruous as it feasted at the foot of the pyramid,
what would he have thought of a party of present-day tourists?

Wilde's friends indulged in a well-earned siesta, but nothing
of the sort for him. He had come to climb the Great Pyramid,
and nothing was going to stop him. He could rest enough
when he returned to Cairo. He, therefore, engaged two Arabs
to conduct him to the top. His object was explained to them
by an interpreter, but they apparently thought he had been
of the party which had ascended the Great Pyramid earlier in
the day, and that he now wished to attempt the second. This

T. G. WILSON

was a most hazardous undertaking, as the coating or outer
layer of stones is still smooth and perfect for a hundred and forty
feet from the top. It has been successfully scaled by few
Europeans, and its ascent is now forbidden even to natives,
so many lives have been lost in the attempt.

The lower part, where the outer casing has disappeared, is
formed by steps of enormous stones, the climbing of which,
although laborious, presented little difficulty. Some of the lower
stones are larger than those on the pyramid of Khufu, and Wilde
had to clamber over them on hands and knees. In this he was
assisted by his agile guides, one an old man, the other about
forty years of age. They turned from the east to the northern
aspect, and finally reached the casing on the west side. Here
was an obstacle Wilde thought even his guides could not surmount, for the smooth polished stones of the casing formed
a dangerously inclined slippery coping above their heads.

Wilde was made to remove his hat, shoes and coat. The younger man then placed his raised hands against the projecting edge, which reached above his chin, and the elder picked up Wilde like a child, and placed his feet on the younger man's shoulders. His body lay flat on the polished surface of the casing stone, at an angle with that of the guide, and in this position he remained for two minutes. The older man contrived to get over the projection, and creeping along the line of junction of the casing, took Wilde's hands and drew him up to where he was. He then lowered his scarf and assisted the younger man over the coping.

One man then mounted to the next junction of the casing, by climbing on the other's shoulder, and Wilde followed suit. In this way they climbed upwards, often having to creep some distance sideways to find a handhold. All the stones had a span of four or five feet, smoothly polished, and set at an angle of less than forty-five degrees. They were four hundred feet above the ground, and if one man had made a slip they must all three inevitably have been dashed to death long before reaching the ground.

Finally they reached the top, which is not more than six feet square. The guides gave vent to sundry demonstrations of satisfaction, clapping Wilde on the back, patting his head, kissing his hands, and uttering a low growl which presently took form in the less musical cry of 'baksheesh'. Looking down, he saw his friends waving their hats and cheering, and 'I began to think something wonderful had been achieved'. Well might he think so, for he had performed a feat of hardihood few others would attempt. It is true he did not know what he was in for when he started, but he might easily have turned back. In that nightmare climb over the casing he had done the most daring deed of his life.

He looked round and took stock of his surroundings. He saw two or three names scratched on the central rock, to which, of course, he added his own; which shows how environment alters our habits, for nobody was more contemptuous of people who scribble their names on ancient monuments than Wilde. Looking down, he saw a scene of intoxicating grandeur. The green-edged silver ribbon of the Nile wound its way through massive rocks amidst the Libyan desert, until it was lost in the union of sand and sky. The thousand pinnacles of Cairo rose beyond the land, the pyramids were below amongst groves of waving palms. In another age Memphis and Heliopolis would have been within his view.

The heat became intense, and the stones so hot that it was very uncomfortable to sit on them. Standing was too daring an experiment to try. The descent was safely effected by the guides, who tied a sash under Wilde's arms and let him slide from course to course. It was even more dangerous than the climb up, but much less exhausting.

The rest of the expedition became an anticlimax. Wilde rejoined his friends, and they explored the chambers of the Great Pyramid, firing a pistol in the Kings' Chamber to hear the echo, and in general behaving in true tourist style. A hasty glance at the recently opened third pyramid, and soon they were once more on donkey-back, bound for Cairo, the Nile and Alexandria.

I

FOR WILDE the visit to Egypt was probably the most important part of the tour, not only because of his experiences amongst the relics of a long-dead age, but also because it was there that he first became interested in diseases of the eye, which were to become an important part of his life's work.

There is no space here to give more than an outline of the rest of the *Crusader's* voyage. From Egypt she went on to Rhodes, and to Telmessus, famous of old for wine and for augury. Here Wilde spent many days wandering amongst the tombs, for there is no place on earth which contains more ancient sepulchres, or so many different kinds of sepulture. Every variety of tomb is there, from the simple barrow to elaborate mausoleums carved in solid rock. They wandered on along the coast of Asia Minor, encountering much bad weather, and on one occasion losing their bowsprit. Finally, they were forced to shelter in the roadstead off Tyre, that famous city of antiquity. It was now but a heap of wretched hovels perched on ancient tottering towers, and far removed from the magnificent, joyous city of old, the city whose merchants were princes, whose silver was heaped as the dust, whose gold was as mire in the streets. Wilde had ardently anticipated his visit to Tyre, for he had long wished to find how the ancients made the famous Tyrian purple, and in particular from what form of shell-fish it was derived. He was fortunate enough to find in the almost perpendicular face of the beach whole strata of tessellated pavement, which gave him the level of the original city. While investigating these remains he found what he thought to be the vats or mortars in which the Tyrian dye was made. In these he found shells which gave him the information he sought, for he was able to identify them as those of the *Murex trunculus*.

Wilde spent much time trying to make out the topography of ancient Tyre. He came to the conclusion that most of the old city had become submerged. 'For saith the Lord God, when I shall make thee a desolate city, like the cities that are not inhabited; when I shall bring the deep upon thee, and great waters shall cover thee; when I shall bring thee down with them that descend into the pit . . .' (*Ezek.* xxvi. 19 and 20). On his return home, Wilde expounded his views with great vigour at the next meeting of the British Association, and exhibited a map he had made of ancient Tyre. His theories were new at the time, but in the succeeding hundred years they have been abundantly confirmed.

Leaving Tyre, they sailed southwards to Jaffa, where they disembarked. They were now approaching the climax of their journey, for this was their point of departure for Jerusalem.

They wasted little time in procuring horses and guides, and made a formidable cavalcade, all fully accoutred and armed, as they left on their four-day journey. They passed through the Garden of the Hesperides, among orange groves and lemon trees laden with fruit and flowers, tall waving cypresses, corals and mimosas, and prickly pears with the scammony in flower twining through their armour. Soon they came to the lovely Vale of Sharon, whose fields were decked with thousands of flowers. The scarlet anemone, the phlox and the iris, with the asphodel and the lily formed an enamelled carpet which perfumed the air. Next day they entered the wild hill country of Judea by the pass of Ladron. Here they found themselves in a very different terrain with dreary bleak hills arising in concentric circles one above the other. For the first time in Wilde's travels he met the hawthorn white with blossom, to remind him of his Irish hedgerows in mayfly time.

As the cavalcade advanced the features of the country became still more wild and barren, the steeps more harsh, and the descents more precipitous, until at last they neared their journey's end. Soon they saw the Holy City—a wall flanked by two or three square towers above which could be distinguished a few domes and minarets. Beyond it rose a three-capped hill of brown and rugged aspect—the Mount of Olives.

II

During a stay of less than a month in Jerusalem, Wilde's activity was immense. He visited the Mount of Olives and Gethsemane, Bethlehem and many other places familiar to him in the Bible narrative. He went daily to the Holy Sepulchre, and visited the alleged tombs of the Blessed Virgin Mary, of Lazarus, and many other places, and from the material gained he made a map of Jerusalem showing its boundaries, ancient and modern.

Wandering one day through the Vale of Kedron, he came to the Mount of Offence, or Hill of Evil Counsel, once desecrated by the High Places erected to Ashtoreth and Molech. Near the foot of the hill he was pointed out the Aceldama, or Field of Blood, said to have been purchased by the Jewish priests with the thirty pieces of silver that Judas had received for betraying his Master, but which he afterwards returned in remorse and went and hanged himself. 'And the chief priests took the silver pieces, and said, it is not lawful to put them into the treasury, because it is the price of blood. And they took counsel, and bought with them the potter's field to bury strangers in. Wherefore that field was called The Field of Blood, unto this day.'

Close at hand he was shown a tomb, which had been generally described as that bought by Judas Iscariot. Wilde did not believe this as he thought its structure to belong to a much later date. This opinion was soon confirmed by his discovery of what he took to be the real Field of Blood. Here, in a tomb, lying amongst layers of whitewash, he found a number of skulls which he thought belonged to members of many different races, Ethiopian, Mongolian and Indian, but not a single Jewish or well-marked Caucasian head. From this remarkable circumstance he concluded that this was the real Strangers' Field. Wilde's description of the quantities of human remains he discovered, and the way in which the tombs were white-washed, this being the first instance to be found of that ancient Jewish custom, is most valuable, for possibly his claims were true. Nobody who is interested in Biblical archaeology should neglect the account he gives of his stay in Jerusalem.

To the antiquary, perhaps the most absorbing story he tells is that in which he describes how he stumbled on the entrance to King Hezekiah's tunnel. This was the water conduit Hezekiah's men made as Sennacherib's army was approaching, in order to sidetrack the waters of the Virgin's Fountain to a pool inside the city of Jerusalem. Isaiah gives an account of the work which is graphically eloquent of feverish preparations against attack, but he supplies no exact details of the nature of Hezekiah's work.

Fortunately, archaeological excavations in modern times have shown us exactly what he did. His workmen extended the pre-existing Jebusite tunnel right through the rocks under Mount Zion, to convey the waters of the Virgin's Fountain to a newly-made pool in the Tyropœon Valley, which by King Hezekiah's time had become enclosed within the boundaries of the city. This tunnel served a double purpose, for it not only brought a fresh supply of water into the city from the camou-flaged Virgin's Fountain, but it removed a valuable water supply from the approaching army.

The tunnel is no less than 1,750 feet in length. It was obviously made by two parties of men, working towards each other from either end. It bears evidence of having been made in great haste, for it winds in a serpentine manner and shows great differences of height and width. There are several false cuts where the tunnel goes in the wrong direction for a couple of feet, and then resumes its proper course. One can picture the men of those ancient times listening in a moment of per-plexity for the sounds made by the other party as they 'picked the hard rock with iron'; and then once more resuming in the right direction.

In spite of the speed with which the work was undertaken and successfully concluded, somebody found time, then or subsequently, to cut an inscribed tablet in the tunnel giving an account of the work. In Hebrew characters it reads as follows: 'Behold this excavation. Now this is the history of the excavation. While the excavators were lifting up the pick, each towards his neighbour, and while there were yet three cubits to (excavate, there was heard) the voice of one man calling to his neighbour, for there was an excess in the rock on the right hand (and on the left). And after that on the day of excavating the excavators had struck against pick and pick, one against the other, the waters flowed from the Spring to the Pool for a distance of 1,200 cubits. And a hundred cubits was the height of the rock above the excavators.'[1]

Hezekiah's tunnel was known in Wilde's time, but the inscription was not discovered until much later, in 1909. When Wilde explored the village of Siloam he found the fifteen hundred Arab inhabitants 'a vicious, quarrelling and dishonest set of people' who had been the principal ringleaders in a recent rebellion at Jerusalem, when they emulated Joab's exploit by gaining access to Jerusalem through the tunnel, where it rose to the surface in the enclosure of the Mosque of Omar. He poked around amongst the tombs until, on sticking his head into one of the crypts, he was scared almost out of his wits by the wild unearthly scream of an old Arab crone who inhabited it. The noise she made became the signal for a general outcry; the other cave-dwellers rushed out to find its cause. Arabs rushed in every direction, and curses fell fast and heavy on the Nazarene and the Giaour. The whole troglodyte population of this living cemetery became as much alarmed as if he had got into the harem of the Pasha. Wilde beat a hasty retreat, and never again ventured into Siloam. What a pity he did not take his courage in both hands, as he had done in Egypt, and explore the fountain and tunnel! If he had done so, what a reward would have been his, in splashing through the pot-holes and shallows of that lonely conduit, with the pick marks of King Hezekiah's workmen on either side. If he had dis-covered, as he well might have done, the tablet and inscription, his name would have gone down in the archaeological history of Palestine as it has in that of Ireland.

[1] Translation by Professor Sayce, with words in brackets filled in from conjecture, as quoted in *Palestine*, by W. H. Bolton, London, Sampson, Low, Marston & Co., Ltd.

So excited was Wilde by the scenes he witnessed daily, and so perfectly absorbed his mind, that he felt himself insulated from the rest of the world. He felt the charm which is always felt by those who have seen Jerusalem from its surrounding hills, or stood beneath its ancient portals and mingled with its mourning, worshipping and quarrelling children.

On 25th March, 1838, they left Jerusalem, and soon the gravid _Crusader_ was headed for home. For Wilde it was really the end of this memorable tour, for although they stayed in Greece for a time on their way home, Egypt and Palestine had obviously been his Mecca.

On the morning of the 3rd of June the _Crusader_ entered Kingstown Harbour. The hour was early; the inhabitants had not yet stirred. A thick mist hung over Killiney Hill, and everything looked lonely and deserted. Still, it was to Wilde

'More dear in its storms, its clouds and its showers,
Than the rest of this world in its sunniest hours.'

CHAPTER VIII   D U B L I N

> '*Dublin is the second city in his Britannic Majesty's dominions, and may rank with the very finest cities of Europe for extent, magnificence, and commerce.*'
> James Malton, *A Picturesque and Descriptive View of the City of Dublin*—1792–9.

> '"*You came by the railroad?*" enquired Lord de Mowbray mournfully of Lady Marney.
> "*From Marham, about ten miles from us,*" replied her ladyship.
> "*A great revolution!*"
> "*Isn't it?*"
> "*I fear it has a very dangerous tendency to equality,*" said his lordship, shaking his head.'
>
> (Disraeli—*Sybil.*)

I

WHEN WILDE stepped ashore at Kingstown he realized at once that his own country compared favourably with any he had seen on his travels.

By this time he and the Meiklams were thoroughly tired of ship's fare, and no doubt their first act was to go to Hayes' Hotel and order breakfast. While eating they could enjoy almost as fine a view as any they had seen in Europe. About a hundred yards away the pier and harbour of Kingstown sheltered numerous sailing ships of various shapes and tonnage. The black hulk of a convict ship lay sullenly amongst them, sentinels pacing its deck to guard the unfortunates below decks, doomed to servitude in a foreign land. In perfect contrast was the Lord Lieutenant's yacht, and the *Crusader* herself, from which he had just landed. A fussy little paddle-steamer passing out of harbour he recognized as the mail-packet bound for Holyhead. In the Bay beyond, a fleet of merchantmen courted the morning breeze with wide-spread canvas, while

F

directly opposite lay the Hill of Howth, hazy blue in the pearly morning mists. It was a beautiful, busy and happy scene.

Breakfast over, Wilde and his companions made their way to the railway terminus, and took their seats in the train for Dublin. This railway, which had been designed by de Lesseps of Suez Canal fame, was one of the earliest in the United Kingdom, and consequently in the world. It was 'substantially and elegantly built' even to the provision of bathing-boxes for both sexes at Blackrock.

Crossing the old harbour of Dunleary they passed first through the rocky coast-road, under the bridge connecting the severed lawn of Sir Harcourt Lees, and through a tunnel under Lord Cloncurry's demesne of Maretimo, and beneath his lordship's

beautiful granite pavilions. Then Blackrock, followed by isolated sea embankments, until Old Merrion was reached. From here they went through rural country as far as Serpentine Avenue Station, after which the railway leaped across granite bridges and past distilleries and warehouses until finally they reached the city terminus at Westland Row.

This may have been the first time the Meiklams had visited Dublin. If it was, we may be sure that Wilde took great pleasure in acting as their guide. Architecturally, Dublin at this time was at its peak, a city almost entirely Georgian in character, as yet unspoilt by the dreadful desecrations of the following century. As now, its principal features were the Liffey, which divides it, and Trinity, the ancient university of one College, a walled city within a city.

Georgian builders had the grand conception, for they built streets and squares; not houses, isolated or in groups. Dublin Georgian can compare with any. Sackville Street, lying to the north at right angles to the seaward end of the Liffey, was then one of the finest streets in Europe. Travellers of the time say that London's Regent Street, although smarter in appearance owing to the houses being whitewashed, was nothing to it, and had no building to compare with the Post Office, with its portico of six fluted Ionic columns. Nelson's Pillar was considered to be at least equal in beauty to the Duke of York's column, although to our eye its square pediment seems incongruous. Sackville Street leads across the Liffey to Westmoreland Street and Grafton Street, the crowded and tortuous counterpart of Bond Street, with which in Wilde's time it could court comparison. All these streets were then as truly Georgian as the residential districts and slum areas are now. They bear testimony to the Wide Street Commissioners, who controlled the development of the city from 1757 to 1841, and to whom we owe most of the good qualities of the present city.

The quality of the public buildings dotted here and there amongst them did much to justify the claim that Dublin, then the second city of the empire, was, for its size, a more beautiful city than London. The Custom House is still Dublin's architectural masterpiece, but the Bank of Ireland, which not long before had housed the Irish Parliament, is a close rival. Situated in College Green, opposite the handsome front of Trinity, its chaste classical colonnades still give the heart of the city an air worthy of any capital in Europe. And there are many other buildings worthy of notice—fine cathedrals and churches, the Castle, with the old Bermingham Tower, Leinster House in Kildare Street, and the many town mansions once occupied by a resident nobility.

The residential parts of the city in Wilde's time were of corresponding quality, and here the wisdom and art of the Georgian builders was, and is, equally apparent. Great wide streets, of uniformly built houses, so long that the farther end is lost in the distant mists, intersecting to form magnificent squares, are the feature of Dublin. Most of the interiors were beautifully embellished with the cream of the eighteenth-century house-builder's art. Beautiful ceilings in rococo and Adams style, Bossi mantelpieces, and fine mahogany doors were everywhere. What a pity it is that so many of these fine streets are now slums, and that gasometers and cranes now ruin many a splendid vista! To stand in Mountjoy Square and gaze at the Custom House far away downhill is still an intellectual and artistic pleasure, but one sadly marred by the realities of the present day.

A revenant from the twentieth century would feel very strange in Wilde's Dublin. The buildings in the shopping streets would be as Georgian in character as the private residences still are. Ladies dressed in bonnets and flowing skirts, gentlemen in tall hats and tight-waisted coloured frock-coats pass by, some on foot, some on horseback, some riding by in their carriages. Our stranger would be struck by the number of carriages, and by the multitude of jaunting-cars, so characteristic of the country. He would at once notice the quality of the horses drawing them. Everywhere he would see an ostentatious display of handsome equipages, with servants in gaudy liveries, and in Grafton Street or College Green he might find a traffic block equal to anything of our modern times, in everything except smell and raucous noise.

But there was an obverse to the medal. In Merrion Square, St. Stephen's Green, or the recently built Fitzwilliam Square, he would see ragged wretches sitting on the steps, in melancholy contrast to the splendid houses with their magnificent carriages waiting outside. If he passed from Grafton Street into the Liberties beyond Great George's Street, he might fancy himself in the slums of mediæval Spain. Beggars, indolent for want of work, in rags, bare head and feet, wandering about or lying on the pavement, fit subjects for the brush of a Murillo. If he went to one of the Royal Dublin Society's cattle shows in Kildare Street he might even see the ragged urchins fighting for and eating the remnants of the turnips upon which the cattle had been fed. If he were of an inquiring disposition and wished to find the homes of these unfortunate creatures, he would find hovels and cottages in the Liberties and back lanes, where they lived in indescribable squalor and wretchedness. And, sad to relate, things are not much better to-day.

Dublin has undoubtedly declined during the last hundred years, although its population has increased slightly. This decline certainly started at the time of the Union in 1800, before which the presence of the two houses of Lords and Commons ensured that no less than two hundred and seventy Peers and three hundred Commoners were at least in occasional residence.

When, after the Union, the wealthy landlords departed to England, their place in the social life of Dublin was taken in part by the merchants and professional classes. If there was less real wealth, it was not at first apparent, for Dublin's citizens contrived to make a show of riches, of country houses and carriages with liveried servants, on a capital which in London would not have been considered sufficient for the purpose. The city grew larger, her streets and squares mellowed, but were not as yet allowed to moulder. The intellectual society, to which Wilde was soon admitted, was equal to anything which had gone before. Maria Edgeworth, Lever, Stokes, Graves, Colles, Hamilton—all are names which denote high achievement. And so it continued until well past the middle of the century.

II

On his return to Dublin, Wilde took rooms at 199, Great Brunswick Street, and started to practice general medicine and minor surgery. His health was still far from good, but no doctor starting in practice at the age of twenty-three is over-burdened with work for the first year or so.

In spite of his physical frailty, he had already developed a tremendous mental energy, a fierce intellectual urge which was to carry him to great heights before its fire died down, all too soon, in another twenty years. When patients were slow in coming, it was almost a necessity for him to find another outlet for his powers.

Fortunately, this was not far to seek. When he had been about to join the *Crusader*, Sir Henry Marsh had pointed out to him that the voyage offered an excellent opportunity for climatic and meteorological research. Not very long since, the famous London physician, Sir James Clark, had acquired a considerable reputation in this way. The book Sir James had written on the subject had brought him wide-spread recognition, and had given him a valuable fillip at the beginning of his career in London.

With the success of Clark's book in his mind, Wilde set to work as soon as he was settled in his new abode. In digesting the elaborate mass of materials he had collected he found much that was more suitable for scientific than for general consumption, and accordingly he prepared papers and lectures which he gave to various learned societies, including the Royal Irish Academy and the British Association. In this way he began a lifelong connection with these two bodies.

For Wilde the more important of the two was the Royal Irish Academy, a body which is in many ways the Irish counterpart of the Royal Society, but which includes polite literature and antiquities as well as science in its scope. During the whole of his career he took a leading part in its activities, and if, during his lifetime, his relations with the Academy were sometimes uneasy, he is now recognized as one of the greatest ornaments in its history.

III

The mental torpor which had affected Dublin after the passing of the Act of Union had not spared the Royal Irish Academy. Now, however, there was a renaissance of intellectual activity in Ireland, and the Academy shared in the general awakening. In the year 1827 two men had joined its ranks. They were both men of rare genius, and Wilde was fortunate enough to become closely associated with both of them for the rest of his life. One was George Petrie, a great archaeologist; the other was William Rowan Hamilton, an even greater scientist.

Rowan Hamilton was a man of colossal brain-power. At the age of seven he could read Hebrew; a few years later he had mastered Latin and Greek, four European and five or six Oriental languages. When he entered Trinity he had sent in an essay written in no fewer than fifteen languages, but by this time he had also developed a taste for mathematics. At the age of seventeen he had discovered in Laplace's *Mécanique Celeste* an error in the reasoning upon which one of the propositions was based. The writing of poetry was another of his interests, and he was awarded the Vice-Chancellor's Prize for English verse soon after his entrance to Trinity. Mathematics, languages, metaphysics, natural philosophy—nothing was beyond his powers. At the age of nineteen he read a paper to the Royal Irish Academy on the 'systems of rays' and predicted conical refraction. It was truly said that this paper had made a new science of optics.

While still an undergraduate, he was elected Professor of

Astronomy in Trinity College, and shortly afterwards he became Astronomer-Royal. He was knighted at the age of thirty, and twice received the Gold Medal of the Royal Society. He is now chiefly remembered as the discoverer of quaternions, a term which he first formally defined in 1844. His first book on quaternions was published in 1853, and the only man then living who could understand it was Professor Tait of Edinburgh.

In spite of Hamilton's great intellect he was a very human person. In those days the Academy met for dinner before the meetings, and Sir William could be at times a source of difficulty and trouble to the other members. He was one of those people who have, for some reason, a bad head for alcohol. Why

William Rowan Hamilton

some people can drink a bottle of whisky, or more, a day without showing it, and others not only become maudlin, but eventually find an early grave from half as much, is a mystery. Sir William Rowan Hamilton did not come into either of these categories, but what little he did drink on occasion went to his head. He often became violent when he was intoxicated, and some of his exploits when 'fighting drunk' are traditions in the Royal Irish Academy.

His domestic life was brightened by children to whom he was devotedly attached, none the less because his affection for them was sometimes combined with a detached speculative interest. 'That little boy,' he once said, pointing to a boy of about five or six years old, 'ran up to me the other day and cross-questioned me about the mysteries in the doctrine of the Trinity. "How," he demanded, "can there be three, and yet only one?" I answered: "You are too young for such matters; go back to your top." He flogged it about the passages a score of times, then returned to me and said: "I have found it all out—this is the explanation," and propounded his theory. "You are wrong," I answered. "You are too young to understand the matter; and go and play." He returned three times more, successively, and each time propounded a new explanation, and received the same answer. But now listen! His four explanations of the mystery were the four great heresies of the first four centuries! He discovered them all for himself. I did not give him the slightest assistance. What an intellect!'

Petrie, the leader of the antiquarian group in the Royal Irish Academy, was older than most of the men whose activities he directed, and twenty-five years older than Wilde.

By profession he was an artist, and a very successful one. Although he never painted in oils, his contemporaries thought very highly of him, and even compared him with Turner. He was elected a full Royal Hibernian Academician in 1828, when he became the only Academician who confined himself entirely to water-colours. In his later years he became President of the Academy. Yet, if the truth be told, he was not a great artist. His smaller works, pencil sketches and pen and sepia drawings, are charming, but his elaborate water-colours were deficient in design and limited in technique and execution. They appear stiff to modern eyes, with their bright chrome foregrounds and hard backgrounds of distant blue.

His archaeological reputation, however, rests on solid ground. His antiquarian and artistic interests developed on parallel lines. 'He was wedded to Art, but caused that lady considerable anxiety by his constant flirtations with her great-grandmother, Antiquity.' In his various sketching tours he found himself irresistibly drawn to the portrayal of ruined churches, dismantled castles and ancient crosses and dolmens, and the drawings he made are very valuable records. He was, above all, a careful and meticulously correct observer, and what his drawings lack in artistic merit, they certainly regain in archaeological value.

The chief of his many archaeological achievements was his essay on the Irish round towers. Before he wrote, all sorts of fantastic views were held as to the origin and uses of these towers, which are such a common and characteristic feature of the Irish countryside. They were supposed to be Phoenician fire-temples, observatories, gnomons, temples of Vesta, phallic emblems, centres for religious dances, and even homes of Persian Magi! Petrie demolished all these theories and showed that the towers were Christian bell-towers which could also be used as watch-towers and places of refuge. In some cases he found the actual year of their building from the chronicles. His evidence is abundant and conclusive, and beautifully arranged. The essay was published in book form, with many additions, under the title of *The Ecclesiastical Architecture of Ireland*. Its importance can only be appreciated by examining previous writings on the same subject.

Petrie had a third talent—music. In addition to his artistic

and literary work, he was also interested in the collection and preservation of old Irish music. He had sufficient musical ability to be able to note down Irish airs as they were sung or played to him during his journeys. He began this work in his youth, kept it up during his long life, and devoted his closing years to bringing out a volume of Irish music which was published in 1855.

His portrait, as a young man, shows a dark, sensitive face, with large lustrous eyes, and a sensitive mouth. A photograph in later life shows a small figure, with white hair and grizzled beard, but still the same luminous eyes. In his character the enthusiasm and the imaginative powers of the artist competed with the candour and caution of the man of science. These qualities are mutually antagonistic, and in Petrie it was the artist who became submerged. He was a kindly, lovable character, a little weak perhaps, and to some extent the puppet of factions, particularly in the restless and temperamental world of art. His memory rests securely upon his archaeological achievements, for he was as great an antiquary as Ireland has produced.

IV

Wilde's relative, the Rev. J. Wills, the literary-minded rector of a parish in County Wicklow, was an old and fast friend of Petrie. This association led to an event of the utmost importance for Wilde, for soon after his return from abroad Petrie invited his assistance in the investigation of a bone-heap at Lagore in the County of Meath. The bone-heap proved to be the first lake-dwelling to be found in Ireland, and the result of their researches led to the establishment of the crannog as a settlement type for Ireland. Wilde came back to the subject time and again. He excavated sites all over Ireland, and it is partly on the work he did on this subject that his reputation as an archaeologist depends.

The earliest Irish crannogs date from the late Bronze Age, although in Switzerland and other parts of central Europe dwellings built in lakes on a foundation of piles were used as early as the Stone and early Bronze Ages. In Ireland, according to Macalister, their structure was somewhat different. Here the foundations were made artificially by heaping stones and earth on a wickerwork raft. When this raft and its load sank to the bottom of the lake, more stones and earth were heaped upon it until an island arose in the midst of the water. Upon this island dwellings were built, probably for use by the more anti-social members of the community.

The Lagore crannog was, however, much more complicated in structure than this, for Wilde and Petrie discovered its framework to be composed of great oak beams accurately mortised and nailed together. It was sub-divided into compartments which contained vast quantities of bones, and various antiquities, warlike, culinary, and ornamental. This in spite of the fact that upwards of a hundred and fifty cartloads of bone had already been sold to Scotland for manure!

The site was indeed a rich one, and it is not surprising that it is still being investigated. Petrie and Wilde made arrangements to publish their results. Petrie was to describe the antiquities and Wilde the bones. Petrie, however, published nothing, and Wilde's paper was very short, 'owing, as it would appear, to some quarrel,' says Dr. Macalister. In spite of this, the Lagore finds provided material to Wilde for many years. The remains were, for the most part, placed on exhibit in the old Royal Irish Academy house in Grafton Street, and formed the nucleus of the present splendid collection of antiquities. When the Academy moved to its present premises in Dawson

The old R.I.A. House in Grafton Street

Street in 1851 they were dumped in subterranean cellars. The task of classifying and arranging them came to Wilde eventually, and they are now to be seen in the National Museum.

Following this, at the meeting of June 10th, 1839, with Sir William Rowan Hamilton in the chair, Wilde was admitted to membership of the Royal Irish Academy, a great honour for so young a man, but one which he had fully earned.

v

In considering Wilde's development at this stage one is immediately struck by his great versatility; not only by the depth of his knowledge, but by its scope. For a young medical man of twenty-four, his knowledge of the botany and zoology of his day was astonishing. Had his career been in Natural Science, it is certain that he would have made major contributions to the subject. During his travels in the Near East he had made careful and penetrating observations on the natural history of the countryside, and on the anatomy of the various animals he had encountered. Occasionally his nature led him into offering dogmatic opinions, subsequently proved to be incorrect, as when he argued that the *Amphioxus lanceolatus* belonged to the Mollusca, in opposition to William Yarrell, who correctly classified it as an archaic vertebrate in his *History of British Fishes*. On the whole, however, the biological papers he wrote at this time contained much that was new and important, and it is rather curious that in another year or so he gave up the subject completely, never to return to it.

One of his most interesting essays was on the subject of suckling in whales and other marine animals. It is common knowledge that whales are mammals, and that, like other mammals, they suckle their young. Their nipples are placed on the under-surface of the body, near the tail, and are in consequence usually submerged. The question therefore arises— how do the young ones breathe while they take the breast? For if they do not breathe they will drown.

Various solutions to the problem have been offered. Many people have seen porpoises gambolling along in front of ships, and have seen one or two young ones trailing behind them, holding tightly to their mother while she describes graceful arcs and curves, now in, now over the water. It has been suggested that the young ones breathe during the aerial part of their ambit. There may be some truth in this, although such activity hardly corresponds to the ruminating restfulness which is associated with suckling in most mammals. Others have stated that the humpback whale inclines her body to one side during the process, and lies in a relaxed condition with the posterior part of her form almost out of the water. But to this day nobody knows the real answer, at least in the case of whales.

Wilde approached the problem from the biological angle. He had dissected numerous porpoises while on board the *Crusader* (how his cabin must have stunk!) He recognized, as other anatomists had done before him, that the mammary gland of the whale consisted of a long central tube, which dilates widely before passing on to the nipple. This dilatation has always been understood to be used for the purpose of storing large quantities of milk, which could be rapidly injected into the young one's mouth. Wilde discovered that this injection was made by active muscular action on the mother's part, and he described the special compressor muscle she used for the purpose.

Wilde's work has since been confirmed, and his theory accords to a considerable degree with recent work on this interesting

subject. A modern description of the anatomy of the mammary glands of humpback whales is given in the *Natural History Report of the Terra Nova Expedition of* 1910, by M. D. G. Lillie, which clearly shows the position of the dilatation and compressor muscle described by Wilde. Further, Mr. Arthur F. McBride of the Marine Studios, Marineland, Florida, who has unrivalled opportunities of observing the habits of porpoises in an enormous glass-sided tank, has been able to prove Wilde's statement that the act of suckling is of short duration. He has watched the development of baby porpoises from their birth onwards, and is able to state definitely that when they are feeding they never stay below the surface for more than thirty seconds without coming up to breathe. In a personal communication he says: 'When nursing the young porpoise holds the end of its snout for about five seconds over the inverted nipple, which lies hidden in a fold in the blubber. By contraction of specialized muscles of the abdomen the parent forces the milk, which has collected in sinuses running lengthwise through the mammary tissue, into the mouth of the offspring. The whole operation can take place quickly, an obvious necessity, because the young porpoises very rarely remain submerged, at least here in the oceanariums, for more than thirty seconds.

'The peculiar structure of the mammary glands has been known for some time and it was believed that the modifications made possible the speedy ejection of the milk. This belief has been substantiated by the observations made here.'

The whole process and its mechanism is a wonderful example of the way in which these animals have adapted themselves to a marine existence, and it is no wonder that Wilde was interested in it.

VI

As well as reading scientific papers to learned societies, Wilde gave lectures to more public audiences at the Royal Dublin Society, and proved himself to be a ready and fluent speaker, who could put scientific facts in a popular way, and was not afraid to break a lance with any opponent, however eminent. He discoursed on such subjects as the anatomy of the chimpanzee, the gizzards of fish, and the unrolling of mummies. These might not be a great popular draw at the present time, but in the scientific renaissance of the early nineteenth century they excited great popular curiosity, and suited the spirit of the age. There was great scope for a lecturer in those days. The entertainment of the public had not become the vast organized business it is to-day; picture-houses and modern games as we know them were non-existent, and a lecturer of personality was assured of a hearing and an adequate reward.

Much of the literary activity of the day, particularly amongst the younger set, centred around Trinity College. *The Dublin University Magazine* had been started in 1833 by six 'Collegians', four of them undergraduates. Its ambition was to be the political and literary rival of *Blackwood* and *Frazer*, an ambition which was fully realized during the fifty or sixty years of its existence. In political feeling it remained conservative throughout its life, although many of its contributors, amongst them Wilde himself, gradually became more Nationalist in their leanings. As a literary organ it attracted all the important Irish writers of the early and middle Victorian periods. It had no official connection with Trinity, and there was nothing to prevent Wilde becoming a contributor, and he soon published in its pages the first of a long series of essays and articles. This was a plea for the removal of Cleopatra's Needle to England. Isaac Butt, the future 'Father of Home Rule', was then editor of the journal, and he extended much kindness and encouragement at the beginning of Wilde's career in Dublin. They were to meet under more sinister circumstances towards its close.

It was natural that Wilde should take his place in this circle. His friend Lever was then in Brussels, spending 'whole mornings discussing chalybeates and sulphurets with all the scarlet and pimpled faces that Harrogate and Buxton have turned off incurable', but 'thankful that the same faces were all suffering from the fat, grease, filth and acidity of German cookery', and that they were 'all, more or less, in need of me before they get their passports from Antwerp'. In spite of this he found time to send *Harry Lorrequer* in monthly parts, *à la Pickwick*, to the *Dublin University Magazine*. Lever's absence was a loss, but there were many others, many of whom were members of the College Historical Society. This body had first been founded in Edmund Burke's time in Trinity, and it had numbered amongst its early members such men as Thomas Addis Emmet, Wolfe Tone, Plunket, Bushe, Shears, and later, Robert Emmet. After the '98 rising it had disappeared, but a new College Historical Society was formed in 1839, while Wilde was still working on the manuscript of his *Travels*.

The nucleus of this society was formed by an extra-collegiate gathering which used to assemble at Radley's Hotel, in a large upper room with a bar across the middle, inside which non-members were not allowed. Within the bar were usually about thirty members, some Whigs, some Tories, and outside it perhaps double that number.

Amongst those inside the bar Wilde must have seen many times a short, thick-set young man of shambling gait, usually wrapped in a reefer coat. This was Thomas Davis. He must also have met many who were later to achieve lasting fame—Joseph Le Fanu, Ball, Jellett, and O'Hea. Although Davis was an infrequent speaker his companions already thought much of him, and when in March 1839 the College Historical Society was once more given an official status in Trinity, he became Auditor and delivered the closing address of the session in June 1840.

VII

Social circles in Ireland are always quick to acknowledge ability, and in Wilde's case his success was immediate. He was lionized by Dublin society, and was received everywhere with great attention, particularly perhaps by the women, who were always attracted to him. Why this was the case is hard to say, for his was by no means the figure of a Don Juan. It was about this time that the Victorian fashion for beards began. Whiskers began to sprout in every direction, starting as Dundrearies, amalgamating under the chin, and finally appearing on the lower lip as Imperials. Wilde went the whole hog, and grew a full beard, but no moustache, thereby concealing a weak chin which was no index to his character, but leaving exposed a sensuous mouth of which the same cannot be said.

If women were drawn towards Wilde, the attraction was mutual. Towards the end of 1838 his first child was born, without the usual social preliminary of wedlock. Who the mother was, or what her rank in life, is not known. The boy went by the name of Wilson, in this instance commonly supposed to derive from Wil(de's) son. He was educated and well provided for by his father, from whom he inherited much ability, but none of his parent's genius. He became a well-known and popular oculist in Dublin. He was received everywhere, but never married and died at the age of forty.

Wilde formed many other less clandestine female friendships, amongst whom were Mrs. Bowdick Lee, an adventurous lady of the period, celebrated for African exploration, and the famous authoress, Miss Maria Edgeworth. Miss Edgeworth was then in her seventieth year, a small, sprightly and entirely charming person, whose intellect was by no means dimmed. She came of a family which had been established in the County Longford since Elizabethan times, and she had, therefore, a territorial connection with Wilde, who hailed from the neighbouring county of Roscommon. Maria was then at the height of her fame, and universally beloved. She knew all the prominent literary people of the day, and her patronage was of great value to young Wilde.

In May 1839, Gideon Ouseley died, and was buried with much pomp in the family vault at Mount Jerome cemetery in Dublin.

January of the same year had seen the publication of Wilde's story of his Eastern journey. Its full title was very descriptive, if ponderous—*The Narrative of a Voyage to Madeira, Teneriffe and Along the Shores of the Mediterranean, including a Visit to Algiers, Egypt, Palestine, Rhodes, Telmessus, Cyprus and Greece. With Observations on the Present State and Prospects of Egypt and Palestine, and on the Climate, Natural History, Antiquities, etc., of the Countries Visited.*

It proved an immediate success. In the *Dublin University Magazine* Lever represents himself at a bookstall:

'Our book club in Castlebar wish to have—what the deuce is the name of it?—that new thing, you know, just come out.'

'*Traits and Stories?*—*The Commissioner?*—*The Mess?*—*The*——'

'No, no, we don't want those. It's a book of travels.'

'Wilde's *Madeira?*' . . .

It was published in two volumes, at the high price of twenty-eight shillings. Nevertheless, the public received it enthusiastically, and the first edition of 1,250 copies was soon sold out.

The success of the book was well deserved. In its pages we get a vivid picture of many sides of its author's character, for it is stamped strongly with his personality. It shows a young man whose eager courage enables him to surmount many obstacles of physical infirmity and danger, who allows nothing to stop him in his pursuit of knowledge. His material collected, he analyses and digests it until his opinions are crystallized, when he expresses them with all the vehemence of youth. His self-confidence is such that no authority is too high for him to attack if he thinks the views expressed are incorrect. Some of his conclusions have proved wrong in the light of subsequent knowledge, but at least he depends upon personal observation and has his facts right as far as he himself can observe them.

G

In spite of many scientific divagations, the book was really addressed to the general educated public rather than to the scientist. It is still delightful reading, and now has an added interest as an historical record.

When he started to keep a diary on board ship, Wilde intended it primarily as a commentary on the climate of the countries visited, and their suitability as resorts for invalids. The book brought him, in consequence, considerable fame as a meteorologist. It had, however, spread far beyond this, touching upon many subjects in a clear and penetrating way, and showing a shrewd, kindly appreciation of human character.

VIII

Wilde was obviously at the outset of a brilliant career. Although only twenty-five years of age, he had a distinguished academic career behind him, he had published a number of scientific articles, each of which was a genuine contribution to its subject, and he was well known as a public lecturer. Now he had published a highly successful book, for which he had received £250 from the publishers, a very reasonable sum of money at the currency value of the day, when the pound was worth about twice what it is worth to-day.

Three careers were open to him. The easiest was to continue writing travel books and lecturing, to give up medicine and embrace the profession of literature, as Lever was soon to do. The second was to become a pure scientist, and had he done so he would undoubtedly have been successful. He had, however, a contempt for 'closet zoologists', and loved the human side of his profession. He determined, therefore, to continue the practice of medicine, and to devote the proceeds of his book to post-graduate study. His attention had been drawn to ophthalmology by what he had seen in Egypt, and now he determined to specialize in diseases of the eye and ear. To this end he arranged to study in London and on the Continent.

Before doing this he joined the British Association and attended the meeting held in Birmingham in the summer of 1839.

He was introduced to the Association by two friends, the celebrated Dr. Pritchard of Bristol, with whom he had corresponded about the skulls he had found at Jerusalem, and Macartney, one of Trinity's most famous sons. Macartney was an old United Irishman who had taken up the profession of surgery to harden his heart and cure himself of lovesickness. Later, after his lady had relented and married him, he became Professor of Anatomy in Trinity College. Under his aegis Wilde read three papers at Birmingham on material gathered in his travels. One described an original method he had devised for the preservation of fish in their natural shape and colours, the others dealt with the ethnology of the Guanches of Madeira, and with the physical geography of the coast of Tyre. No less an authority than Sir Charles Lyell joined in the discussion on the latter subject, and he gave Wilde high praise.

Wilde enjoyed himself hugely at Birmingham. The scientists were on holiday, and nobody appreciates a party, good food and wine, more than your scientific man when in the mood for relaxation. The hospitality shown to the British Association was notorious. Some of the younger naturalists, led by Forbes, repaired daily for refreshment to an inn known as the Red Lion, Wilde amongst their number. This was the origin of the famous Red Lion Club, which still flourishes. Forbes gave them a constitution—the chairman was the Lion king, new members were cubs, those who organized the proceedings jackals. On rising to speak, sing or recite, members must roar and flourish their coat-tails. Other similar manifestations on the part of the audience showed approvement or the opposite. On a later occasion the famous Sir Joseph Hooker drank a wine-glassful of red ink at a Red Lion dinner before he appreciated the fact that it was provided for the purpose of signing the attendance book! Wilde attended the first session of the club, which was a tremendous success.

When these activities were over, Wilde proceeded to London. He took rooms in Carthusian Street, near Charterhouse Square, so as to be near the famous Moorfields Hospital, which stands to ophthalmology as the Rotunda does to midwifery.

CHAPTER IX

LONDON

*'My special breeding has been in the general skill of Chirurgerie. . . .
I left the greatest masses of that unmeasurable mysterie, as a heape
too heavy for my undergoing; to take up onely some particular pieces,
wherein I might the better proceed to some perfection; choosing to
walk in a right line, whose very beginning points to a certain end;
than to run in a ring, whose mazefull compasse foretells much paine
with little progresse, or a long journey without an Inne. . . . And
finding some defects in mine owne eyes, I chose their cure for my care,
that I might benefit my selfe first, and others after by mine owne
experience: unto this also I adioyned the helpe of Hearing by the
instrument, the cure of the Hare-lip, and the wry Necke.'*
Richard Barnster's *Breviary*, 1622 (as quoted in *A Short History
of Ophthalmology*, by Arnold Sorsby).

I

THE ROYAL London Ophthalmic Hospital, better known as
Moorfields, was founded in 1805, principally through the efforts
of John Saunders, aided by Richard Battley and John Farre.
Saunders had been assistant to the great Sir Astley Cooper.
Before he came to London his interest in the eye had been
awakened by Dr. Hill of Devonshire, to whom he had been
apprenticed, for Dr. Hill had the fortitude to remove cataracts
in those pre-anæsthetic days. After spending some years in
London, Saunders, in spite of his close association with Sir
Astley Cooper, found the way to promotion barred because
of his provincial apprenticeship. He, therefore, determined to
specialize in diseases of the eye and ear, and to this end he founded
Moorfields.

The time was ripe for his project. Napoleon had invaded
Egypt in 1799. After the destruction of his fleet by Nelson at
the Battle of the Nile, English troops were landed at Aboukir in
1800. Almost to a man they were attacked by 'Egyptian
Ophthalmia'—a mixture of purulent ophthalmia and trachoma.

Many regiments were so crippled that they were rendered unfit for service.

Egypt was evacuated by the British in 1803, and the disbanded troops spread the disease throughout Great Britain and Ireland. The medical men and hospitals at home were badly prepared to deal with such an immense increase in the number of cases. There was little provision for eye cases in the hospitals, students were taught little or nothing of the subject, and most cases were tacitly abandoned to the quack 'oculists'.

Thus, when Saunders established himself in practice in London there was a tremendous increase in the incidence of eye disease, but very few medical men competent to deal with it. Saunders and his associates filled the gap very adequately at their new hospital.

Saunders soon decided that diseases of the eye were more interesting and, incidentally, more profitable than those of the ear, and as a result, Moorfields became solely an eye hospital from the year 1807.

In making this decision, Saunders bequeathed an almost completely unexplored field of research to others. Wilde saw this, and profited by it, and eventually became the first and, in many ways, the greatest of English-speaking ear surgeons.

II

When Wilde attended the practice of the hospital it was a fine new building some eighteen years old. Tyrrell was at this time senior surgeon to the hospital, and Wilde worked principally with him and his brilliant junior assistant, Dalrymple. Tyrrell had achieved great fame as an eye-surgeon, but 'not without prayer and fasting'. It is recorded that when first attached to Moorfields he was such a clumsy and unlucky operator that he was debarred from performing major operations for a year. By steady, unremitting perseverance he became an excellent surgeon, capable of operating with either hand, an important matter in those days.

It is interesting to look at the practice of the hospital in Wilde's time. Operations on the eye itself were practically confined to the removal of cataracts and the making of artificial openings in the scarred and deformed pupils resulting from inflammation.

The old operation for cataract was the practice of 'couching'. This consisted in pushing the opaque lens downwards into the substance of the eye, leaving a transparent area for the passage of light through the pupil. This procedure, although it gave brilliant immediate benefits, was attended by grave after-results, usually involving the loss of the eye. It was, of course, beloved of the quacks, but not by reputable practitioners who had to abide by the results of their handiwork. They preferred the more difficult method of total removal of the lens, and extracted it in almost exactly the same manner as to-day.

Another method of treatment still in use in certain cases is what is called 'needling'. This consists of scratching the capsule enclosing the lens with a needle to admit the aqueous fluid which bathes it in front. This fluid then dissolves away the opaque lens. Much of the credit for the development of this operation goes to Saunders, who used it mostly in the case of children.

Removal of the eyeball was a most formidable procedure, only resorted to in the case of malignant growths. Hulke has left a description. 'The first excision of the eyeball that I saw, was to me, a novice, so horrible and distressing a scene that the impression it made still lingers in my recollection. No anæsthesia. The surgeon first passed through the eyeball a strong needle armed with stout silk, and knotting the ends, formed a loop. Next, with this he dragged forward the eyeball, and then scooped it out of its socket with a double-edged knife curved on the flat of the blade. This done, an assistant, who stood ready with a large brass clyster-syringe, checked the profuse bleeding by squirting into the orbit iced water. How different this from enucleation as now done!'

These operations, with other work such as the treatment of conjunctivitis, 'ophthalmia', trachoma and other superficial diseases of the eye, constituted the major part of the work of Moorfields in 1840. Prior to the invention of the ophthalmoscope in 1850, the interior of the eye was as black as the inside of one of Wilde's tombs. Nothing was known about diseases of the back of the eye during life, although questioners were seeking the cause of the luminosity in the eyes of animals and children, and beginning to doubt that animals with lustrous eyes could see in the dark. Glasses, as an aid to vision, had been known for many centuries, but were still not considered worthy of the attention of a physician. Consequently, most people had their glasses prescribed in the opticians' shops or by the quacks.

III

Wilde worked diligently for many months at Moorfields, but he did not forget his other interests. He found time to write a lengthy biographical sketch of Sir Thomas Molyneux, the first Irish medical baronet, from material supplied to him by Sir Henry Marsh. Molyneux was an interesting personality, and Wilde did him full justice in the memoir, which was published serially in the *Dublin University Magazine*. Molyneux had been a contemporary and friend of Dr. Steevens, of Sir Patrick Dun, of Newton, Hally and Evelyn, and of all the learned society of Dublin and London, and later of Holland and France. He wrote copiously on many subjects, including natural history and antiquities. Many of his works are very interesting, notably those on the structure of the Giant's Causeway, on the influenza epidemic of 1693, and on the Irish Elk. He held that no species of animal ever became extinct, but as he wrote before nineteenth-century geologists had unearthed the remains of ichthyosaurs, dinosaurs, and pterodactyls, and long before Darwin or Lamarck, we must forgive him.

Molyneux also wrote on 'Danish' monuments, on the London Pride, on Sperm Whales, and on the Irish Wolfhound—a subject which Wilde regretted he did not treat more fully. 'A sort of dog,' said Molyneux, 'peculiar to this country . . . being of the greyhound kind, and of so beautiful and large a make that for it's . . . goodly size it far surpasses all other dogs of the creation, and if compared to a *common* greyhound, shows itself of a truly *gigantic breed*; and we may further add concerning it, that the giant's stock of old is extinct, at least in these countries, so this gigantic dog is now so rare that in a few generations more I doubt not but 'twill be quite lost in these parts, and the species perish, for ought I know, off the face of the earth.'

In this prediction Molyneux was only too accurate, for the old Irish wolf-dog *has* disappeared from the face of the earth, and not a piece of its hair, skin or body-skeleton remains. Wilde had, however, already found a number of skulls in the Lagore crannog which proved the animal to have been of immense size, with a head about twelve inches long, and standing at least three feet high. It was, as Molyneux had said, a gigantic greyhound.

While in London Wilde spent much time at the Hunterian Museum, working on zoology and comparative anatomy with a tall, gaunt, clean-shaven young man with a massive head. This was the famous anatomist, Owen, who was then conservator of the Museum. Wilde found his companionship elevating and stimulating, as indeed might be expected, for he was a most lovable personality and the friend of Cuvier and many other great men.

Another young doctor with whom Wilde formed a lasting friendship was Robert Todd, who, like himself, had been a pupil of Graves. He had gone to London, as he himself said, 'without a sixpence to help himself', but he soon became one of the leading physicians in London. Years later, Thackeray wrote in the *Roundabout Papers*: '. . . As I am in this cheerful mood, I will tell you a fine and touching story of a doctor which I heard lately. About two years since there was, in our or some other city, a famous doctor, into whose consulting room crowds came daily, so that they might be healed. Now this doctor had a suspicion that there was something vitally wrong with himself, and he went to consult another famous physician at Dublin, or it may be at Edinburgh. And he of Edinburgh punched his comrade's sides; and listened at his heart, and lungs; and felt his pulse, I suppose; and looked at his tongue; and when he had done, Dr. London said to Dr. Edinburgh: "Doctor, how long have I to live?" And Dr. Edinburgh said to Dr. London: "Doctor, you may last a year."

'Then Dr. London came home, knowing that what Dr. Edinburgh said was true. And he made up his accounts, with men and Heaven, I trust. And he visited his patients as usual. And he went about healing, and cheering, and soothing and doctoring; and thousands of sick people were benefited by him. And he said not a word to his family at home; but lived amongst them cheerful and tender, and calm, and loving; though he knew the night was at hand when he should see them and work no more.

'And it was winter time, and they came and told him that some man at a distance—very sick, but very rich—wanted him; and though Dr. London knew that he was himself at death's door, he went to the sick man; for he knew the large fee would be good for his children after him. And he died; and his family never knew, until he was gone, that he had been long aware of the inevitable doom.'

We know that 'Dr. London' was Todd, but who 'Dr. Edinburgh' was, we do not know, although it most probably was Stokes. It was not Graves, for Graves predeceased Todd in 1853.

Another of Wilde's medical friends in London was the celebrated Sir James Clark, who was much in the public eye on account of the unfortunate case of Lady Flora Hastings. This young lady, who was one of the Queen's maids of honour, was noted for her acidulous tongue. She had aroused considerable resentment by her comments on the intimacy which existed between the Duchess of Kent and Sir John Conroy, the Duchess' Irish major-domo. Sir John was naturally annoyed, and when one day he noticed an alteration in Lady Flora's appearance, he commented crudely upon it, drawing the worst conclusions, for Lady Flora was unmarried.

Soon the rumour was public property. Lady Flora consulted Sir James Clark, and he gave it as his opinion that she was pregnant. Unfortunately both Clark and Conroy were wrong, for poor Lady Flora was suffering from a malignant abdominal tumour, which proved fatal in a few months' time.

The furore which ensued may be left to the imagination. Lady Flora's relatives, outraged and incensed, demanded that Sir James should be disgraced and relegated from his position as Court physician. But the Queen retained his services. After all, as somebody said, he had been a naval surgeon and therefore could not be expected to know much about these matters! A few years later when the Prince Consort died of typhoid, he was once more in trouble through his failure to make the diagnosis.

Clark has been portrayed as a futile, doddering old Court physician, trusted implicitly by the Queen, and refusing aid from his fellow-doctors. Nevertheless, he was no fool, as his record shows. He made no addition to medical knowledge, but he was an accomplished 'medical politician' like so many fashionable London physicians of later days. He helped in the foundation of London University, and in the reconstruction of the University of Aberdeen, and influenced Prince Albert, with whom he was on the most confidential terms, in making valuable alterations in the medical curriculum at Oxford and Cambridge.

His life was dogged by calamities. He first took up medicine because of his lack of success as a Writer to the Signet. He became a naval surgeon, and his first two ships were wrecked off the American coast. In the first of these shipwrecks many men were lost, and Clark, amongst the rest, suffered great privations. Then there was an interval during which he travelled widely on the Continent, accompanying a consumptive patient, much as Wilde had done. Later came the two cases we have just described. Yet he triumphed over all these catastrophes, and died, aged eighty-two, in 1870 in Bagshot Park, which the Queen had lent him for life.

He cannot be called a failure, for he made full use of the talents which had been given him. His writings make it quite clear that his greatest disability was a lack of brains, for which he cannot be blamed. In his early days, Sir James had made his name in much the same way as Wilde, by publishing an account of the climate, diseases, and medical schools of the countries he visited as medical attendant to his patient. Shortly afterwards, he settled in Rome, where he practised for five years. In the summer months he visited the mineral springs and universities of Germany and enlarged his acquaintance with the wealthy members of English society who congregated on the Continent for the sake of their health. When Clark returned to England, he soon became an F.R.S., a baronet, and physician to the Duchess of Kent. Queen Victoria made him physician-in-ordinary on her accession in 1837.

It is highly probable that the great success of Clark's publications on climate and disease had influenced Sir Henry Marsh in advising Wilde to follow his example. Wilde had, however, gone one better, for his *Madeira* was not only an interesting contribution to the subject of climate, on which little had at that time been written, but also an interesting and original travel book such as Sir James, for all his great success, could never have written. In his works on climate and on consumption, Clark had been assisted by a young man named William Farr, who was later to become famous as a pioneer in the infant science of vital statistics. There is no proof that Wilde knew Farr, but it is more than likely that he did, and indeed it is highly probable that Clark and Farr originally stimulated Wilde's interest in this subject. Twenty years later Wilde and Farr were acknowledged as the chief authorities on medical statistics in Ireland and England respectively.

Whether or not he was acquainted with Farr, there is no doubt that Wilde was on intimate terms with Sir James Clark, who was not slow to recognize the ability of the young man who had followed in his footsteps. With Maria Edgeworth, Sir James sponsored Wilde's entry into the exclusive London society of the time—the society of Blessington D'Orsay, of Lady Gore, and of Lady Morgan, the 'Wild Irish Girl'. They were an incongruous pair—the heavy, illustrious Scotsman of fifty-two with his brilliant society practice, and the quick-witted young Irishman of twenty-three or four who had already made a name for himself in both science and literature.

IV

After some months Wilde had seen enough of London, and he determined to move on to the Continental clinics. He went first to Vienna, which was already a famous centre for post-graduate teaching.

CHAPTER X

VIENNA

I

A HUNDRED years ago the population of Vienna was only about three hundred thousand, much the same as that of Dublin. Since then the number of its inhabitants has swollen to almost two millions, while the size of Dublin has remained more or less stationary. Vienna was then the capital of a vast, lumbering and ramshackle empire, for, after Russia, Austria was the largest state in Europe, bounded on the south by Turkey, who still held the Balkan countries, on the east by Russia, and on the north by Poland, Prussia and Bavaria. On the west the Austrian territory included the Italian provinces of Milan, Venice and Dalmatia. This enormous heterogeneous empire had a population of thirty-five million people, of every creed, race and language; Christians, Jews, Moslems, Croats, Slavs, Magyars, Italians, Bohemians and Germans. The whole state was ruled by a monarchy of the most absolute description. At the time of Wilde's visit the Emperor was Francis II, but Prince Metternich was the power behind the throne.

Vienna in 1840 had little of the baroque splendour of the modern city, and architecturally compared badly with the other European capitals. It was divided into the old, rather mean, fortified town, and the splendid new suburbs. The old town, or *Stadt*, was compact, more or less circular, and surrounded by a wall, with fosse and bastion. The court, with its impossibly haughty aristocracy—the *'crême de la crême'*—dwelt here, and amongst them some others not quite so exalted, perhaps even a wealthy banker or two. Here were situated the churches and museums, with the *Chancellerie de l'État*, the residence of Prince Metternich, and the embassies of Bohemia, Austria, Transylvania and Hungary. The palaces of the *'haute noblesse'* were here also, to be recognized by the coroneted coats of arms over their doors—the arms of Lichtensteins, Esterhazys, Starhembergs, Schoenbarns, Palfys, and many others. The focal point of old Vienna was formed by the cathedral of St. Stephen, rather than by the Chancellerie of the Empire in the *Burg Platz*, the residence of the Royal Family.

All these buildings were more interesting than magnificent, and they all suffered from being badly 'sited', as the architects say, because they were crowded too closely together. The university was also situated in the *Stadt*, but its buildings were not in any way remarkable. The most obvious outward sign of its presence was the numerous groups of students in flowing gowns to be met with daily on the ramparts.

The old town was surrounded by a green grassy belt, the *Glacis*, intersected like a spider's web by avenues and thoroughfares. Here the light-hearted Viennese spent their summer afternoons drinking lager beer and listening to the strains of Strauss and Lanner, just as their descendants do to-day in the *Prater*. The military manœuvred on the sward, marching and counter-marching in the quaint uniforms of a hundred years ago. Building was not then permitted in this green belt, but the city's growth has since swallowed it up. To-day the *Glacis* is represented by the *Ringstrasse*, a noble circular thoroughfare, whose beauty to some extent compensates Vienna for the loss of a lung.

Beyond the *Glacis* lay the *Vorstadt*, or suburb, far more populous than the parent city. This was the residence of the middle classes, the bourgeosie, the tradespeople and manufacturers, and the canaille,' said Wilde. In the *Vorstadt* was situated the *Allgemeine Krankenhaus*—the famous General Hospital of Vienna. It had been established towards the end of the eighteenth century by the Emperor, Joseph II, son of Marie Theresa, who in doing so had amalgamated most of the smaller hospitals.

Wilde took lodgings in the *Hohen Markt*, or *Am Hof* as it is now called. He found himself in a very different capital to that which he had just left. Winter was coming on, and preparations were going on on all sides. Outside every house lay logs of wood, and all day long the inhabitants were sawing them up. Heaps of sawn wood piled up, while the streets became almost impassable with tree-trunks lying in every direction.

As soon as he had established himself in his lodgings, Wilde visited the *Allgemeine Krankenhaus*. He found it to have three main divisions—the general medical and surgical hospital, the maternity institute, and the lunatic asylum. In general plan it was much the same as it is to-day, a vast quadrangle enclosing about a dozen minor squares. These squares contained gravelled walks, and were pleasantly planted with flowers and shrubs. A fountain played in the centre of each, and seats and benches were placed in the shade of the trees for the use of the patients.

The hospital had over a hundred wards, and contained well over two thousand beds. Up to twenty thousand patients were cared for annually. It contained the residences of the doctors, priests and professors, the pharmacy, chapels and libraries; the mortuary, museum, theatres and baths. Two or three hundred people availed themselves daily of the latter—not a bad proportion, even by present-day standards. The medical staff amounted to seventy-six persons, drawing salaries ranging from the equivalent of three hundred pounds per annum down to practically nothing. In addition, there were about fifty male nurses, and five times that number of female nurses, all of whom lived in the hospital.

When accompanying the doctors on their rounds of the wards, Wilde found much at which to wonder. The wards were cleanly, and heated by large iron stoves in the walls. He was surprised to find the beds were not curtained off, as at home, and that the nurses slept in the wards. When the principal doctor, the director, entered the ward, he expected the patients and nurses to kiss his hand. A servile habit, Wilde thought this, and he was glad to see that some of the younger men were satisfied if their inferiors did so verbally, by muttering '*Küss' die Hand*'. Bedside conversations between doctor and student were conducted in Latin, a practice which caused him some discomfiture for a time. Austrian students were very fluent Latin speakers, and he found their German pronunciation of the language disconcerting at first. Over each bed an account of the patient's illness, with his temperature and pulse-rate, was written on a tablet in flour and water each day.

Wilde thought the Viennese system of clinical instruction wholly admirable. It was only approached in the British Isles by Graves and Stokes, who had indeed originally brought their methods from Germany. No student could attend clinical lectures until his fourth year, by which time he had a solid grounding in the theory of his profession. Each student then in turn publicly undertook the examination and treatment of a case, under the watchful and critical eyes of the professor and the rest of the class, and he followed it daily through its course, the professor modifying his treatment if necessary. At the end of each six months' course the professors held public examinations, and gave or withheld certificates of proficiency to the students according to the results.

In theory this form of instruction was excellent. In practice it had the disadvantage that a class of two or three hundred were often crowded into one small ward. The resulting atmosphere is best left to the imagination. Wilde also noted, with disapproval, that the students were not encouraged to roam at will through the wards without supervision.

Associated with the surgical clinique was the Operators' Institute. Its object was to educate certain physicians and surgeons as operators, for curious as it may seem, one could apparently be a surgeon and not operate. The number of students in this operators' clinique was limited to fourteen. They were paid by the state, and did a two-year course of training on the dead subject. On receiving their special diploma they in most cases returned to the province of their origin, where they were compelled to serve the state gratuitously for some years. Sometimes, however, they were destined for higher promotion, either to the rank of professor, or to some position under the government.

Being blessed, or afflicted, with a curious turn of mind and keen observation, Wilde saw many differences in the clinical material in the wards to that with which he was familiar at home. He thought the fever mortality too high, for one-third of the patients died. Syphilis was milder in form than in Steevens', where he had seen the disease in a more malignant and fatal form than anywhere in his travels. Surgical operations were fewer, stone in the bladder was not so common as in Ireland, and industrial accidents were rare, because of the lack of machinery and heavy wheeled traffic in Vienna. These were the principal indications for surgery a hundred years ago.

The famous Professor Skoda had a private clinic where he taught diseases of the chest, which he studied by the new instrument, the stethoscope. Wilde took great interest in this, being, of course, familiar with Stokes' pioneer teaching on the same subject in the Meath Hospital. He thought Skoda was unrivalled as a diagnostician, but that he failed badly in treatment. His criticism was that Skoda's treatment was 'purely antiphlogistic'—consisting in blood-letting, leeching, blistering and purging, together with 'the use of a few simples'—digitalis and antimony. In this he was quite right, for although Skoda advanced our knowledge of diagnosis in chest diseases, he could not be compared to Graves or Stokes in the matter of treatment.

The great Rokitansky was in charge of the pathological department. Wilde said of him that he would soon have a European reputation. In fact, it was soon world-wide. Rokitansky was probably the first modern whole-time pathologist, for he never attended patients during their life. The body of every single person who died in the *Allgemeine Krankenhaus* was removed to the mortuary, the *Todtenhaus*. Here to the dead-house at eight o'clock in the morning came the professor, his two assistants, and his class. In the allotted space of two hours it would be impossible to examine one-half of the bodies sent down, but most of the interesting cases would be investigated carefully. Usually from four to six bodies were opened daily, the professor himself performing the postmortem, while one or other of his assistants sat at a desk taking notes to be preserved in the archives of the museum. Rokitansky was a forceful and explicit teacher. He was the leader of the young school of Viennese doctors, and with Skoda and Semmelweiss was about to place Austrian post-graduate teaching on the pinnacle which it has occupied ever since.

Progressive as Viennese medicine was in some ways, it was sadly behind in others. The treatment of lunatics was even worse than the treatment of women and infants. In Dublin, Swift's asylum had been from the first a humane and admirably conducted institution. In Vienna the madhouse was comparable only to the nightmare dungeons Wilde had seen in the Orient. It was divided into two sections, one for the harmless lunatics, the other, considerably larger, for the more violent cases. These latter were housed in a circular building, five stories high, with a courtyard in the centre. It was built, as Wilde said, with the object of securing the greatest number of insane within the smallest possible space. It remained a wretched, filthy prison, ill-ventilated and stinking. Of its two hundred and fifty frantic inmates, all were chained, and many were naked. The public was admitted at certain times to gaze on these wretched creatures, and human nature unfortunately being what it is, the show was never without an audience. Wilde went along with the rest, and was almost sickened with the horrors of what he beheld, as the brutalized warders lashed the apathetic maniacs to a frenzy in order to gratify the mob. It is to the credit of German medicine that in his subsequent travels in Prague, Berlin, and elsewhere, Wilde found the lunatic asylums to be models of humanity, order and cleanliness. The dreadful state of affairs in Vienna was probably due to the fact that lunacy was not a subject of medical teaching in the city.

It was about this time that Heinrich Hoffmann, medical officer in charge of the asylum at Frankfurt, wrote and illustrated *Struwwelpeter*. Can one imagine a better form of 'escapism' from an occupation such as his?

II

Wilde had gone to Vienna 'chiefly to improve his knowledge of ophthalmic and aural surgery'. The latter subject was even more neglected in Austria than at home, and otology in Vienna was a non-existent science. But the ophthalmic school of Vienna was already world-famous, and as soon as possible he introduced himself to Professor Rosas, who was then in charge of it.

Rosas was a Hungarian, and a worthy follower to the great Beer. The arrangement of his two wards was interesting. Each of these had twenty beds, each bed being curtained off and constructed in two halves, like those already used for fractures, the upper half being made to raise. The windows gave a soft light, and the walls were painted green, now recognized to be the colour most restful to the eyes. The patients bathed their eyes in a running jet of lukewarm water, and in this way cross-infection from one to another was avoided. Wilde recognized that this was a great improvement on the Dublin practice of using sponges common to all patients, which often resulted in infection of a man by his neighbour's disease.

Next door to the wards was the *Auditorium* or operating theatre. This was a large room with a raised platform railed off at one end for the examination of patients: it was, however, too small for the hundreds of students who congregated there, and in Wilde's opinion was inferior to the theatre at Moorfields.

H

Before an operation was performed, the unfortunate student in charge of the case, the *Ordinarius*, had to read a dissertation in Latin upon the case, its history, the object of the operation, and the hoped-for result. After operations were over the professor and his class visited the wards, and at other times they examined patients in the *Ambulatorium*, or extern department.

Wilde was impressed by the methods in use in this clinic where, as he very pertinently observed, the eye was treated as a part of the body, and not as a chemical preparation to be acted on by various chemicals and drugs without considering its relationship to the rest of the human frame. He found Rosas a 'steady and dexterous operator'. He made the old and comparatively easy downward section through the cornea in cataract extraction, in spite of the fact that his colleague Jäger had popularized, and was then practising, the upward incision which Santerelli had invented and which is in universal use to-day.

Jäger operated in the ophthalmic clinic of the neighbouring military hospital, the Josephinum Academy. Here the patients were the soldiery and their wives, and the students were future military surgeons. Latin was superseded by German as the colloquial language in this hospital. Wilde conceived a great admiration for Jäger, and in this he was right, as Jäger was a greater man than Rosas in spite of the inferior status of his appointment. Wilde may have been influenced to some extent by finding that Jäger agreed with the ideas he had expressed in the *Madeira* as to the causation of trachoma.

Jäger was the first to popularize the use of the phantom, or model, in teaching eye operations. On it he demonstrated the use of surgical instruments by manipulations as definite and accurate as those in use in engraving or in playing the piano. Each joint of every finger had to be in an exact position at every stage of the cataract operation, and every motion must be delicate and unembarrassed, and follow in its correct sequence. By this system he made the removal of the opaque lens almost a geometrical science. He was ambidextrous, and could complete the incision in both eyes within fifty seconds. It is interesting and curious to note the care which these early surgeons took to avoid pricking the side of the nose with the cataract knife—interesting because it demonstrates that the eye is less sensitive than the skin, and curious because it would seem an almost impossible thing to do if any sort of care was exercised to prevent it. Jäger's knife was particularly long and fine. He practised a form of treatment for pannus, a complication of trachoma. Wilde had never seen this treatment, although it had been employed for many years in Germany. It was based upon the old observation that an acute infection supervening upon a chronic sometimes results in the cure of the latter. Jäger's method consisted in nothing less than the inoculation of the pus from cases of ophthalmia neonatorum in the patient's eyes. The underlying idea is somewhat similar to the principle of vaccination, where cow-pox is given to prevent small-pox, but a more accurate analogy is the present-day system of giving malaria to a patient as a cure for general paralysis of the insane. General paralysis of the insane is a late manifestation of syphilis, and a very fatal one. The high temperature produced by the malarial parasite kills off the syphilitic organism in a number of cases, the patient is cured of G.P.I., but left with malaria. It is surely a justifiable procedure

'To jump a body with a dangerous physic,
That's sure of death without it,'

but when we reflect that the cause of ophthalmia neonatorum is now known to be the gonococcus, Jäger's physic seems just a little too dangerous.

Wilde saw Jäger treat two patients by this method; an officer and a private, both 'of scrofulous habits' and in low health. In each case the cornea was so greatly inflamed as to resemble a piece of red cloth, and very raised and swollen. Both had been blind for months, or years. Jäger infected them by placing a tuft of camel hair soaked in pus from a case of ophthalmia neonatorum between the eyelids. By the following day both patients had a tremendous reaction, with great swelling of both lids. The conjunctiva swelled to such an extent that its turgescence had to be relieved by snicks with scissors; each cornea became dull, grey and sloughy. The lids became purple, and the upper swelled up and overhung the lower. Pus squirted out in all directions when the lids were forcibly drawn apart. It was a truly heroic treatment. Leeches, purging, blistering, fomentations, and the other usual 'antiphlogistic' remedies were resorted to, and three months later, after several fresh attacks of inflammation, both men were discharged, 'although much broken in health, free from pain in the eyes', and with a certain limited amount of vision, which was probably soon lost. Wilde spent much time with Jäger and Rosas, and did practical courses in eye surgery with both of them. The work done and the methods employed met with his hearty approval, as indeed they well might, for the Vienna school of eye surgery was already world-famous.

It was, however, otherwise with the midwifery department, which compared very badly with the corresponding school in Dublin. The organization of Viennese midwifery at this time was extraordinary, and well worth a detailed description.

The *Gebäranstalt*, or maternity hospital was a self-contained department of the *Allgemeine Krankenhaus*. It was freely availed of by all grades and classes, from the patrician to the serf. Private rooms were provided for those who could pay for them, and for those who could not afford a room to themselves varying degrees of luxury were provided, according to their means. There were also free wards, to which women were admitted without paying anything whatever for their upkeep. In this, the *Maternité* differed from the other departments of the hospital, where every patient had to pay his way, or else be provided for by his local authorities.

The strictest secrecy was observed about every admission to the house. The entrance into the paying wards was at the end of a passage between two high blank walls. At the end of this cul-de-sac was a small door, with a porter in attendance by day and night. Ladies might present themselves masked, veiled or disguised in any way they liked. They might enter at any period of their pregnancy, and remain as long after delivery as they wished. No awkward questions as to identity were asked, but every woman had to write her name and address upon a sheet of paper, which she folded over and sealed —this being before the use of envelopes. The physician in charge then wrote the number of her room and bed upon the folded sheet, which was then placed in the locker beside her bed. It remained there until she was about to leave hospital, when it was returned to her unopened. Its purpose was to prove evidence of her identity to her friends and relatives, or to the police, in case of her death.

Once in the paying wards, the woman found complete

sanctuary. The law itself could not enter. Nobody but the doctor could come in, except at the patient's desire—not a husband or father, not even a nurse. The patient might, if she wished, remain veiled during the entire period of her stay in the hospital, so that if she wished she might enter the hospital, be delivered, and depart without her name being known, or even her face being seen by the physician or attendants. On the other hand, if she cared to, she could bring in her own servants and linen, or be attended by a consulting physician unconnected with the hospital. After delivery she could carry her baby away with her, but if not disposed to do so she could send it to the foundling hospital.

The free part of the *Maternité* was remarkable in that it had two wards set aside specially for those actually being delivered. In this Vienna anticipated Dublin, where the Rotunda had as yet no special labour ward. These wards contained eleven beds each. There were also three large wards containing, in all, one hundred and ten beds for women awaiting delivery, eight wards with altogether two hundred and fifteen beds for those who had had their babies, and two wards, with thirty-seven beds, for cases of fever and other puerperal complications. In all, there was the very respectable total of three hundred and eighty-four free beds, and fifty-seven private beds. The number of cases delivered annually was about four thousand five hundred.

It was laid down that all unmarried pregnant women who wished free treatment in the hospital must get it, on the production of a certificate of poverty. Not only this, but if they wished to be admitted secretly they must be admitted even without this certificate; and secrecy was observed quite as rigorously as in the pay wards. For married women, on the other hand, a certificate of poverty was necessary if they wanted free admittance, which was rather hard on the more respectable mothers. Ladies who left things a bit late, as ladies are apt to do, were admitted immediately and their circumstances inquired into after the emergency was over. Wilde said that 'females' were frequently delivered on the *Glacis* on their way to hospital, but this need not have surprised him. Human nature does not really change much in a hundred years, and when a student he must, at least occasionally, have done a like service for the ladies of Dublin in the neighbourhood of Nelson's Pillar.

Each woman delivered in the free wards, except those whose children had died, was compelled to go into the foundling hospital for two months, to nurse her own and one other baby. The second child was usually an unwanted baby from the paying wards, but occasionally one whose mother had died.

Why was all this secrecy observed? Obviously to protect unmarried mothers, and check infanticide. The number of illegitimate births in Vienna at this time was truly amazing—the proportion of illegitimate to legitimate births being 1 to 2.24. In the provinces the proportion was less. Carinthia, where the number of illegitimate births is still the highest in Europe, led the way with 1 to 3.2. These figures were, however, easily surpassed in Munich, where, in 1838, the number of illegitimate *exceeded* the legitimate births by 270! And this in a city so prudish that smoking in the streets was prohibited!

From the humanitarian point of view one cannot but approve of the way in which the unfortunate unmarried mothers were looked after in Vienna. Nevertheless, it does seem to have put a premium on illegitimacy. The laws of the time in Austria put every sort of obstacle in the way of poor people who wished to get married, and consequently single women, even of the more well-to-do classes, were hardly blamed for becoming pregnant. In the sixth or seventh month of her time the woman applied to the Lying-in Hospital, alleging her poverty. If she was unmarried, she was received without further ceremony. She was given clothes to wear, and her own were carefully kept for her until her departure. In the summer she had handsome gardens to walk in, in the winter she lived in a comfortable, well-heated ward. Here she spent a couple of months as pleasantly as might be, and no work was required of her, except to assist in keeping her ward clean. If she escaped the very real perils of childbed and puerperal fever, she was sent to the foundling hospital to perform her nursing duties for two months, and given more clothes to wear while doing so. On her departure she was given a small amount of money, and assisted to find a post as wet-nurse in some aristocratic family, for very few of the high-caste Viennese ladies could be bothered to nurse their own children. It is small wonder that many of the women found their way back to the hospital, time and again. Most of them were low-class, ignorant peasant girls from the provinces, scavengers and female labourers—the majority employed as mason's assistants, 'hod-women', according to Wilde.

III

Connected with the non-paying part of the *Maternité* was the Practical Obstetric Clinique, for the education of accoucheurs and midwives. This was divided into two separate departments, one for the education of students, the other for the nurses. No stranger was allowed into the nurses' department, but any physician could enter the first and attend the professors' classes.

The fearful ravages which puerperal fever made annually did not escape Wilde's notice. 'The doctors did not consider it as infectious,' he said, 'and, therefore, no precaution is ever taken to prevent its spread by cleansing, fumigating, whitewashing, or shutting up certain wards where it has particularly prevailed for any length of time. I myself have seen a newly-delivered woman placed in a bed scarcely yet cold, in which a death from puerperal fever had taken place not two hours before!! From my own observations I am inclined to attribute the frequency and fatality of this terrible scourge to the want of proper ventilation, in addition to the necessarily crowded state of the wards, and to the most unjustifiable practice that I have just detailed. In order to preserve the proper temperature during the cold season, it is necessary to keep a great number of stoves lighted; there are also double windows to the wards, and as every chink and crevice that might admit the cold (and with it a fresh supply of good air) is closed with the most scrupulous attention, the air must become in a short time exceedingly impure; and the fact that puerperal fever appears epidemically, and generally in the winter and spring of the year, confirms this idea of at least one of the probable causes of its destructive influences.

'I have constantly remarked four and five bodies in the dead-house, for several successive mornings, that had died of puerperal fever: these the stranger may at once recognize by the extensive and deep blister-marks on the inside of the thighs. The bodies of these poor females, many of whom were young and handsome, present a sad spectacle even among that vast throng of breathless carcases. Vesication of the thighs by the most powerful means forms one of the chief remedies in practice for this disease; and had it proved effectual even in mitigating these maladies, or lessening their mortality, one could not well object to it, but I believe it has not had this effect, while the torture it inflicts is of the severest kind, as blister over blister is frequently applied. In those who have recovered I have seen some of the worst sloughing sores I ever beheld from its effects.'

When we consider that these words of Wilde's were written long before the advent of antiseptic surgery, we realize how remarkable they are, although it was not the first time the contagious nature of puerperal fever had been pointed out. At the age of twenty-four Wilde already had an insight into the realities of his profession, not only beyond his years, but far ahead of his time.

He thought little of the Vienna midwifery school and did not hesitate to say so. 'The present professors in the midwifery clinique are Doctors Klein and Bartsch, neither of whom have done much to advance the science they profess, although so vast a field for observation and research lay open to them.'

There can be no doubt but that Wilde's strictures on Viennese midwifery and its exponents were quite justified. To the honour of the school it can be said that this state of affairs was soon changed. The manner in which the reform came about forms one of the most fascinating chapters in medical history.

Amongst the more junior Viennese maternity specialists in Wilde's time was Dr. Ignaz Semmelweis. Wilde knew him well, and afterwards corresponded with him for many years. He it was who was destined to discover the cause of puerperal fever, although not until seven years after Wilde's visit to Austria. We have seen how the Practical Maternity Clinique in Vienna was divided into two parts, one for medical students, the other for midwives. The midwives were at least socially clean, but the students often came into the wards with their hands covered with all the detritus of the dissecting room. And the mortality in the students' department was much greater than that of the midwives' wards.

A colleague of Semmelweis' died of blood-poisoning resulting from a dissecting wound. As Semmelweis watched the *post-mortem*, he realized that the appearances presented were exactly the same as those he had seen in patients who had died from puerperal fever. It was not long before he realized that many of the puerperal patients in the students' wards must have been infected by material carried from the dissecting room.

In this extraordinarily fortuitous way the cause of puerperal fever was found. Viennese midwifery had quite accidentally performed a full-scale experiment with a control. One may feel that with such a wealth of clinical material as Vienna unfortunately possessed the truth was bound to come out in time, yet it took the genius of Semmelweis to discover the obvious.

He immediately insisted upon the strict personal cleanliness of the students and on making them wash their hands in chloride of lime, just as Wilde had recommended. In this way he reduced the puerperal mortality by the very considerable margin of six per cent. In spite of this achievement, and notwithstanding the logical nature of his argument, the doctors of Vienna and elsewhere did not believe in his teachings. With the exception of a few men such as Oliver Wendell Holmes, his views were not accepted until the coming of Pasteur and Lister. He died, disillusioned and insane, in 1865. Many brilliant obstetricians came after him in Vienna, but he is still the greatest of them all.

High as the mortality was in the *Maternité*, that of the Foundling Hospital connected with it was far worse. It had been founded in the same year, 1784, with the object of caring for illegitimate children, and removing as far as possible the social disabilities under which they suffered. It also received poor children whose parents could not afford to keep them, and unwanted children of the more well-to-do classes.

Wilde found the hospital clean and orderly, but insufferably noisy from the crying of the children. 'As soon as one infant commences crying, it is the signal for a general squall from all in ear-shot of it.'

Epidemics, mostly of gastro-enteritis, created great havoc in this hospital. The mortality was terrible. No less than seventy-three per cent of the children admitted in the five years before Wilde's visit died. It had been worse, for at the beginning of the century the mortality was actually ninety-five per cent.

Wilde saw two practices which he, very properly, thought contributed to this state of affairs. During the first year or eighteen months of life the unfortunate children were swathed like Egyptian mummies, by bandages bound round their pillows, so that it was impossible for them to move arm or leg. Each child, in addition to its ordinary feeding, was provided with a comforter consisting of a piece of linen stuffed with bread and milk. The food in this was supposed to be changed every twenty-four hours, but human nature being what it is, in many cases it was only renewed after many days. This piece of fermenting filth was stuffed into the child's mouth at every opportunity. Hot one minute, cold the next, and always saturated with saliva, no wonder it was a most efficient means of propagating disease.

In this hospital there was no basket or trough outside the building in which unwanted and unknown babies were clandestinely deposited before their admission. Although strict secrecy was observed, the identity of each child was known, and a receipt for it given to the mother. If she wished, she could see it again at any time, if the child survived. There was one exception to this—no Jewess could ever again see or hear anything of her child.

Should a child manage to survive, its future was looked after by the state. Most of the males found ready foster-parents among the peasantry. According to the conscription laws, each family must provide one soldier, but an adopted child was acceptable. Wilde thought the Austrian army must be composed almost entirely of illegitimates!

Before condemning the Vienna Foundling Hospital too hastily, there are a few facts which must be taken into consideration. The first is that the institution was founded with philanthropic motives to remedy the great public evil of infanticide. Foundling hospitals are an impracticable idea. If institutions on the same scale existed to-day, the mortality would still be tremendous. The difficulties of dealing with epidemics in children's hospitals are considerable, as many of us know to our cost, and it must be remembered that children's hospitals are not foundling hospitals. High as the mortality statistics were in the Vienna institution, they did not nearly come up to those in the Dublin Foundling Hospital, where in the twenty years before 1796, of 10,272 children sent into the infirmary, only forty-five came out alive. And we have heard grisly tales of asylums in wintry Russia, of barns stacked high with tiny corpses, waiting until the snow melted and the ground became sufficiently soft for them to be buried.

IV

Viennese society at this time was the most exclusive, autocratic and snobbish in the world. Naturally enough Wilde did not see much of its stratosphere; nevertheless he met many interesting people. With the *Madeira* as his passport, he called upon the famous Orientalist, the Baron Hammer-Purgstall, who was one of the old nobility and a protégé of Metternich. Baron Hammer had had a successful career as a diplomatist in the East, where he had been sent because of his knowledge of the Turkish, Arabic and Persian languages. He later became court interpreter, but resigned this post in 1837 on inheriting various estates. When Wilde met him he had just finished his famous *History of the Ottoman Empire*. His work is said to be slipshod and inaccurate. He has been called a charlatan, and a 'witty driveller', but he must have been more than this, for during his life he published nearly three hundred volumes, writing in Greek, Latin, Italian, French, English, Spanish, Russian, Turkish, Persian and Arabic!

The Baron received the young man with due hospitality, and although the two really had little in common, they saw much of each other for a time. What they talked about, goodness knows, for Wilde was really an anatomist and oculist, and Baron Hammer was so steeped in the East that he lived more like an Asiatic than a European. Wilde was much impressed with the beautiful binding of his Persian and Arabic books and manuscripts, but their contents must have been double-Dutch to him. Most likely a bottle of wine and capacity for listening were the bonds between them.

Wilde, as usual, had lady friends, the more respectable being his countrywoman, Lady Talbot, and the celebrated Madame Ottilie von Goethe. In their company he attended many balls and carnivals, resplendent scenes of gaiety with ladies whose *décolletage* was brilliant with diamonds, and men in every variety of uniform, naval, military and diplomatic, from every country in Europe and many of those in Asia.

Wilde was still but twenty-five, and was really more at home with the students than in the more sophisticated society of his elders. Austrian students were a quieter lot than his friends at home, for the repressive government controlled them with a heavy hand. The *Burschenschaft* society of students, which Lever admired so much in Germany that he introduced it to Dublin, was not permitted.

There was, however, plenty of cheap amusement for the students and the masses. Dancing and smoking provided the most of it, in the *Goldenen Biern*, the *Volksgarten*, or the *Eliseum*. The *Eliseum* seems to have corresponded to the basement of the modern *Rathaus*, for it consisted of a vast number of cellars excavated beneath several streets. These cellars were fitted up to resemble various quarters of the globe, and were capable of entertaining several thousands of people each night. The decorations, bands, dresses, and even the temperature of each of these fairylands was adjusted to correspond with the original. Here the music of the fiddlers, the jesting of the clowns, the clink of glasses and the beaming good humour in the faces of the light-hearted Viennese and their ponderous *Frauen* and buxom daughters made a most attractive scene. Admission cost but fourpence, and yet Wilde seldom went there without seeing some of the nobility—perhaps even a royal archduke.

As to dancing—Orpheus himself must have been a *Wiener*, or at least have started them off, and if he should return to earth, he will find they have never stopped since he left. Everywhere and always, but particularly during the Carnival season, they danced incessantly and well, pausing but to eat and drink, which they did with equal fervour. One feels that in those days it needed but the sound of the first scrape of the fiddle of Strauss or Lanner in any place or season to start all who heard it dancing—the coachman would leap from his carriage, the butler from his pantry, the laundress would desert her basket, and all—peers, priests, professors, waiters and washerwomen, Turks, Jews and Gentiles—would rush into each other's arms and waltz themselves into a jelly.

This is not a typical picture of an oppressed people, and yet the rulers of the land were riding for a revolution. Trouble was brewing, because the government thought the best way of ensuring peace was to keep the people in the darkness of ignorance. Scientific knowledge, thought Metternich and his ministers, was dangerous for the multitude, and allied to subversive doctrines of equality and liberty. Consequently, in spite of the magnificent collections in the galleries and museums, art and science were at the lowest ebb they had been for years.

The scientists of Vienna recognized their plight. They saw that one of their chief disabilities, with the discouragement of travel, was the lack of an Academy of Science, but the government set its face strongly against this, thinking that by encouraging the progress of science they would foster a revolutionary spirit in the country. Wilde saw the folly of this idea, and commented forcibly upon it.

v

When Wilde had completed his six months' course of practical eye surgery, he set off to visit the German capitals before returning home. His first visit was to Bavaria, which was then an independent state. He found a lovely country, of wooded mountains and rushing streams, in the midst of which a worthy capital was rising, for King Ludwig I of Bavaria was rapidly transforming Munich from a homely German town into one of the most elegant cities of Europe.

Ludwig I was the first of the three mad Ludwigs of Bavaria, the last members of the Wittelsbach dynasty, which had ruled the country for a thousand years. His son, Otto, was King of Greece, having accepted the crown which Byron refused. The national colours of Greece are still the blue and white of Wittelsbach, but apart from this there are few reminders of the reign of King Otto to be found in the country.

King Ludwig I was more than eccentric. He had a passion for the antiquities of Greece and Rome, and when Wilde visited Munich he was busy pulling down the old houses in his capital and replacing them with grandiose buildings in the classical style. He ransacked the east of Europe for ancient marbles and statuary, grudging no expense to pay for them and for his extravagant building schemes. And yet, while the *Ludwigsstrasse* was being laid out, and magnificent palaces were springing up around Munich, in his private life he was miserly and sordid. He dressed in the oldest clothes, and went about amongst his workmen unrecognized. He loved his children, but was niggardly enough to feed them on black bread. He was an affectionate husband, yet, like Wilde, he ran after women all his life. He was a just and benevolent ruler, who loved his country and his people, and yet he was weak enough to throw both away for the sake of Lola Montez, the Irish-born courtesan who was the last of his many mistresses.

Wilde found much to interest him in Munich. He would have found more had he been able to visit the *Schönheits-Galerie* in the Royal Palace. He would have found portraits of no fewer than thirty-six young ladies whom Ludwig was interested in. They show the catholicity of Ludwig's taste, for the sitters vary in every conceivable way, in shape and size and social standing. They may be dark or fair, peasant or patrician, Lady Milbanke or a tradesman's daughter, but they have one common factor, for all are young and beautiful. Nobody who visits Munich should miss the *Schönheits-Galerie*.

Wilde went on to Prague, where he stayed with Count von Thunn, whose friendship he valued for years. From there he proceeded to Dresden, where he was received by the famous anatomist, Carus, and by Seiler, the physiologist. He then studied for a month or two at Heidelberg before going on to Berlin.

At Berlin he studied surgery under Dieffenbach, who has been called the 'father of plastic surgery', for his speciality was the making of new noses, lips, cheeks and eyelids. Many of his achievements were really remarkable, for, of course, he operated on fully conscious patients without anæsthesia, but not all his work was sound. Wilde saw him performing a particularly brutal operation he had devised for the cure of stammering in children. It consisted in excising a wedge-shape portion of the back of the tongue. The mutilation may have cured the stammer, but, as somebody has said, so also can the hangman cure indigestion.

In Berlin Wilde found his letters from Maria Edgeworth opened every door. He read a paper on Irish Ethnology to the Berlin Geographical Society, where it attracted considerable attention. Amongst the distinguished audience, which included von Buch and Carl Ritter, was no less a person than the Baron von Humboldt, then living in high favour at the Prussian Court. Humboldt at this time was writing his *Asie Centrale*, but he found time to show much kindness to Wilde, and introduced him everywhere. Wilde also met the British Ambassador, Lord William Russell, elder brother of Lord John Russell, who was still Prime Minister of England. Wilde made the best of the meeting, but they had little in common and he felt much more at home with the old Baron, who had done so much and travelled so much, whose interests were so much more like his own.

Before leaving Berlin, Wilde, at Humboldt's instigation, sent the King of Prussia a copy of the *Madeira*, which was acknowledged by an autographed letter of thanks. It remained ever after one of Wilde's most treasured possessions.

On his return journey he visited Brussels in order to visit Lever, who had temporarily settled there. Lever was in the middle of writing *O'Malley* at the time, and after a first delightful day of reunion he pushed Wilde into an enormous four-poster, and threw a bundle of proofs at him for his opinion. It is recorded that Wilde's opinion was soon shown by the ponderous bed shaking in every joint from his immoderate laughter at O'Malley's freaks.

Wilde now set his face homewards to begin his life's work in Dublin. Before taking him finally back again, let us look at the changes wrought by a few years in the actors and setting of the scene through which he has just passed.

By 1848 there were mutterings of revolution in Austria. Metternich had fled for refuge to England, but before his flight he had been compelled to establish the Academy of Science for which Wilde had pleaded so strongly, with Baron Hammer as its first president. Semmelweis had made his pioneer observations on the cause of puerperal fever. And poor Ludwig of Bavaria had been tumbled from his throne by the people he loved so well, for the sake of a beautiful dancing-girl with Irish blue eyes. Poor, ineffectual Ludwig! And poor Lola!

CHAPTER XI   O C U L I S T   A N D
                 A U R I S T

' *That the age we live in is one fraught with interest, and hastening
us to the dawn of great events, is a fact the most apathetic must admit.*'
                    Wilde's *Narrative of a Voyage, &c.*

I

THESE SENTIMENTS would come naturally enough from
any young man at the outset of his career. In Wilde's case
their truth has been proved by history.

It was not until the beginning of Victoria's reign that the
modern world began to emerge from the ashes of the squalid but
extraordinarily picturesque eighteenth century. The most obvious
sign of the change was the extensive network of railways which
had spread over the British Isles.   The *Great Western* had
crossed the Atlantic under steam, and the propeller, later to
reach its apogee in aeroplanes, had made its first appearance
in a small steam launch on the Regent's Canal.   Mining and
other industries were progressing in a manner which forecast
the industrial revolution, which was so greatly to alter the
relative wealth of England and Ireland.

Drama, literature and art were flourishing.   Landscape painting
in particular entered on a glorious phase of activity.   Constable
and young Bonington, whose limpid, luminous colour alone
stamps him a master for all time, were gone, but Turner, de
Wint, Copley Fielding, Prout, Cotman and David Cox were
at the height of their powers, and their work furnishes a complete
answer to those who think of early Victorian art as typified
by Landseer and Leslie.   In literature Tennyson, the Brownings,
Disraeli, Lytton, Matthew Arnold, and a host of others were
beginning their work, while Maria Edgeworth and Carlyle
remained to form a link with Regency days.   Dickens had
his first great success with the *Pickwick Papers* in 1837, and
Lever's *Harry Lorrequer* came a year or so later, although

Thackeray's *Vanity Fair* did not appear until 1847. Curiously enough, there was a dearth of musicians. Composers were scarce, and executants more so.

It was a young and fresh and vigorous world, and many traces of the ribald past remained. Duelling was still common, and bull-baiting was occasionally practised. Cockfights were attended by noisy crowds, and public executions were still looked upon as a form of amusement. The old-time prize-fights, with bare fists and unlimited rounds, were still popular with the people. All these things are very coarse and cruel, no doubt, to our eyes, but after all what right have we to criticize our ancestors?

The feminine costume of the period was entirely charming.

In many ways it is farther removed from modern fashions than the dresses of the Regency, but to us this makes it all the more picturesque. There are many delightful portraits in existence of the young ladies of the time, often painted in water-colours, carefully drawn and delicately coloured. The subjects all have a gracious old-world fragrance, of ringlets, old lace, ribbons and bows. Tight, low-cut bodices and short sleeves lengthened by flounces of lace were the vogue. Skirts were full and long, although crinolines did not make their appearance for ten or twelve more years.

Masculine attire was gradually approaching the drab sobriety of mid-Victorian times, which has remained with us ever since, in spite of Oscar Wilde's extravagant reaction in the '80's. The peacock splendour of the eighteenth century was gone for ever. The buckskin knee-breeches of the beginning of the century had been replaced, first by pantaloons, and then by tight trousers, often of a wild check pattern. Brocaded waist-coats and stocks remained for a time as reminders of the past, but they too were doomed to be sacrificed to the rush and bustle of the machine age. The only exception is the top-hat, the universal head-gear of Victorian times. Then it was worn by everybody, chimney-sweep and clubman, aristocrat and errand-boy alike. Now it is produced on state occasions, the only survival from the male wardrobe of last century.

II

When he came home again Wilde set up in practice as an eye and ear specialist at No. 15, Westland Row, where his mother and his sister, Margaret, kept house for him.

He felt at once the lack of hospital facilities for the treatment of his poorer patients. The only institution which catered for the eye ailments of the poor was the National Eye and Ear Infirmary in Cuffe Street, which was quite inadequate to deal with the volume of work available.

He determined, therefore, to establish a hospital, which he proposed to model on the lines of Moorfields. He wisely started in a small way. From a dentist friend, Mr. Grimshaw, he acquired the lease of a stable at 11, Molesworth Street, which had an opening into South Frederick Lane. At his own expense he fitted up this stable with a few fixtures and instruments.

The poor of Dublin soon flocked to him for treatment. Servants told their masters of his skill, and maids their mistresses, and they in turn came to him at Westland Row. He was appointed lecturer on diseases of the eye and ear at the Park Street School, where he joined his old teachers, Cusack, Graves and Stokes, Carlyle, Hamilton and Fleming, on the staff. With the almost unanimous backing of the medical profession in Dublin, Wilde soon came to have a large and lucrative practice at a time when most young doctors are still struggling for existence.

His hospital proved an unqualified success. At the end of the first year he found the number of patients had grown far beyond his expectations, and was more than he could support without help. He did not wish to apply for public aid at this stage, so he determined to try what was then a new idea. This was to make the hospital pay for itself by a monthly subscription from each patient. The plan succeeded fully, and by March 1844 he had treated over two thousand cases in the little stable dispensary.

By this time he felt the need of beds for operation cases and other in-patients, and he began to look round for new premises. The old general 'Hospital of St. Nicholas, or the New Charitable Infirmary', which had been established in Cole-Alley, off Meath Street, in 1745, the same year as the Rotunda, had fallen on evil days. When the Meath Hospital was founded it had encroached on the district served by St. Nicholas', which was therefore moved to Mark Street, off Great Brunswick Street,

Eheu fugaces!

The first St. Mark's Hospital to-day

where it was re-established in an almshouse beside the Widows' House of St. Mark's Parish.

In spite of the move the hospital, now called St. Mark's, continued to decay, until finally it was closed, and the building was still unused when Wilde began to cast around for new quarters. He realized at once that it was what he was looking for. It was centrally located, had two wards each capable of accommodating six in-patients, a good surgery and a large waiting-room, in addition to a kitchen and apartments for nurses.

In February 1844, he reopened St. Mark's as an 'Ophthalmic Hospital and Dispensary for Diseases of the Eye and Ear'. The furniture of the Frederick Lane dispensary was moved in, additional material supplied when funds allowed, and soon the hospital was working at full pressure.

Before long the finances of the new St. Mark's were in a satisfactory position. Part of the funds of the old general hospital had been realized to pay off debts when the hospital had first been closed, but a substantial remainder still existed, and was made available. In addition, Wilde applied for, and was given, a grant by the Grand Jury. A subscription list was also opened, which realized the respectable sum of £120 for the first year. Lord Mountsandford was amongst those who gave donations.

During the eight or nine years Wilde worked at Mark Street he made a great reputation for himself and the hospital, a reputation which was sustained when later another move was made to more commodious premises. For many years Wilde was the sole regular medical attendant, although he had Graves as consulting physician, Sir Philip Crampton, picturesque but able, as consultant surgeon, and Grimshaw as consulting dentist. He attended night and day, attending out-patients three days a week, operating on two mornings, and giving a course of lectures every winter. For a long time Wilde's was the only hospital in Great Britain in which aural surgery was taught, and post-graduates and students flocked to it from all over the world—particularly from America.

III

When he started in practice the science of otology, like that of ophthalmology, was in the hands of quacks and nostrum-mongers, galvano-therapists, mesmerists and their ilk. Accurate diagnosis of ear conditions was not attempted, and treatment was utterly primitive. A popular remedy for a discharging ear was to insert a piece of 'rusty bacon'. Another was to insert some wool from the left forefoot of a six-years-old black ram, a superstition which has an easily recognized descendant to-day. All sorts of fluids were used as ear-drops, and it was even recorded that about this time a child died near Newry from the effects of strong nitric acid drops in the ear.

Wilde determined to end this ignorant empiricism. In his teaching in his new hospital he would help to divest this branch of medicine of its shroud of quackery and superstition. He would do this by 'taking as basis the principles of pathology, and by reducing treatment to recognized rules of modern therapeutics and scientific surgery'.

To Wilde's eternal credit it can be said that he succeeded in his object, and placed his chosen subject on a scientific footing. In so doing he proved himself one of the two greatest English-speaking aurists of his time, for the supremacy he attained in the specialty during his lifetime was challenged only by the great Toynbee.

When Wilde qualified as a doctor the ear-drum was a structure the majority of doctors never even saw. Those who attempted to see it used daylight or lamps which could only throw an oblique light on the external opening of the ear, and consequently they could only see the drumhead, which lies at a depth of more than an inch, when the external opening was particularly wide and the passage very straight.

Wilde, who preferred daylight for illumination, must have failed to see the drum on many occasions, although he introduced to English practice an instrument which made it more easily visible, and which is still universally used. This is the trumpet-shaped tube, or speculum, inserted to straighten the passage and hold the hairs aside, which replaced the forceps-like speculum previously in use in these islands. It had been invented by Gruber of Vienna, in whose hands Wilde had first seen it.

Wilde taught that the best light by which to examine an ear was sunlight, and the best time 'between the hours of eleven and three'. One feels that he must have seen more of the sun than we moderns do. He believed in 'a well-managed light, natural not artificial, a practised eye, and delicate manipulation'.

When forced at times to use an artificial light, he preferred the lamp devised by Thomas Buchanan 'an intelligent surgeon, of Hull'. As somebody said, Hull was the very spot where one might expect such an instrument to be invented. There were many such lamps on the market in the 1840's. Buchanan's lamp, which was a development of Miller's, was in construction very like a magic lantern. It was a tin box with a strong lamp and powerful reflector, opposite which was a tube containing two convex lenses. In using this apparatus a disc of strong light about an inch in diameter was thrown upon the ear.

Having inserted the speculum in the ear, and directed light rays, natural or artificial upon it, and having managed to keep his head out of the light, Wilde next inspected the auditory canal most minutely. He noted any wax, or pus, and removed it if necessary, so as to see the skin of the passage more clearly. He next turned his attention to the drum, looking for perforations, polypi and other abnormalities, making notes which described the conditions most accurately.

If the patient came complaining of deafness, his hearing was assessed by the degree of his ability to hear the human voice, shouted, spoken and whispered. Wilde also used 'a loud-ticking watch', but at this time the use of tuning forks had not been thought of. Dr. Schmalz of Dresden had invented the sonometer, an anticipation of the modern audiometer, but Wilde did not see any virtue in it.

Miller's Lamp and Gruber's Speculum

His next procedure was to persuade the patient to perform what is called Valsalva's experiment. This somewhat dangerous procedure consists in holding the nose, shutting the mouth, and making a forced expiration, so that air rushed into the ear-drum from the back of the nose and mouth, via the Eustachian tube. Watching through the speculum, Wilde closely observed the results of this manœuvre. If it was performed successfully, he saw the drum redden and bulge, and he might see a mucous discharge coming through the lips of a perforation so small that he had previously overlooked it, to the accompaniment of a 'squeeling', hissing noise. He might see thick pus coming through a larger perforation. Finally, he removed the speculum and listened with a stethoscope or by applying his ear directly to the patient. From the noise made by the air rushing through the Eustachian tube he diagnosed whether or not it was partially obstructed.

In some cases Valsalva's experiment failed because the patient could not force the air through. When this was the case Wilde resorted to mechanical methods to open the passage between the back of the nose and the ear. He passed a Eustachian catheter, a hollow silver tube, along the floor of the nose until he could engage its curved end in the mouth of the Eustachian tube at the back of the nose. This is just what is still done to-day, but at this point the similarity ended. Instead of simply applying the nozzle of a rubber ball to the free end of the catheter and blowing air through, he had recourse to a much more elaborate procedure. First, he secured the catheter by a small clamp depending from a band round the forehead. He then got up pressure in an air-pump, which he had designed, and connected this by means of a rubber tube to the catheter. When all was in position he allowed air to escape from the pump into the tube and catheter, regulating the pressure by means of a stop-cock.

This may sound a radical and troublesome procedure, but it was nothing compared to what some others practised upon their unfortunate patients. Kramer also had a pump of his own design, through which he injected ether and various other medicated vapours—'fumigation', according to Wilde.

If both Valsalva's method and the air-pump failed to restore the hearing, Wilde proceeded to pierce the ear-drum, if he thought the deafness of Eustachian origin. This operation had, of course, often been done before since the time of Degravers, who first performed it, and it had been considerably popularized by Sir Astley Cooper. All sorts of punches, gouges and trocars had been invented for the job, but Wilde would have none of them. 'Having brought the membrane fairly into view under bright direct sunlight, I introduce this small, sickle-shaped knife . . . and having made the patient inflate the tympanum so as to make the membrane tense and pressed outwards, I gently introduce the knife into its inferior, thin, vibrating portion. . . . Occasionally I make a crucial incision. So simple is this, and so little pain does it give, that the patient is often unconscious of its performance until he hears the air rushing out through the aperture.' He found considerable difficulty in keeping the perforation open. 'For this,' he said, 'there is nothing like silver nitrate.'

For the new science he was developing Wilde invented all sorts of instruments—probes, 'porte-caustics', specula and goodness knows what. His aural snare is still a standard instrument, illustrated in all the catalogues, and to be found in the armamentarium of most aurists, as is Gruber's ear speculum, which he popularized in this country. His most useful invention, however, is the aural dressing forceps with which his name, for some reason, has never been associated, although he appears to have been the first to design it. It is a simple forceps with an angle in the blade—that angle, now standardized, which he insisted must be in the shaft of every aural instrument.

IV

In treatment he was, on the whole, very sound. The ordinary running ear he treated by syringing, afterwards instilling *liquor aluminis* or *liquor plumbi*, and by preaching the doctrine of

Wilde's Snare

cleanliness. In treating catarrhal deafness he was not, perhaps, on quite such firm ground. 'When there is redness and relaxation of the throat and nose, with much "stuffing in the head" and mucous engorgement of the middle ear, the moderate use of tobacco smoke inhaled from a *good* cigar, and gently puffed out through the nose, will be found beneficial. I understand soldiers are in the habit of forcing tobacco smoke into their ears when they become deaf.'

Wilde concluded that most of the diseases of the ear are inflammatory in origin—therefore 'depletion is strictly enjoined'. He did not often practise general bleeding, but thought that to bleed locally was essential, either by cupping or by leeches.

When he wished the apothecary to apply leeches he first

plugged the ear with cotton-wool. This was a very necessary precaution, for if a leech found its way inside the ear passage, it would cause excruciating pain. He marked the places with ink where the leeches were to be applied. The apothecary then came along with a cylindrical leech glass, in which he placed each leech so that he could accurately place it upon the chosen spot. Usually he put as many as five or six around the external opening of the auditory passage, sometimes putting a few more behind, in front of, and below the ear. Free bleeding resulted, the cotton-wool always becoming saturated with blood, and the leech-bites often continued bleeding so long that the haemorrhage had to be stopped by the application of caustics.

He also employed counter-irritation freely. In acute cases, common fly-blisters were most often used. At other times he used croton oil, strong iodine, or tartar emetic ointment, rubbed on twice daily until the ear became angry and irritable, and a copious eruption of purulent blisters produced. These irritants, Wilde said, must be continued for a considerable time, long before the end of which both patient and doctor would be heartily sick of each other!

Wilde disapproved of the use of stimulating or sedative ear-drops, so common at the time. 'Why,' he asked, 'are not these essential oils, this turpentine, creasote, tincture of cantharides, oil of origanum, etc., poured into the eye, or injected into the urethra? Why do not surgeons prescribe a roasted onion, or a boiled fig, for inflammations of other parts as well as the ear?' Of medicines to be taken internally he said, somewhat cryptically, 'potassium and the iodides were just as useful as in affections of other parts of the body.' Quinine —'Peruvian bark'—he also used, and the only drug he ever found of use in tinnitus or head-noises, was 'leopard's bane'—otherwise arnica, the familiar remedy for bruises and sprains. He taught that mercury had a specific effect in controlling inflammation and removing its products. He employed it in moderate dosage, but found that amongst his private patients there was considerable prejudice against its use. There was an idea prevalent that it was difficult to 'get it out of the bones'. That this idea was commonly held is shown by the gentleman who swore at the trial of the quack, St. John Long, that he had seen the mercury taken several years previously appear in globules of pure quicksilver upon the forehead of a nobleman, drawn forth by that ingenious charlatan's prescriptions! Wilde watched his patients very carefully, for they varied greatly in their reactions, some tolerating the mercury well, others developing profuse salivation, enlarged glands in the neck, a white slimy, swollen, protruding tongue, and a stinking foetid breath. He observed, however, that those who naturally suffered from bad breath were always cured by salivation with mercury, and even on occasions prescribed mercury in order to cure this trouble.

Wilde could remember Steevens' when, from the quantity of mercury used, the wards were virtually vapour baths, in which the smell of foetid breaths contended with the stench of sloughing ulcers, and the effluvia resulting from mercurial diarrhoea. Consequently, he thought little of an occasional overdose. 'The abuse,' he said, 'which one comes in for in practice, because a patient has suddenly got a sore mouth, should be borne with philosophic indifference.'

At the outset of his career Wilde was considerably influenced by the work of Wharton Jones, who, amongst other places, had practised in Cork for a time before settling in London. Jones was an able man who did much good and original work. In later life he became very pedantic and critical, so much so that on one occasion he accused Sir Joseph Lister of 'an illogical proclivity to hasty excogitation'! Wilde constantly quoted his works, but did not hesitate to criticize him when he thought fit. Jones was really more interested in physiological obscurities than in the care of his patients, in marked contrast to Wilde, who was gifted with a capacity for the minute observation and digestion of detail which stamped him a true follower of the Dublin school.

v

The work of the eye department of the hospital was quite as active as that which dealt with the ear. Wilde introduced many innovations from English and Continental practice, the most important of which was the use of atropine for corneal ulcer and in the extraction of cataract. At the end of two years he was able to refer to one hundred and twenty cases which he had operated on for squint. He claimed complete success in eighty-five per cent of these cases, but we may perhaps be permitted to doubt the accuracy of this statement. The operation he practised consisted in the division of the internal rectus muscle of the eye, a thin strip of muscle tissue about an inch and a half long, and not half an inch wide, which pulls the eye inward. After dividing the muscle he completed the operation by putting a stitch through the tendon stump to maintain divergence.

To do this required no little dexterity, particularly without anæsthesia, but it is a bad operation, and even then had its critics. Its principal fault is that the turning inwards of the eye for which it is performed is almost invariably followed by divergence, so that an inward squint is turned into an outward one. Bernard Shaw's father was amongst those upon whom Wilde operated in this way, and he certainly squinted outwards for the rest of his life. Wilde said that in no one case had he observed a relapse: but this was before any length of time had elapsed since operation, and, of course, strictly speaking, the conversion of one type of squint into another is *not* a relapse. In trachoma he practised the expression of the granulations by squeezing them between his thumbnails, which must have been an excruciatingly painful procedure, and he also performed various plastic operations for lid deformities. In cataract extraction he followed Jäger's technique, using the upward incision. In spite of the fact that little could be done for congenital ocular abnormalities, he was keenly interested in them, and made many drawings of them to illustrate his work.

The impact of social conditions on his hospital practice made a profound impression on him. 'This country, I regret to say, affords but too many opportunities for studying diseases of the eye, owing to the peculiar variableness of our climate, the reckless character of our population, the very great prevalence of scrofula, the poverty, dirt, and misery and destitution of our people, particularly in large cities like this, the bad feeding, the bad clothing, the exposure, and late hours, and the overworked condition of some of the feeblest part of our community, whose minds and bodies are enslaved and chained to the god of wealth. . . . Go into any ophthalmic institution, look around you there and see how many seamstresses, milliners and shirt-makers, stand around, of all ages, but chiefly young women from eighteen to twenty-five, pale with watching, haggard with working sixteen hours a day for 3s. 6d. or 4s. per week, cold, and perhaps hungry, and nearly blind with stitching for the votaries of fashion.

'In these days of forced education on the one hand, when unhappy children are compelled, both by parents and teachers, to pore over books, often of very small type, for hours and hours together, with the head bent, the shoulders stooped, the abdomen compressed, and the legs often dangling in the air, in crowded, badly illuminated and ill-ventilated apartments;— when young ladies in the upper circles, and those girls in the middle ranks who are preparing to be governesses and teachers, are obliged to "practise" and read music for five and six hours a day;—when young gentlemen are induced, either by threats or emulation, to read for eight and ten hours a day, and in addition several hours of the night, under the glare of a strong gas light, in order to uphold the character of a school or master at the risk—often at the expense of sight and life—when on the other hand, unfortunate tradesmen are compelled by low wages, the high price of provisions, and scarcity of work, to support their almost starving families by working in dark, damp cellars and garrets for fourteen or sixteen hours a day;—and when poor seamstresses and milliners are necessitated by the fashionable luxuries of the upper classes to work for no less than eighteen hours out of the twenty-four;—and when we add to this the various factories and private trades which require the continuous application of the eye to minute objects, we wonder not that near-sightedness and impaired or altered vision should be now so common amongst us.'

CHAPTER XII CENSUS
COMMISSIONER

I

IN 1846 Wilde's mother died at Westland Row, at the age of sixty-four. Little is known about her, except that she was one of the Fynnes of Ballymagibbon, and that she had three sons and two daughters. She was buried in a vault at Mount Jerome, where Wilde himself was to join her in thirty-two more years. The vault stands on the edge of a broad walk in the cemetery, and its covering obelisk is overshadowed by the towering monument which covers the remains of Gideon Ouseley and his brother, the Major-General.

The year before she died Wilde's name had again come before the public as an author when he published an account of part of his Continental tour under the title of *Austria: Its Literary, Scientific and Medical Institutions. With Notes on the Present State of Science and a Guide to the Hospitals and Sanatory Establishments of Vienna.*

This book is still the standard work in any language on the Vienna of the period. It was much smaller than the *Madeira*—'by no means prolix', as one reviewer said—but it was very well received. 'Another of the many instances of how agreeable a book can be made on apparently the least amusing topics, by a clever man, particularly when that clever man is a clever physician,' said the *Dublin University Magazine.*

It excited considerable comment for several reasons. At this time little was known of the internal workings of the Austrian Empire, in much the same way as we really know very little to-day about Russia. Wilde's comments were very outspoken. He did not hesitate to condemn what he disliked—the bureaucracy, stupid officialdom, the feudal tyranny under which the country laboured. He hit hard, as always, but right was on his side, and his revelations were everywhere received with surprise and indignation, not least in Austria itself.

Apart from this, the book contained a quantity of tabulated information compressed into a small space. This information, naturally enough, was mainly concerned with medical matters, but it spread into many other fields of public life. It was obvious that the author held high rank amongst those peculiar men who delight in the study of statistics. The immediate result was that at the instance of Lord Elliott, the Chief Secretary for Ireland, and Captain Thomas Larcom of the Ordnance Survey, Wilde was appointed Medical Census Commissioner, an appointment which he retained for the rest of his life.

In 1841 this appointment was no sinecure, for the census organization was still young and ill-developed, and there was as yet no registry of births, deaths, and marriages. Wilde threw himself into the task with his customary energy, compiling vast numbers of tables, adding, subtracting, analysing and recording, and doing a great quantity of what another would have thought unnecessary work.

Wilde's published observations are very interesting. We learn that smallpox, although it had decreased by half since the previous century, still accounted for about one in seven of all fever cases. The Vaccination Act had been recently passed, but still inoculation of infants with virulent pus from smallpox eruptions was practised by itinerant quacks. The incidence of smallpox in the country districts was double that of the towns where vaccination proper, with material from cases of cow-pox instead of with 'the natural Pock', was practised. Measles caused 30,739 deaths in the ten-year period, compared with 7,886 from scarlatina. Wilde referred to the prevalence and severe nature of scarlatina in the middle of the previous century, when, however, it is probable that a number of fatal cases really died from other causes. Those in which 'the sick died, as though suffocated by the deluge of phlegm which descended, as it were, upon the tonsils, uvula and larynx', probably suffered from diphtheria.

'Hooping cough' was the fifth most fatal epidemic disease, accounting for no less than 36,298 deaths in the ten years reviewed. Pemphigus killed 17,799. 'Intermittent and Remittent Fever, as well as true Quotidian, Tertian and Quartan ague, the effect of Marsh Miasmata' accounted for only 518 deaths. Most of these occurred in labourers who had become infected in the fens and marshes of England. Wilde thought that the disease was transmitted by drinking infected water, in which decomposition of vegetable matter had occurred. He believed the comparative freedom of Ireland from malaria was due to the presence of tannin in the bog water, which gave it preservative properties and prevented vegetable decomposition.

Of all the epidemic diseases cholera was, as might be expected, much the most fatal. He commented upon the fact that syphilis, like scarlatina, was already decreasing greatly in virulence, a decrease which has continued to the present day.

Of the other diseases, consumption, which alone accounted for 135,590 deaths, was by far the most fatal. Cancer was very prevalent, and, Wilde thought, on the increase. The 'iliac passion', a term used for any obstruction or stricture, ulcer, cancer or inflammation of the gullet and intestines, was only given credit for forty-two deaths in ten years. Kidney and bladder stone, according to the returns, was a very rare cause of death in Ireland. Diabetes—'increased discharge of urine containing saccharine matter, attended by a morbidly increased thirst and appetite', caused death in only 118 instances.

Leprosy was supposed to cause death in seventeen cases, but as Wilde remarked, many other skin diseases might have been labelled leprosy in error. That this disease was once very common in Ireland there seems no doubt, and is attested to by the number of old leper houses (*cf.* Leopardstown) which once existed. There was an old superstition that it was due to eating 'boiled salmons, hot out of the kettle, in great quantity'. Wilde thought that this was a legend fostered by some ingenious mind to prevent the eating of salmon in the spawning season. The 'almost leprous' look of a spent salmon suffering from furunculosis probably gave credence to this report.

The recorded deaths from violence speak plainly to all. Homicide accounted for nearly 4,000 deaths, of which almost a thousand were cases of infanticide. Coroners' inquests returned verdicts of wilful murder in 890 cases, which resulted in 197 executions, a large enough number in all conscience.

This census report brought Wilde much further kudos, and deservedly so, for his return was clear, succinct and exhaustively tabulated, with no conclusions from false or unproven premises. It was so fully worked out that he even added a map of Dublin, beautifully engraved, and coloured so as to illustrate the first, second and third class residential and shopping districts.

II

In spite of his other activities, Wilde still found time for antiquarian research. In the retrospective science of archaeology he found an ideal foil for the more vital and creative labours of his everyday life. Physically he still was far from strong; mentally he was so active that a change of work was a relaxation. With George Petrie as his guide, he delved deep into Irish prehistory. He found much to interest him, for Ireland is particularly rich in prehistoric remains, and far excels England or Scotland in this respect. Not only in Meath, but in Sligo, Mayo, Galway, Kerry—almost anywhere in the country, every knoll and hill-top tells a story of the hazy distant past. Cairns and earthworks remind us of the time when our savage ancestors lived their primitive hunting and agricultural lives amongst rich undergrowth and luxuriant forests.

Wilde was one of the first to undertake the study of these early peoples in a precise and scientific manner. His accurate, tidy mind, his capacity for clear thinking, and his genius for classification were ideal qualifications for archaeological research of this type. He soon became the leading Irish prehistorian of his period, while Petrie's principal interest remained in the early Christian period.

Wilde's chosen study was far-reaching and fascinating, and one which may never reach finality. Our knowledge of the customs of our aboriginal ancestors is still far from complete. Some of the dead were disposed of by placing the cremated ashes in an urn, which was then placed upside-down in the ground. Of these, many survive. Cist burials are often found, and in his time Wilde excavated several of them. Here the urn is placed inside a cubical cavity formed by flag-stones. Sometimes a tightly-bound body is placed inside the cist, with an urn, presumably a food vessel, to keep it company. These cists may be clustered together to form a cemetery, and one cist may be superimposed upon another.

The most distinctive type of Irish prehistoric monument, however, is the dolmen, or cromlech, as it was called in Wilde's day. A dolmen is in essential a large flat stone supported by

K

three upright stones. Some of them are gigantic, as for instance the enormous monument at Mount Browne in Carlow, the largest European dolmen outside Spain, of which the coverstone is estimated to weigh a hundred tons. Three is the most usual number of supporting stones, although a greater number is not unusual. As Macalister says, Ireland is pre-eminently a land of dolmens. No fewer than 780 have been described in Ireland, not counting fifty chambered tumuli and 68 megalithic monuments of doubtful character.

In his student days Wilde had assisted at the excavation of the tumulus of Knockmaree, in the Phoenix Park, the central cist of which is now re-erected in the Zoological Gardens.

Knockmaree Tumulus

This tumulus was originally 120 feet in diameter, and fifteen feet high. The central cist was four feet long and two feet deep, and contained the uncremated remains of three people, a 'fibula' of bone and a shell necklace. Secondary cists of later date contained urns filled with human ashes. Many variations of tumuli such as these have been described.

An outstanding example of megalithic monument building in Ireland, and indeed in north-west Europe, is undoubtedly the great chambered tumulus of Newgrange, in which Wilde delighted, and which he must have visited scores of times during his lifetime. It lies a few miles inland from Drogheda, and near the battlefield of the Boyne. This great tomb is situated in the midst of one of the greatest cemeteries of pagan Ireland, for here, within an area of a few miles, are upwards of twenty tumuli of varying sizes. Of these, Newgrange is easily the largest, with Dowth and Knowth, which flank it on either side, coming next in point of size. Newgrange is the masterpiece of megalithic Ireland. The architect who designed it did his work well, for after three or four thousand years it is still perfect. Wilde was fond of likening it to the Pyramids. In this he was more or less correct, for in function and plan it is similar. Its appearance differs because it was built of apparently unhewn stone.

The principal feature of Newgrange is the length of the passage which leads to the sepulchral chamber. Armed with a torch or candle, stooping through the narrow doorway less than five feet high, one finds oneself in a passage no less than sixty-two feet long. In some places it is possible to walk upright, at others it is necessary to squeeze through on hands and knees. The stones which form the walls of this passage are from five to eight feet high, standing on their ends, and it is roofed with flag-stones of great size. The course of stones which line the passage is continued into the central chamber, which has a lofty domed roof of corbel construction. Three recesses open off this central chamber, one opposite the passage, and one on either side, so that the ground plan, when the passage is included, takes the form of a cross. On the floor of each recess is a rude stone basin or sarcophagus.

It is a most eerie experience to stand in this cavern for the first time. With flickering candles half lighting up the immense stones of the hive-shaped dome and surrounding crypts, one cannot wonder at the flights of fancy the scene has evoked. Then as one's eyes grow accustomed to the half-light, it becomes possible to pay attention to detail. Then it is seen that spirals, cup-and-ring marks, circles, and lozenges, all are carved in profusion on the stones, sometimes pocked, sometimes carved in relief.

Nobody really knows what these carvings represent. The most reasonable explanation seems to be that they are degenerate symbols which have evolved from what were once realistic drawings of human beings. We know that our primitive ancestors could draw well at one time—as is shown by the rock carvings and paintings of men, reindeer and oxen made by early men in other countries. Suppose that the artist's skill deteriorated, or that it was only permitted to a certain caste of priest or witch-doctor to execute them. We can well imagine that in the course of time a combination of lines once easily recognized as a human figure eventually came to be unrecognizable except as a magic symbol, even to those who executed it. A similar reaction in art may be going on at the present day. The camera can now produce a pictorial image more accurately than any but the most painstaking artist. The latter, therefore, retreats. He says he has no interest in realistic art, as Leonardo had, and Rembrandt, and Phidias, but that he is solely concerned with the abstract. The result is Surrealism or some other movement, the products of which may be good, perhaps even great art, provided they are well conceived and executed. Nevertheless, they may be quite as unintelligible as the Bronze Age man's spirals and circles are to us, and possibly were also to him.

Dr. A. Mahr has put forward an ingenious hypothesis as to the origins of these people. He holds that during the great Ice Age, when all Europe was covered with a sheet of ice; when the red deer careered through fields of snow on the shores of the Mediterranean, and the Sahara was covered with luxuriant ferns, the original inhabitants of Europe were gradually driven to seek refuge in more temperate lands. They finally arrived in the Southern Islands of the Pacific. When the ice began to melt, and the weather became more temperate, they started on the return journey.

A great mountainous spine extends throughout Asia and Europe. In Asia this spine is formed by the Himalayas and the mountains of Tibet and Turkestan, in Europe by the Carpathians, the Alps, and the Pyrenees. When this ancient people started on the return journey to Europe, some of them took the northern route through China, and Russia, to Germany. Others, perhaps more fortunate, travelled by way of India, Egypt, Asia Minor, to France and Spain and England. In the long ages occupied by this percolation, the two streams of population developed different cultures. The southern stream, blessed by temperate climes, did not require to work overhard to get their food, and so they developed great empires and had time on their hands for artistic work. In this way the megalithic culture was developed. The Egyptian Pyramids, the great rock-tombs of ancient Greece, and the chambered tumuli of Italy, Spain, France and the British Isles, are all equally expressive of this megalithic culture, and so also is Stonehenge, whatever its purpose was. The northern race, on the other hand, developed an entirely different culture, of which one difference is that they buried their dead, not in cists or tumuli, but in urn-fields. There are, of course, urn burials on the southern side of the mountain barrier, but they are usually isolated, and megalithic monuments do not occur in the northern countries.

The northern and southern streams of population finally came to rest face to face on opposite banks of the Rhine. They had grown widely apart during the ages, and came to hate each other. They have done so ever since, and the world has known no rest. Since the time of Caesar and before it, they have spent inestimable brains and money, trying to annihilate each other. If only the energy thus expended had been used to fight disease, the common enemy, how much a better place this world would be. As it is, it looks as though the southerns may win, for statistics show that cancer is almost twice as common amongst the Nordic peoples as it is in the Latin races.

III

With such a wealth of material on his doorstep it is no wonder Wilde soon became an enthusiastic archaeologist.

The first-fruits of his researches were seen when he addressed the King's and Queen's Colleges of Physicians in Sir Patrick Dun's Hospital, on the subject of the ethnology of the ancient Irish. This was the 'second soirée of the 1843 season', and the occasion was a notable one. A 'very numerous assemblage of literary and professional gentlemen' were present to hear this young man, only twenty-eight years of age, but already famous by virtue of his two books.

It was natural enough that Wilde should be interested in ethnology, for his medical training and archaeological tastes led him straight to it. Ethnology deals with the natural history of man, his form and stature, his physiognomy and habits, moral and physical, ancient and modern, and ethnography with his geographical distribution.

In the case of our early ancestors these facts are not always easy to determine, but much can be deduced from the shape of the skull. In this lecture, which was the first of Wilde's many contributions to the subject, he classified the various kinds of skull found in different types of Irish prehistoric burials. He described three forms in particular—a small globular brachycephalic head, a markedly long-headed type, and a well-proportioned broad head which approached the higher form of the Indo-European race. Unfortunately, he then attempted to identify the races to which the owners of these skulls belonged with the Fir Bolgs and Tuatha de Danaan of the ancient Irish annalists.

In doing so he was following the old manuscript book of MacFirbis, thereby complicating his subject with an unnecessary side-issue, for ethnology is best studied as an exact science from objective findings. He did not mention the Milesians, who traditionally succeeded the de Danaans, and were the favourites of the patriots—Davis was always weaving romances about Milesian maids and Cromwellian settlers, and about this time O'Connell was crowned at Mullaghmast with the famous Green Cap, supposed to be a replica of an ancient Milesian crown. It actually was a replica of a Bronze Age urn, but O'Connell did not know this, and wore it contentedly on big occasions until he died.

This was Wilde's first excursion into ethnology, and his second serious work on archaeology, the first being the paper on crannogs written before he went to Vienna. These two subjects retained his interest always, and it was upon them that he did his most important original work in archaeology.

The paper on ethnology was published in the *Dublin Literary Journal*. This was a short-lived journal, which only lasted three years, but it was a delightfully gossipy paper, and most interesting now as an index of the lives of ordinary people. It gave us reflections from many facets of Victoria's first decade, 'this age of Universal Improvement', as the journal did not hesitate to call it. Reviews of books, at great length, or rather a series of lengthy extracts in the fashion of the time formed its chief feature. The second edition of the *Madeira* was noticed in no fewer than five numbers. Indeed Wilde featured largely in the journal. Apart from the lecture on ethnology and reviews of his books, his name keeps cropping up in various places, in records of his activities as a member of the Archaeological Society and of the Council of the Zoological Society. Amongst others on the Council with Wilde were Dr. Dominick Corrigan, another of Dublin's famous medical sons, and F. W. Burton, the artist. The pushful Isaac Butt had already become a vice-president, with Marsh and Crampton and others.

Isaac Butt

CHAPTER XIII

LITERATURE,
ART AND POLITICS

I

SHORTLY AFTER Wilde had visited Lever in Brussels,
McGlashan had persuaded the latter to return to Dublin as
editor of the *Dublin University Magazine*, at a salary of £1,200
a year, together with half the profits on all he wrote. This was
a very comfortable figure in those days, with income-tax at
sixpence in the pound. If it did not suffice Lever's needs, we
must blame his lavish hospitality at his residences at Templeogue
and Stillorgan.

His dinner-parties were attended by the best of the literary
and professional society of Dublin. These two groups indeed
merged into one another, for most of the men who wrote for
the *Dublin University Magazine* were churchmen, barristers or
doctors. Lever's entertainments lost nothing by this, for it
meant that there were few of the jealousies and rivalries which
beset men who seek distinction by the same road, while on
the other hand there was great contrast of experiences from
the diversity of daily occupations.

Wilde already had his place in the social life of Dublin. He
had attained distinction in scientific and literary circles, and
had also gained a reputation as a ready wit. Being an old
friend of Lever's he was a frequent guest at his house, with
Isaac Butt, Petrie, McGlashan, the publisher, and others. He
was often accompanied by his consulting surgeon at St. Mark's,
Sir Philip Crampton, the Surgeon-General—'a general in the
lancers' as some humorist defined him. Sir Philip was tall
and elegantly proportioned; his slight figure was 'as elastic
as corkwood'. In spite of a weakness for dress, he ranks
amongst the greatest of English-speaking surgeons and scientists.
Amongst his many activities he found time to keep his own
pack of hounds and hunt them three days a week. He shone

in convivial company, and was a great talker, and, like Wilde, he was in great demand at Lever's parties.

After a time Wilde began to find Lever's hospitality a little overpowering. His increasing practice made his time more limited, and, besides, there were 'too many monkeys in the menagerie' as Lever himself confessed. But Lever did not let him go without an effort. One afternoon he called several times at Westland Row in order to ask Wilde to dinner, but was denied admission—'the doctor was too busy'. Finally, he tied a bandage over one of his eyes and called once more. This time he had no difficulty in gaining admission, and of course

the meeting ended with uproarious laughter, followed by dinner at Templeogue.

The fact was that Lever, like Walter Scott twenty years before, was trying on a moderate income to lead the life of a country squire with unlimited means and leisure. He had little enough to spare of either. He was spending considerably more than his income, and to make ends meet he had to work far into the night, while at intervals his fat German factotum, Kieffer, would bring him coffee and curaçao, or a grilled bone.

Kieffer figures in a story told by Wilde. 'One evening,' wrote he, 'I arrived in my green gig to spend a few hours with Lever; and while I and other friends were sitting together enjoying Lever's sallies, another gig, driven by Mr. Kildahl, the house-agent, came to the door. He wished to see Lever regarding the rent of the place, and sent in his card with that object. The Teutonic man-of-all-work was at once deputed to mind the gig, while Mr. Kildahl joined the group within. In a few minutes the fat German entered the room, and, making a profound obeisance, said impassively: "*Das Pferd ist durchgegangen,*" which means, of course: "The horse has run away." Lever laughed immoderately, so did I; and so infectious was the merriment that Kildahl laughed immoderately too, though without the remotest idea that the laugh had been at his own expense. Kildahl's consternation at discovering the real facts may be conceived. The run-away horse and gig dashed down the steep hill of Stillorgan until all came to a dead smash at Galloping-Green, the fragments being there gathered up and sent back to Dublin on a float. The German, who was perhaps more *au fait* as a cook, we found to be a great proficient at making a woodcock-pie. He never appeared to such fine advantage as when submerging ten or twelve of the birds in a rich gravy of truffles, and serving up the dainty dish for supper.'

Lever left the editorial chair of the *Dublin University Magazine* in 1843, and was succeeded by Joseph Sheridan Le Fanu. Le Fanu was an almost exact contemporary of Wilde's, for he was born in 1814, and was in Trinity during the time Wilde was a medical student at Steevens'. At this time the two young men were on intimate terms, although in later life Le Fanu's upright, retiring nature caused him to shrink from Wilde.

In spite of the tremendous popularity he enjoyed amongst his contemporaries, Lever's books are now seldom read. His characters have too much of the "stage-Irishman" in them, and his works savour too much of a generation that is past. Le Fanu, on the other hand, is still widely read. The reason is not far to seek, for Le Fanu is probably, after Edgar Allen Poe, the greatest of all writers of tales of mystery and horror. He tells a story with effortless simplicity, building up an eerie supernatural atmosphere, which grips the reader with increasing tension until it reaches a climax of uncanny horror. His stories are steeped in a sense of foreboding awe, developing into a sense of the unearthly which is so strong that it is almost realistic. Nobody could tell a tale with such strength and simplicity unless he was a man of great scholarship. Like Wilde and many others of his time, Le Fanu was widely read in archæology and science, and a deep knowledge of nature is reflected in his work. It is not surprising that M. R. James is one of his greatest admirers.

Le Fanu's first novel, *The Ghost and the Bone-Setter* was published in the *Dublin University Magazine* when he was twenty-three years of age. Soon afterwards he wrote the famous ballad *Shamus O'Brien*. Many macabre tales followed, of which *Uncle Silas* and *The House by the Churchyard* are best known. *In a Glass Darkly*, recently re-issued, is a collection of masterly short stories. It opens with *The Familiar*, a tale of haunting terror, and ends with *Carmilla*, a weird vampire story in a wild continental setting which is surely the fore-runner of *Dracula*. It has recently been dramatized on the Irish Stage. *Green Tea* is a masterpiece of quite different type.

Most of these stories were written in what is now No. 70, Merrion Square, where, after his beloved wife died, Le Fanu lived in seclusion, keeping the world at bay. As time went by he became almost a hermit, only venturing forth by night. Coming home early, he retired to bed, and wrote far into the night by candle-light, at intervals brewing himself strong coffee or black tea. It is no wonder that when he did sleep awhile, his rest was disturbed by horrifying dreams. He recorded them faithfully on waking, and many of them eventually formed themes for his stories. He rose late in the forenoon, and in his dark study downstairs sat down to write once more, at a table which once belonged to his great-uncle, Richard Brinsley Sheridan. When he felt the need of exercise he would go through the french-window into his tiny garden. Filling his pocket with stones, he paced the garden, dropping a pebble each time he reached a certain corner. When his pocket was empty he returned to his fantastic, imaginary life with

'The dark folk who live in souls
Of passionate men, like bats in the dead trees;
And with the wayward twilight companies.'

The last book he published, shortly before his death in 1873, he called *Willing to Die*.

Le Fanu remained editor of the *Dublin University Magazine* until 1869, and he was, therefore, in charge of it during the whole time of Wilde's association with it, and for most of Lever's. In the end Le Fanu became so eccentric that he even refused to see Lever when he called to see him on his last visit

to Dublin, and for a long time before this he had had nothing
to say to Wilde.

But we have gone too far ahead. In the 1840's these three
young men were still close friends.

II

Another almost exact contemporary of Wilde's was the artist,
Frederick William Burton. Burton had received his earliest
artistic education from the famous Brocas brothers, but soon

came under the influence of Petrie. He was, however, a much
greater artist than Petrie, and even in his earliest work shows
an artistic perception and sense of colour much beyond Petrie's
limited range. Like Petrie, he never painted in oils, but confined
himself to water-colours and chalk drawings.

In the early '40's Burton and Wilde became rivals for the
hand of the beautiful Helen Faucit, the most famous actress
on the Irish stage. She was talented as well as beautiful. Like
many great actresses she had literary as well as histrionic ability,
which may to some extent account for Wilde's interest in her.
About this time she was appearing as *Antigone* at the old Theatre
Royal. At every appearance she was greeted with enthusiasm,
as she came on the stage attired in classical garb embroidered in
crimson and gold, the music of Mendelssohn blending with the
silvery inflexions of her voice. She had a great vogue in the

Dublin of those days, and it is no wonder Wilde and Burton both were fascinated. Burton must have been a formidable rival for Wilde, for in appearance he was much more prepossessing. Wilde was small and ugly, with simian arms and restless, uncertain temper: Burton was extremely handsome and had considerable charm of manner. The lady, however, would have nothing to say to either, and eventually married Sir Theodore Martin, a man of many gifts, poet, satirist, critic, and the biographer of the Prince Consort. It was said that Martin valued his prize less highly after it was captured than before.

Wilde, if his intentions were serious, afterwards consoled himself with his Speranza, but Burton never married. He left Dublin and went to Bavaria to copy pictures for Ludwig's gallery, and soon took up his residence in Munich for a number of years.

It is a pity Wilde and Burton crossed each other. If this had not happened he would almost certainly have painted Wilde: but the only portrait of Wilde at this time was executed by Bernard Mulrenin, a much inferior artist. It was exhibited in the Royal Hibernian Academy in 1846.

III

Amongst others whom Wilde met constantly at this time in the 'snuggery' of the editor of the *Dublin University Magazine* were Waller, Stanford and Butt. Two of these men were to become lifelong intimates, the third he was to meet later under less auspicious circumstances.

The great archaeological undertaking of the day had just been discontinued. This was the Ordnance Survey, which had been carried out by a staff of scholars under the supervision of Captain Larcom, R.E., afterwards Sir Thomas Larcom, Bart., K.C.B. Wilde had many friends amongst its members, principally in the branch which Petrie supervised. The duty of this department was to collect all available information, antiquarian or topical, about the particular part of the country which at the time was being surveyed. Petrie's staff numbered many of the greatest Gaelic scholars of the age—O'Curry, John O'Donovan, O'Keefe and O'Connor. They met in a back parlour in Great Charles

Street, and here Wilde had been a constant visitor, and also poor Clarence Mangan, with his queer puns and jokes, his odd cloak and wonderful hat, just like that traditionally worn by witches on broomsticks. He wore a flaxen wig, false teeth, and carried invariably a bottle supposed to contain tar-water, from which he would sip away all day. He affected a pair of enormous dark-green spectacles, which made a most effective contrast to his waxen cheeks.

He was a great poet, the only authentic lyric poet of his day in Ireland, a skylark amongst blackbirds. Like many other great poets, he died young, and destitute. Had he but confined himself to tar-water—if that black bottle had contained nothing stronger—his end might have been happier. The story is told how, in the year 1849, Stokes was doing his rounds in the Meath Hospital, when he came to a miserable-looking mortal who had just been admitted in the last stages of cholera, which was ravaging a body already harassed by drugs and drink. He was shocked to find this poor wretch was the once famous, long-forgotten, Mangan. Stokes treated him with every care and kindness, but he died within a week.

As he lay dead, Stokes paid a last tribute to him by sending for Burton, who made several studies of his head, which are now in the National Gallery of Ireland. He was followed to his grave, in those days of tremendous funerals, by three mourners. only. He had sunk to depths to which no friend could accompany him.

IV

Most of these men were young, like Wilde himself, and they also were, in most cases, on the threshold of brilliant careers, in various and different walks of life. All had a common interest in love of the ancient lore of their native land. They were, however, soon to split into two streams. One was conservative and Unionist, the *Dublin University Magazine* coterie, in whose current Wilde was carried. The other was a more revolutionary, separatist group, whose fortunes were associated with a new publication ever since famous, the *Nation* newspaper.

In the year 1840 the great Dan O'Connell had re-opened the campaign for the promised Repeal of the Union between England and Ireland. But O'Connell, although still a power in the land, was no longer the powerful tribune of the Catholic Emancipation movement of 1832. The elections of 1841 resulted in a complete débâcle. Less than a dozen Repealers were returned, and O'Connell lost his own seat in Dublin. When the Nationalist party was reorganized after the elections, a number of new recruits appeared. They were mostly young barristers recently called, and half of them were Protestants—the first of their religion to join the National cause since Wolfe Tone. The most important of the new men were Thomas Davis, a Protestant, and John Blake Dillon, a Catholic from the west of Ireland.

These young men joined the Repeal Association and were welcomed at first by O'Connell, who found work for them to do. But they soon went beyond O'Connell in their ideas. O'Connell advocated some sort of Home Rule, Repeal of the Union by consent, while Davis and Dillon were prepared to use physical force, if need be, to secure the independence of their native land.

Early in 1842 another young journalist-barrister, Charles Gavan Duffy, came from Belfast to keep terms as a law student. He had met Davis and Dillon the year before, and had been much impressed by both of them, and convinced that they would be a power in the future. He met them again, by chance this time, in the hall of the Four Courts, and the three young men went for a stroll up the Liffey's quays and into the Phoenix Park.

Duffy has described how they sat down under a noble elm near Parkgate, and how he put a proposition to them. This was that the three of them should establish a newspaper. It was to be published weekly, and mainly written by themselves. In this way the *Nation* came to be founded, in the year 1842, by three young men whose ages ranged from twenty-six to twenty-eight.

They rapidly attracted others to their banner—MacGee, Smith O'Brien, Clarence Mangan (not yet sunk to the depths), and many others. Some of them—John Mitchel, Thomas McNevin, and Torrens McCullagh—had been contemporaries at Trinity. They became known as the Young Ireland party, whose first and last aim was 'national independence', an ideal for them beside which Irish grievances and English concessions were equally insignificant. They were full of the romantic liberal nationalism of the time, the ideals which animated such men as Garibaldi and Kosciusko. They drew their inspiration from far back in the Gaelic past. Like many of the educated people of the day they were keenly interested in archaeology, and the ancient history of Ireland. Clarence Mangan, Davis and the other poets of Young Ireland became inspired to translate this scholarly interest into patriotic passion by their stirring ballads. The *Nation* soon gathered a tremendous circulation, and carried this poetry into every village in the land.

One would have thought that Mangan, with his intrinsic genius, would have became Young Ireland's principal voice in poetry, but he was completely supplanted by Davis, who never wrote a line of verse until he became associated with the *Nation*. The reason is not far to seek. Mangan was often

indolent and unproductive, while Davis was always energetic, even-tempered and enthusiastic.

Davis was far from being a mere versifier, and in the three following years he wrote many virile ballads on heroic historical themes. Propagandist verse, as J. M. Hone points out, is by no means easy to write, for it must, without offending, stir the pulses and incite to action. Davis could write good poetry which was also good propaganda.

There can be no doubt that much of what Davis wrote *was* good poetry. Some of it was not propaganda at all. In the sixth number of the *Nation* appeared the '*Lament for Owen Roe O'Neill*'. Of the '*Lament*' W. B. Yeats has written: 'It has the intensity of the old ballad, and to read it is to remember Parnell and Wolfe Tone, to mourn for every leader that has died amongst the ruins of the cause he had all but established, and to hear the lamentations of his people.'

There were, of course, many other writers on the staff of the *Nation*, for besides poetry, the journal contained reviews, literary articles and news items, even 'Army and Navy Intelligence' not being excluded. For Davis and Duffy its purpose was to lead public opinion into a single national groove, and thus achieve the union of Protestant and Catholic interests. O'Connell's object was to 'raise the passions', the *Nation's* to do the same, and in addition to provide a reasoning background of logic. The paper from the first was tremendously successful, and its circulation soon rose to 250,000 copies. It was widely read in every provincial town. A copy never grew obsolete, but passed from hand to hand until it fell into rags.

In September 1845 Davis became ill with what he thought at first was a mild attack of scarlatina, but which may have been an attack of the cholera which was shortly to decimate the land. Seven days later he was dead. It is said that his death was due in part to a rash visit to his fiancée before he had properly recovered from the first shock of his illness. His death came as a crushing blow, not only to his friends, but to the whole country.

It has been said by many that Robert Emmett and Davis are the most beloved of all Irish leaders. Certainly Thomas Davis has left a sweet memory. Although he was not destined to bear arms for his country, his political views were unequivocal, and yet he was mourned by his opponents in public life, who respected him because of his upright and forthright nature. Strong and vigorous as he was, he never said a bitter word in controversy.

To his followers and associates, his loss was indeed bitter, for in the three years of the *Nation's* activity he had become the acknowledged leader of the Young Ireland Group. They carried on without their strong man, and in time went on to greater strength, but for the moment the loss appeared irreparable.

Those were the days of vast public funerals, and a great concourse followed Davis to his grave. O'Connell was there, himself with but two more years to live, members of the Repeal

L

societies and of the '82 Club in glittering uniforms, the Senate
of Trinity College in red gowns, the members of the Royal
Hibernian Academy and the Royal Irish Academy in full panoply.
Wilde may have been there also.

A young girl, recently up from County Wexford, was walking
through St. Stephen's Green that day. The crowd was so
great that she could not pass, and she was forced to take refuge
in a shop. The procession seemed interminable. She asked the
shopkeeper what the occasion was. 'It is the funeral of Thomas
Davis,' she was told. 'Who is Thomas Davis?' she asked.
'I have never heard of him.'

'He was a poet,' the shopkeeper said.

The young girl was Wilde's future wife, soon to become
famous as 'Speranza', poetess of the *Nation*.

CHAPTER XIV

MEDICAL
EDITOR

I

ALTHOUGH WILDE was a keen social reformer, he was
not tempted to enter the political arena, but preferred the rôle
of an interested spectator.

He became a Fellow of the Royal College of Surgeons in
1844. In this year the College was reorganized and given a
Supplemental Charter, and it was decided to grant the Fellowship without examination to all those who had been Licentiates
before January 1845, provided they paid the statutory fee.
Wilde was one of the lucky ones who received the Fellowship
in this simple way.

In spite of the time occupied by the Census reports and his
other activities, Wilde had found time to contribute a number
of articles to the *Dublin Journal of Medical Science*, which was
the most important of the Irish medical periodicals of the time.
When a change in the editorship became necessary in 1845,
Wilde, with his literary experience, was the obvious choice for
the post.

He took charge in July 1845, and at once introduced very
material changes in the journal. Up to this time it had been
issued every two months. He brought this series to a close
after publishing two more numbers, and at the same time
announced his intention of 'raising it to the character of a
quarterly periodical'.

In accordance with this promise the first number of the
Dublin Quarterly Journal of Medical Science appeared on February
the first, 1846, Wilde contributing a masterly preface of forty-
eight pages, in which he reviewed the history of the journal
up to that time, and also gave an admirable summary of Irish
medical history and of the Irish Medical Societies.

The effect of Wilde's editorship was soon evident by the

increased size and circulation of the journal. Much of the new material it contained came from his own pen. The majority of the original articles naturally enough came from the Dublin school, but distinguished men such as Bowman, the London oculist, did not hesitate to contribute to it. Wilde added a new feature in biographical and obituary notices of notable Irish doctors, information which had been conspicuous by its absence in the former series. His keen interest in Irish medical history led to a further development in this direction, and soon he published a series of articles on bygone Irish physicians and surgeons, most of them illustrated by engraved or lithographed portraits. Six of these articles appeared, giving admirable accounts of Sir Patrick Dun; Bartholomew Mosse, the founder of the Rotunda; David McBride, John Rutty, John Oliver Curran, and Sylvester O'Halloran. In the preparation of these articles Wilde had access to materials which have since been lost, and we are indebted to them for much precious information which we should not otherwise possess. The article on Bartholomew Mosse is of particular value, as the manuscript history by Benjamin Higgins on which it was founded has now disappeared, and we are dependent solely on Wilde's article for much of the early history of the Rotunda Hospital. (T. P. C. Kirkpatrick.)

Wilde's connection with the *Journal* was short, for he was able to direct its course for only three years, after which he became so busy in other directions that he was compelled to resign. Nevertheless, the stimulus he gave it had a profound influence on its subsequent success.

A few years before Wilde took over the *Journal* another young oculist named Arthur Jacob, who was the Professor of Anatomy in the Royal College of Surgeons, had been its assistant editor for a short period. Jacob had not been a success, for he had immediately got into hot water by a controversial paper on medical politics, and his assistance had been dispensed with after he had helped to produce two numbers.

This was unfortunate in many ways, for Jacob was a force to be reckoned with, and he was ever after inimical to the *Journal*. He was the only oculist of any importance in Dublin except Wilde, and it was perhaps inevitable that some of the hatred he felt for the *Journal* should be reflected upon his rival. With Henry Maunsell he founded another paper, the *Dublin*

Medical Press, in 1839, and in its pages he gave his polemical proclivities full sway.

Jacob was an active worker in the scientific field, and was the first to discover the 'layer of rods and cones' in the retina at the back of the eye, a structure which for a long time was called Jacob's membrane. He also first described 'Jacob's ulcer', or rodent ulcer of the eyelid. Curiously enough, he anticipated much of Wilde's work on the mammary glands of the whale tribe in an article he had published during his brief career as editor of the *Dublin Quarterly Journal.* He seems to have been a most cantankerous, argumentative individual, and unlike Wilde he had no convivial qualities, for the midnight lamp held him in almost hypnotic sway. His portraits reveal tight-lipped, uncompromisingly ascetic features, a stubborn chin and fine forehead with beetling brows, from under which hard eyes stare through wire-rimmed spectacles. It is the face of a man who could be a bitter and implacable enemy.

II

It is pleasant to know that both the *Dublin Journal* and the *Medical Press* are still flourishing, although their names have been altered slightly, and the head-quarters of the *Medical Press* are now in London. From the beginning the two journals took different lines. The *Press,* although it contained scientific articles, was really a medical newspaper, while in Wilde's quarterly subjects connected with medical politics and organization were taboo.

Nevertheless, Wilde lost no opportunity of tilting at charlatans from the editorial chair. 'The public mind of England is diseased,' he said; 'manifestly, there must be an unhealthiness in that state of national opinion which can afford nourishment to every species of quackery and humbug. When we see fungi abounding on a plant, or parasites preying on an animal, we are led to assume the operation of some cause leading to decay and rottenness; and we are justified in coming to a similar conclusion when we behold such creatures as the Morisons and Holloways battening on the credulity of a nation.'

Wilde was perhaps a little hard on Morison and Holloway, who were amongst the earliest patent-medicine makers. They both advertised largely, and their products probably did little harm. 'The beauty of Morison's pills,' says Bernard Darwin, 'seems to have been that the more you took the better you were. They were infallible, so long as you did not, in Mr. Bob Sawyer's words about hot punch, "fall into the vulgar error of not taking enough".' Wilde's favourite villain, however, was a much more sinister character than the pill-pedlars. This was the notorious Limerick-born quack, St. John Long, whose career of infamy had recently closed in London.

It was indeed a golden age for unqualified practitioners, for the traditions of the eighteenth century died hard. 'Animal magnetism', mesmerism, phrenology, and 'water-cures' flourished, and all kinds of nostrum-mongers were rife.

It seems a pity that mesmerism, or hypnotism, had become discredited in Europe through falling into the hands of these gentry, for in India it had long had a legitimate use in the hands of the Yogis and fakirs. When Colles and his colleagues were using alcohol, opium and tobacco smoke as substitutes for anæsthetics, Indian surgeons were painlessly performing complicated operations while their patients were under hypnotic influence. In this way they were even able to make new noses for mutilated faces out of flaps of skin twisted down from the forehead. It might not have been possible to use hypnotism to this end on Europeans, for Esdaile failed when he tried it in 1846. However, by this time it mattered little, for this was the period of the discovery of anæsthesia, an inestimable boon to mankind, and the greatest advance ever made in medicine until that date.

Simpson of Edinburgh was the man who fought and won the battle for anæsthesia in the British Isles, although he did not discover either chloroform, ether or nitrous oxide. Oliver Wendell Holmes did his share in America. He it was who devised the terms anæsthesia and anæsthetic, and in doing so bequeathed to posterity the worst tongue-twister in the English language, the word 'anæsthetist'.

The development of anæsthesia may be traced in the pages of the *Dublin Journal*. It was received cautiously at first, and occasional unfortunate experiences were recorded, but on the whole the first patients suffered more from too little anæsthetic than from too much. Wilde recognized its value immediately and used chloroform extensively in the plastic operations which he performed on the tear-passages and eyelids to make good the ravages of trachoma. In cataract extractions and squint operations, however, he still preferred a conscious patient, for here he thought co-operation on the part of the patient was necessary for success.

At this time he seems to have occasionally taken cases outside his specialty. In 1849 he recorded 'a case of dislocation of the hip, reduced with great facility by the use of chloroform'. The production of muscular relaxation by anæsthesia, which is a commonplace to-day, was an exciting new discovery in those days. 'The following case is only worthy of notice from the decided influence which chloroform exercised upon it. Upon the 7th of the present month, a gentleman in the prime of life, of great muscular strength, and in perfect health, while walking across a lawn some miles from town, about half-past ten o'clock at night, fell into a sunk fence from the upper side. He was immediately conscious of having experienced some great shock, and said his leg was either broken or dislocated, as, upon attempting to rise, he found it impossible to put the limb upon the ground. I saw him about half-past 11 o'clock, and found that he had dislocation of the hip. I immediately procured the valuable aid of Mr. Ellis; and two gentlemen who resided in the house, together with a small servant boy, were all the assistance which we could then (past 12 o'clock) procure. Having placed the patient lying upon his back upon a narrow lounger with a short arm, the usual extension and counter-extension were made, and kept up, for about a quarter of an hour, without the least impression upon the dislocation. Mr. Ellis and myself then agreed to try the effects of chloroform, as it was quite manifest that, without many more assistants, it would be impossible to reduce the limb, and it would be unwise to allow it to remain unreduced in so powerful a person as our patient until morning. I administered the chloroform in a full dose, and the patient was very soon under its influence; the extension then commenced, and was kept up steadily, Mr. Ellis himself taking charge of the limb and making the proper rotation. In about four minutes after the patient was in a perfect state of anæsthesia, the dislocation was reduced with an audible noise, and upon the patient awaking from the condition of insensibility, he stated his total unconsciousness of what had occurred, and his perfect freedom from pain or uneasiness. He suffered no further inconvenience, and experienced no ill effects from the exhibition of the chloroform.

'This case I think worth recording, as the dislocation certainly could not have been reduced, except for the aid of the chloroform, particularly at so late an hour of the night, and when the usual assistance could with difficulty be procured.'

III

In the August of 1846 Wilde, in his capacity as editor of the *Dublin Journal*, received a letter from Dr. William Mackenzie, the celebrated Glasgow oculist, inquiring whether any new facts were known about Dean Swift's medical history. The letter pointed out that in his old age Swift's 'left eye swelled to the size of an egg, and the lid was so much inflamed and discoloured that the surgeon who attended expected it to mortify'. In particular Mackenzie wanted to know what had been the cause of this swelling, and whether or not it had spread to the brain or its immediate coverings. He inquired as to the state in which Swift's brain was found at post-mortem, and if any tumour or other morbid process had spread from the brain to the eye, or vice versa.

The letter suggested an investigation after Wilde's heart, and he forthwith dived with fervour into a frenzy of research. He read all the biographies, unearthed various unpublished papers and letters, and examined the death-mask of Swift which was then exhibited in the Museum of Trinity College, and is now in the Anatomy Department. In this way he assembled a complete medical history, which he published in parts in the *Journal*, together with his conclusions and the diagnosis he had made from them, and some previously unpublished *Swiftiana*. A year or so later this work was given to the general public in a separate volume, *The Closing Years of Dean Swift's Life*.

The *Dublin University Magazine* hailed the book as 'one of the most chivalrous literary efforts of recent years'. It would have been more accurate to call it one of the most nonsensical, for it must be confessed that Wilde, who was on every other occasion a most accurate and truthful observer, in this instance was led by his enthusiasm to make the most unwarranted assumptions and conclusions.

Nevertheless, Wilde's book ranks as one of the most important works about Swift. Nobody who is interested in the Dean's personality can fail to feel with him for his ailments. The Dean himself was very much concerned about them.

> 'See how the Dean begins to break,
> Poor gentleman, he droops apace,
> You plainly see it in his face;
> That old vertigo in his head,
> Will never leave him till he's dead.
> Besides, his memory decays,
> He recollects not what he says'
>
> *   *   *   *   *
>
> 'The doctors, tender of their fame,
> Wisely on me lay all the blame.
> "We must confess his case was nice,
> But he would never take advice,
> Had he been ruled, for aught appears,
> He might have lived these twenty years;
> For when we opened him, we found
> That all his vital parts were sound."'

Wilde's worst mistakes are the conclusions he drew from examining the death-mask. There is no doubt that the mask is authentic, for it has been kept in Trinity College since it was first made. It has been examined curiously and minutely by very many people, amongst them Sir Walter Scott, who said: 'In the museum of Trinity College, Dublin, there is a plaster bust, or cast, of Dean Swift. It is an impression from the mask applied to the face after death. The expression of countenance is most unequivocally maniacal, and one side of the mouth (the left) horribly contorted downwards, as if convulsed with pain.'

There is, in fact, no 'maniacal' expression whatever to be seen in the mask—the face is quite placid and peaceful. Wilde thought Sir Walter had 'greatly exaggerated', but he said 'there is an evident drag in the left side of the mouth, exhibiting a paralysis of the facial muscles of the right side.'

The cast may still be inspected in the Anatomy Department of Trinity College by anyone who asks to see it, and it requires little medical knowledge to realize that it shows no evidence whatever of facial paralysis. As for the maniacal expression, it just does not exist, for a more placid, peaceful expression never was seen. The head is that of an ordinary-looking, edentulous elderly gentleman, who closely resembles the late Edgar Wallace.

It is extraordinary that Wilde, whose observations in every other case are conscientiously exact, should have misled us in this case. It was particularly unfortunate that he should have done so, for the mistake has persisted until the present day. It has misled later writers, who have not taken the trouble to examine Wilde's evidence at its source—Bucknill, for instance, reviewed Swift's medical history in 1882, and taking the supposed facial paralysis for granted, came to the conclusion that he had suffered a right-sided stroke.

A tremendous amount of utter nonsense has been written about Swift's health. The chronic illness from which he

suffered throughout his life has been ascribed to many causes—otosclerosis, epilepsy, syphilis, alcoholism, and, of course, insanity. There is no evidence whatever that he suffered from any of these conditions.

The truth is that Swift, like Martin Luther, suffered from Ménière's disease, a most distressing ailment which attacks its victims periodically with extreme suddenness, plunging them into paroxysms of giddiness and violent sickness, and leaving them a legacy of head-noises and deafness which may persist until the next attack. Ménière's disease fits Swift's history very well. First, we have the Dean's gloomy introspective mentality and neurotic temperament, exactly what we have come to expect in these cases. Then there are the continual linked-up attacks of giddiness, deafness and vomiting, although Swift did not himself realize that these three symptoms were related. After all, why should he? Giddiness is apparently an ocular manifestation, and vomiting an abdominal one, and it was not suspected for a century after Swift's death that the three symptoms were really caused by a single disorder, and that an affection of the internal ear.

It is interesting to speculate as to the influence of the disease upon his temperament. Would the Dean have had that fierce, extroverted indignation, that savage introspective gloom, without it? If those minute changes were not present in his internal ears would his genius have remained the same, or would his have been the gentler muse of a Barrie or a Lamb? Or, on the other hand, did his temperament affect his disease? We cannot affirm that it did not. Most Ménière patients are highly strung and nervous, like asthmatics and other allergic subjects. Perhaps if they were not so constituted they might not be susceptible to the disease.

It is quite likely that posterity is profiting by Swift's sufferings, for an illness which comes on so suddenly with such extremely unpleasant manifestations is bound to leave an impression, particularly upon a man so stamped with personality as Swift. A disease in which one can fall out of a chair, which may make it necessary to lie prostrate to avoid injury in falling while a world whirling in giddy circles mingles with a background of violent nausea, will leave its mark on any man. Plunged periodically into this violent illness, and immobilized physically and mentally; gradually crawling back to health only to suffer sudden relapse when he felt fully recovered, it is no wonder the Dean became gloomy and morose. But no Ménière patient is stupid, and Swift's brain seems to have been sharpened rather than dulled by his experiences; warped it may have been, but not blunted.

Ménière's disease had not been described when Wilde wrote. Wilde thought the symptoms which it caused in Swift's case were due to 'periodic cerebral congestion', which was reasonable enough in the state of knowledge at his time. Unfortunately, he thought the terminal phase of senility which preceded Swift's death at the age of seventy-eight to be a culminating stage of this 'periodic cerebral congestion', and thereby confused the issue hopelessly for those who came after him.

In spite of all its errors, Wilde's book remains of the utmost importance. There are two principal reasons for this. One is the uncompromising way in which he insisted, against the general opinion of his time, that Swift was not mad. The other is the entirely admirable way in which he marshalled all the known facts of Swift's whole medical history in its pages.

CHAPTER XV THE BOYNE AND
BLACKWATER

I

DURING THIS decade Wilde's practice grew rapidly, and his health improved considerably. His father was dead, many of his ties with Roscommon were gone, and he did not revisit the west for some years. Instead he sought health and relaxation in the countryside around Dublin, sometimes fishing and shooting, occasionally hunting, but for the most part developing his antiquarian interests in the rich fields of Leinster. Sometimes he went farther afield, and on one occasion he went to Scotland with Petrie to look at the round tower at Brechin, but as a rule he confined himself to the counties around Dublin, where he found much to interest him.

A keen angler, he was naturally attracted to the rivers, along the banks of which he found many pagan and Christian remains to interest him when the fish were not rising. In particular, he loved to wander along the sides of Meath's great river Boyne, unlocking its vast storehouse of ancient treasure for those who came after him. For those who have eyes to see, the whole romance of Irish history is spread among the fertile plains of Meath. The earliest abodes of learning and Christian philosophy had their seats by Boyne's margin; parliaments and councils were held in its castles, and kingdoms lost and won on its banks.

When Wilde first visited the Boyne in search of health, he wandered, rod in hand, along its side in the morning freshness of early spring, to catch the mighty salmon for which the Boyne is famous. Later, in the scented air of summer evenings, he stalked the wily trout with subtler lures. When the mayfly's ephemeral existence was no more, and the deep rich foliage of midsummer shadowed the placid pools, his mind turned irresistibly to the past, for in these scenes of sylvan beauty fairy legends of little people and forgotten heroes seem as natural as the soil itself.

II

Being himself a countryman, Wilde was well able to talk to farmer and peasant. It is not hard to picture him, with his dark expressive eyes and wide mobile mouth, exploring and measuring an ancient castle or abbey, while some old farmer clad in sober frieze told him of its early history and inhabitants. In the opalescent twilight, he might sit in an ancient rath listening to the legends of Celtic fairyland. At night, by candlelight, with a bottle of claret at his elbow, he would put down a record of the day's gleanings.

The result was a long article on the Boyne and its tributary, the Blackwater, which appeared in parts in the *Dublin University*

Magazine as one of a series on the Irish Rivers. This paper was notable for the pleasant and yet accurate way in which Wilde discussed historical and archaeological matters. He gave a detailed itinerary, and described minutely the features of the district, and the nature and history of the remains he met with. The article attracted considerable attention and proved so popular that McGlashan soon published an expanded version of it in book form. As Wilde said himself: 'The interest which has been awakened by these rapid sketches of the Beauties of the Boyne was such as to induce the Publisher to request that I would again visit the great river of Meath, make further observations, collect additional information, include the Black-water and publish the materials thus obtained, in the form of an illustrated Hand-book for those charming, but hitherto neglected streams.'

This handbook was *The Beauties of the Boyne and Blackwater*, which was published by McGlashan in 1849. For some reason the book was published in a great hurry, as the following letter shows:

DEAR MAC GLASHAN,

Unless there is some great effort made to-morrow or that the printers worked on Sunday, which I suppose they won't, there will not be a chance of the book being out at all next week, and I intend to go away about the end of it. . . . I have now only about twenty pages to write, being the conclusion of the Battle of the **Boyne,** and the Notice of Drogheda which must be necessarily short. But unless some great effort be made at the **Press Work** there will not be perfect books for at least seven or eight days. If they put two presses at work to-morrow (Saturday) and keep them at it until we are finished it is just possible that there might be perfect books upon this day week (Friday next).

Will you like a good man poke up the Printers and don't leave all the abuse to me for I have enough to do without it. Indeed I cannot complain of them. They are doing for Gill's people wonders, but I want them to do more. I want them to do Miracles, which I am doing at present. If I don't live to see the book finished write my Elegy—Killed by a book—Slain by a Book-seller—Squeezed to Death in a Printing Press—made a Pye of, or anything literary of that description.

I send Sig I. Revise it for the printers at once.

W. R. WILDE.

It is remarkable that, notwithstanding this hurried publication, there is not a misprint to be found in the book.

With the *Lough Corrib*, written twenty years later, *The Beauties of the Boyne and Blackwater* remains Wilde's most popular work. Although it is now almost a century since it first appeared, no other author has equalled it as a regional guide to any part of Ireland.

It contains a wealth of legend and story, tales of the dragon who scooped out the bed of the Boyne; of the coming of St. Patrick to Slane; of Dearvorgaill, the Helen of the Irish Iliad, who was seduced by Dermot McMurrough, the ill-fated King of Leinster; of the de Lacys, the Berminghams, and other Anglo-Normans, of William and James, the last kings who in person staked their crowns in battle on British soil. It is full of information on historical and archaeological matters.

The first edition of *The Boyne and Blackwater* was dedicated to Petrie, 'whose Learning and critical Research have placed the Archaeology of this country on a philosophic Basis, And by whose Pencil its Sceneries and Antiquities have been so happily Illustrated', and to O'Donovan, 'the Irish Historian of the Nineteenth Century', 'in Testimony of public Respect, and private Affection'. A second, and enlarged edition was published within a year. The new volume contains no dedication to Petrie and O'Donovan, but is inscribed instead to 'Thomas Babington Macaulay, in testimony of the Respect and Admiration of the Author.' The great English historian had paid a visit to Dublin during the year in order to collect material for his History. Wilde, who was never one to neglect notabilities, conducted him to Newgrange and Dowth, and to the battlefield of the Boyne. Before coming over an English reviewer had expressed the opinion that Wilde's description of the countryside was overcoloured. Wilde took Macaulay up the Hill of Slane to prove his critic wrong.

CHAPTER XVI   PESTILENCE

*'A whimsical anecdote is related of an Irish potatoe.   An Englishman,
seeing a number of fine florid children in a cabin, said to the father:
"How do your countrymen contrive to have so many fine children?"
"By Jasus it is the potatoe, sir," said he.*
                                    Carr's *Stranger in Ireland.*

I

IN THE text of both editions of the *Boyne and Blackwater* appears
a stanza of a poem.   It is indifferent, if earnest verse, but it is
significant for us in that it was signed *Speranza.*
    Speranza's signature is a reminder that while Wilde was
peacefully pursuing his professional and archaeological activities,
Ireland was passing through years of disaster.   Nobody in the
land could avoid all the implications of the catastrophe.   We,
still in the first half of the twentieth century, pity ourselves
for having to suffer two world wars in a generation.   Ireland
a hundred years ago passed through a greater trial than modern
warfare has brought to any country in Europe.   The great
Irish Famine of 1845-49 produced horrors which would be
quite incredible were they not fully authenticated.
    The primary cause of the famine was the failure of the potato
crop, upon which the poor people depended almost entirely
for their subsistence.   Before the famine agriculture was in a
very neglected state.   Wheat, barley and oats were produced in
small quantity, and green crops, except turnips, were almost
unknown.   The vast peasant population, already on the verge
of destitution, did not even grow potatoes properly.   Although
they lived principally by them, they preferred to sow them
in lazy-beds, rather than in properly made drills.
    Never was a country in a more receptive position for famine.
The population was most dense in the poorest parts, the bogs
and mountains; they lived in wretched mud cabins, often
without chimneys, and lit by tiny windows; without money

M

or reserves, breeding great families of half-naked children, who grew up, built cabins for themselves on the bogside, married and multiplied, scraping a bare existence from the soil.

The completeness of the failure of the potato-crop during the famine has never been equalled, in Ireland or elsewhere. Since it was the main food of the people the consequences were unparalleled. It must not be thought that there had been no practical warnings of the peril of relying for support upon a single root-crop. On the contrary, the potato had failed many times before. There had, in fact, been no less than seven more or less extensive failures of the crop between 1821 and 1842. In most of these visitations the loss was ascribed to excessively wet weather, which so affected the potatoes that they rotted away after they had been placed in the pits in which it was customary to store them. In the five years of the great famine, another cause appeared—the blight. Although its effects were worst in Ireland, it occurred all over the world.

The first symptom of the disease presented itself as small brown spots on the leaf. These enlarged and coalesced, until the whole foliage of the plant was black and withered. The potatoes themselves were rotten, and not worth storing in the pits. In succeeding years things went from bad to worse. The spectres of starvation, destitution and disease stalked across the land, horror mounting upon horror, as in the kaleidoscope of a fantastic nightmare.

Wilde followed the famine closely in his capacity of Census Commissioner. He studied it as a whole, placing its origin just after the first invasion of cholera in 1832, when there was a very fatal epidemic amongst pigs. This was a very serious matter, which continued with intermissions up to the end of 1851, and almost annihilated the only saleable animal bred by the peasantry—'the gintilman that pays the rint'. This was followed by pleuro-pneumonia and foot-and-mouth disease amongst the cattle. Next, sheep got the rot, and soon even domestic fowl began to die mysteriously.

The ground being thus prepared, the blight, the real trouble, came. It was not only the potato which suffered. All types of vegetation decayed. Wheat, oats, turnips, beans and onions were affected, even the hardy race of coniferae suffered, and whole tracts of larches and pine-trees decayed. The air became dank and ominously oppressive, and lightning played in the electrically-laden sky. Whole fields formerly green and luxuriant were now not merely black and withered, but emitted an intolerable stench, like the effluvium of decaying flesh. Even apple trees withered and died. This state of affairs recurred yearly *for five years*.

During the famine, food prices rose excessively. It is said that during the first year sixteen millions worth of produce was destroyed. It is said also that during the first year the landlords and tax-gatherers exported, or sold, enough cereals and cattle to feed twice the population. This may perhaps be true, but it is also true that politicians, to their eternal shame, used the terrible events of this time to stir up unrest, as they always do in Ireland in times of crisis. In other countries a national calamity unites their peoples in a solid resolution of purpose.

In Ireland it produces undercurrents of intrigue, pulling in many different directions.

There was, however, another side to all this misery, which to some extent brings back our faith in human nature. This is the generosity with which the whole world, including England and many of the much-abused landlords, contributed to the relief schemes. The Society of Friends were foremost in the field; the British Association and every other public body subscribed liberally. Wilde's friend, George Henry Moore, of Moore Hall, Co. Mayo, father of George Moore, the novelist, with two of his kinsmen, Lord Sligo and Sir Robert Blosse, chartered the *Martha Washington* and loaded her with a thousand tons of flour in New Orleans. The cargo was duly discharged in Westport, Co Mayo, and involved the three landlords in a loss of nearly five thousand pounds. Some idea of the magnitude of the schemes undertaken, and also, unfortunately, of the destitution which prevailed, is given by the fact that on one day, the 3rd of July, 1847, nearly three million people were fed gratuitously. Road making, pier building and other public works were undertaken, and if many of them were stupidly conceived and unproductive, at least they were undertaken with a good object. Bridges were built where there were no rivers, and piers where there were no harbours. From the shores of Lough Corrib there is a canal which connects the lake with Lough Mask. It was originally intended to bring steamers to Ballinrobe, but when the water reached a certain distance it rushed into the bowels of the earth, for the engineers had completely overlooked the porous nature of the soil. The part of the canal which holds water now provides excellent, if educated, trout with the dryfly.

It must not be thought that all muddle and obstruction was on the part of the Government. Maize was imported in large quantities to feed the people. It was quite good food in the circumstances, but the politicians referred to it as 'Peel's brimstone', and the belief was fostered that it would turn those who ate it black. After all, there may be something to be said for government by despotism.

II

With the famine came pestilence—fever, scurvy, dysentery, cholera, influenza, and ophthalmia. Wilde, as Editor of the *Journal of Medical Science*, addressed a questionnaire to the country doctors. 'The Editor of the *Dublin Quarterly Journal of Medical Science* presents his compliments to Dr. ——, and begs to solicit his co-operation in bringing out a collective Report on the recent Epidemic Fever of Ireland. With this view he takes the liberty of submitting to him the accompanying list of queries, to each of which, he need hardly observe, separate replies are not expected. They have been merely drawn up as indicating some of the subjects on which information is desired by the profession here, and on the Continent', etc., etc. The list of questions was both searching and extensive, consisting of no less than forty-four items.

He received more than eighty replies, and from this drew up a record of the epidemics, which composed the greater part of four numbers of the *Journal*. For the first article he had the assistance of Dr. J. Moore Neligan of Jervis Street Hospital, who succeeded him as Editor in 1849, and of Dr. John Aldridge. Without their aid the numbers for the first quarter of 1849 would never have been published, for Wilde himself was at that time severely ill.

The health of Irish medical practitioners at this time gave rise to serious alarm amongst their ranks. Cusack and Stokes published a paper in the *Quarterly Journal* in which they pointed out that the mortality amongst the dispensary doctors for a period of twenty-five years past, had reached the appalling figure of twenty-four per cent per annum. These are amazing figures. Almost a quarter of the dispensary doctors, men mostly in the prime of life, had died. Curiously enough, cholera accounted for very few deaths, while almost half the number were due to typhus. Typhus is a dirt disease, conveyed by lice, but we need not presume that doctors were as insanitary in their person as the rest of the population, for, as Cusack and Stokes remarked, typhus was permanently present in Ireland at this time.

Dr. Crumpe was amongst those who answered Wilde's questionnaire. His report gives an idea of the conditions under which medical men laboured in Ireland during the famine. He was medical officer to the jail at Tralee, and he said: 'Circumstanced as our jail is, built on a flat from which there is no fall, and the hospital small and ill-ventilated, the sewers and necessaries become quickly choked up. The crowds of poor, starved wretches, hurried in droves to jail for some petty thefts, generally perpetrated for the purpose of being committed to jail to be saved from death by starvation, were quickly taken off by death from disease. These also quickly fell victims to fever, and from them it spread among the healthy classes in the jail, who heretofore enjoyed good health, and never suffered from starvation. The hospital soon became overcrowded, though my call for more accommodation was urgent long before it was attended to.

'In this horrid den those labouring under local disease, those ill from fever, those dying, and the dead from fever and dysentery, were promiscuously stretched together. So insufferable was the atmosphere of the place, so morbidly foetid and laden with noxious miasma, notwithstanding constant fumigation with chloride of lime, that on the door being opened I was uniformly seized, on entering, with most violent retching; and it is singular that I should be so affected, who dissected so much, have opened so many bodies, performed so many operations, and see often such forms of loathsome disease: yet the fact is so. Such was the polluted and contagious state of the air, that the nursetenders were quickly attacked, and some died. In this place my visits were as short and hurried as could be; I was forcibly driven back by the smell. The mortality was enormous, deaths often taking place a few hours after admission; but this occurred in the most exhausted and worn-down subjects. A few cases were seized with vomiting, throwing up large quantities of black stuff from the stomach; some few were jaundiced all over. But, generally speaking, the form was mild, commencing with chills and wearisomeness, followed by heat of surface, slight headache, quick pulse, white tongue, and loathing of food. By confinement to bed, and simple drinks, these symptoms subsided in a very few days, sometimes from three to five, often without any medicine, being succeeded by a ravenous appetite, which it was most difficult to regulate and control. Relapses and re-relapses were most frequent; diarrhoea generally setting in which no medicine or treatment could check. Had these cases occurred among previously healthy well-fed subjects in private life, where proper ventilation could be preserved, and airy apartments procured, recoveries would be more frequent. Many of the jail guards were attacked; none of these died in jail; they were well fed, and had better apartments.

'In the female department cases of fever and dysentery were comparatively few, more cleanliness of person being enforced among them, and they were not so crowded together.

'So foul was the atmosphere, so cadaverous was the smell, that I could not make post-mortem examinations, nor was there any accommodation to do so, though the bodies were numerous, and often no claimants for them. From one post-mortem which I saw in the military barrack, and from the symptoms and appearances—slight, minute ulcers on the mucous coat of intestines—I am convinced the same appearance would be found in all those fatal cases where diarrhoea succeeded fever. Strong, healthy, robust persons, with local disease, who would insist on going to hospital *contrary to all advice*, were quickly attacked by the same fever which their fellow-patients had, and soon fell victims. I do not know any circumstance which is a stronger proof of the contagiousness of the disease than the nursetenders being attacked.'

Wilde's report on the medical aspects of the famine ran through four numbers of the *Journal*, each part running to about sixty pages of three hundred and eighty words. It is a close analysis of symptoms and treatment, and demonstrates Wilde's wide grasp of detail and clarity of thought. It is typical of the best medical work of the period, in which for want of a scientific foundation recourse is had to what would now be considered a great amount of unnecessary detail of superficialities.

III

In the trail of typhus, dysentery and scurvy came trachoma. Wilde and Jacob, the two rival medical editors, who were also rival oculists, were sent to investigate outbreaks of ophthalmia which occurred in the workhouses of Tipperary and Athlone respectively. Their reports are interesting—Jacob's diffident and showing an inclination to hedge a little, Wilde's confident and definite. Dr. Jacob said: 'Of the nature of this ophthalmia, I have to state that when it attacks persons of feeble constitution, or labouring under derangement of the general health, it becomes most destructive. In such case, the eye is either more or less injured or rendered altogether useless by rapid ulceration in the first stage; or it is subsequently injured by protracted disease of the inside of the eyelids.

'The causes which produce it appear to be various. . . . As it is in the present case very desirable that it should be determined whether or not it is propagated by infection or contagion, I have given that point due consideration. There is a difference of opinion respecting this, but without attempting here to reconcile conflicting testimony, I advise the adoption of precautions calculated to prevent the spread of the disease in this way.'

Wilde had apparently been originally invited to examine the outbreak in both workhouses, but had refused to go to Athlone, for what seems an adequate reason. 'I was applied to, in the beginning of December 1849, to visit and report on the Ophthalmia which then raged in the Athlone Union. I did not do so, because I did not consider the sum offered a sufficient remuneration for my professional services.'

The matter of fees seems to have been settled to his satisfaction, for next year he visited the Tipperary Union. What he saw there was enough to make him report quite definitely both on the diagnosis of the disease and on its epidemic nature. 'The disease of the eyes under the effects of which the cases submitted for my inspection here labour, is an epidemic inflammation of the conjunctiva or external coat of the eye, commencing and chiefly having its seat in the inside of the eyelids, but in many instances extending rapidly to the globe, and destroying the cornea or transparent external coat, and so producing complete or partial blindness in one or both eyes. I believe it to be a modified form of the disease, denominated Egyptian Ophthalmia, which I have seen upon a large scale at Cairo and in other parts of the Levant, and which committed such ravages in the British army at the time of and subsequent to its occupation of Egypt in 1803. This disease still exists among the British troops, and a vast number of soldiers, both at home and in the colonies, lose their sight from it, and become pensioners upon the country. It has also lingered in particular regiments for years, notwithstanding every effort made to eradicate it, and such regiments having frequently changed climates. It used formerly to spread in public schools, particularly charter houses, and it has several times appeared in the country parts of Ireland, and spread among the people, not then subject to any particular privation, and apparently in previous good health. So long ago as 1720, an epidemic of this nature broke out near Castletowndelvin, in the County Westmeath, and a vast number of people lost their sight in consequence.

'It is manifestly contagious, as much so as fever, cholera, dysentery, or any other established contagious or infectious disease. . . .'

He told the medical attendants at Tipperary some home truths. 'In the observations which it is my duty to make, and the recommendations which I suggest for the removal of those errors which it appears to me have been committed, and still exist in the general management of your Ophthalmic Hospital, I beg to state that I am well aware that it is not within your power to rectify them. Their removal I will strongly impress on the Commissioners, but, at the same time, it is proper you should always bear them in your recollection. The wards of the hospital are much too low, and far too many patients are crowded into them. The ventilation is both irregular and inadequate. The clothing of a great number of the children is insufficient. During the approaching cold weather some means for heating the wards must be procured, and the unglazed windows must, in inclement weather, be properly secured. Cleanliness is not sufficiently attended to; three sponges are not enough for a ward containing nearly one hundred patients; there should be at least a dozen sponges, and the elder children should be shown how to use them themselves, and compelled to do so several times a day.'

From Tipperary he went on to visit the Athlone Union, about which he had equally pungent comments to make. 'Furnished with an umbrella, for it was raining at the time, I proceeded to the spot, and found two of the adult female paupers, each with a bucket of water before her, standing upon one of the highest and most exposed portions of the yard, and which commanded an extensive view of the adjoining river Shannon, and the damp, swampy ground beyond and around it. The children, according as they breakfasted, crept along an adjoining wall for shelter on their way to the schoolroom, which was at a considerable distance; and as each child came up, one of the washerwomen laid hold of it, pulled down its dress in front and behind, and bending it over the bucket, threw some of the cold water with her hand upon the face, neck, breast and shoulders of the little girl and then gave her a scrub with the open hand. Sometimes the child escaped before the process was completed, and ran off with the water trickling from its hair and down its neck; in other instances the children were dried with their own dresses. There were no towels there and upon inquiry I found that but two had been supplied by the guardians for the entire establishment.

'The patients in this hospital were chiefly cases of dysentery and ophthalmia. Of the latter, there were fourteen; and of these, eleven boys aged from eight to thirteen, presenting the worst cases which I witnessed anywhere, miserable-looking creatures, squalid and ragged, slept on a board laid directly on a damp floor in a sort of cellar or dormitory 33 feet long, 10 broad and 7 high, with unglazed windows facing a yard surrounded by high walls and only 25 feet square. This inclosure was the exercise-ground for these and about twelve other boys located in the same establishment! Of the eleven boys in this apartment, three had lost both eyes, three had lost one eye each, and the remainder had one or both seriously injured.'

IV

Ireland was indeed in desperate straits at this time. In case medical pens do not sufficiently describe the horrors of the famine, let us quote once more, this time from the writings of a layman, John Mitchel:

'There is a green nook, high up amidst the foldings of granite mountains, forty leagues off and more, and there is gurgling through it, murmuring and flashing in the sun, a little stream clear as crystal. . . . At our feet is the clear, poppling water; over our head the birch leaves quivering in the warm June air; and far-off is the sea, smooth and blue as a burnished sapphire.

'Rise, then, and we shall show you the way through the mountains to seaward, where we shall come down upon a little cluster of cabins, in one of which, two summers ago, we supped sumptuously on potatoes and salt with the decent man who lives there, and the dark-eyed woman of the house and five small children. We had a hearty welcome though the fare was poor; and as we toasted our potatoes in the *greeshaugh*, our ears drank in the honey-sweet tones of the well-beloved Gaelic.

'As we come down towards the roots of the mountain, you may feel, loading the evening air, the heavy balm of hawthorn blossoms; here are whole thickets of white-mantled hawthorn, every mystic tree smothered with snow-white and showing like branching coral in the South Pacific. And be it remembered that never in Ireland, since the last of her chiefs sailed away from her, did that fairy tree burst into such luxuriant beauty and fragrance as this very year. The evening, too, is delicious; the golden sun has deepened into crimson, over the sleeping sea, as we draw near the hospitable cottages; almost you might dream that you beheld a vision of the Connacht of the thirteenth century. . . . But why do we not see the smoke curling from those lowly chimneys? And surely we ought by this time to scent the well-known aroma of the turf fires. But what . . . may heaven be about us this night! . . . what reeking breath of

hell is this oppressing the air, heavier and more loathsome
than the smell of death rising from the carnage of a battlefield?
Oh, Misery! . . . had we forgotten that this was the *Famine
Year*? And we are here in the midst of those thousand
Golgothas that border our island with a ring of death from
Cork Harbour all round to Lough Foyle. There is no need
for inquiries here . . . no need for words; the history of this
little society is plain before us. Yet we go forward, with sick
hearts and swimming eyes, to examine the Place of Skulls nearer.
There is a horrible silence; grass grows before the doors; we
fear to look within, though all the doors are open or off the
hinges; for we fear to see yellow chapless skeletons grinning
there. But our footfalls rouse two lean dogs, that run from
us with doleful howling, and we know by the felon-gleam
in the wolfish eyes how they have lived after their masters
died. We walk amidst the houses of the dead and out at the
other side of the cluster, and there is not one where we dare
enter. We stop before the threshold of our host of two years
ago; we put our head, with eyes shut, inside the door-jamb,
and say, with shaking voice: "God save all here." No answer!
. . . ghastly silence and a mouldy stench, as from the mouth
of burial-vaults. They are dead! . . . the strong man and
the dark-eyed woman and the little ones, with their liquid
Gaelic accents that melted into music for us two years ago;
they shrunk and withered together until they hardly knew
one another's faces; but their horrid eyes scowled on each
other with a cannibal glare. We know the whole story . . .
the father was on a "public work", and earned the sixth part
of what would have maintained his family. It was not always
paid him; but still it kept them half alive for three months,
and so instead of dying in December they died in March. And
the agonies of those three months . . . who can tell? . . . the
poor wife wasting and weeping over her stricken children;
the heavy-laden weary man, with black night thickening around
him . . . feeling his own arm shrink and his step totter with
the cruel hunger that gnaws his life away, and knowing too
surely that all this will soon be over. . . . Now he can totter
forth no longer, and he stays at home to die. But his darling
wife is dear to him no longer; there is a dull, stupid malice in
their looks; they forget that they had five children all dead
weeks ago, and flung coffinless into shallow graves . . . nay, in

the frenzy of their despair they would rend one another for the last morsel in that house of doom; and at last, in misty dreams of drivelling idiocy, they die utter strangers. . . .

'No shelter here to-night, then; and here we are far on in the night, still gazing on the hideous ruin. A man might gaze and think on such a scene, till curses breed about his heart of hearts, and the *hysterica passio* swells in his throat. But we have many miles to walk before we reach our inn; so come along with us and we will tell you as we walk together in the shadows of the night . . .'

CHAPTER XVII

REVOLUTION

I

WHEN THOMAS DAVIS died Gavan Duffy chose John Mitchel to be his successor as editor of the *Nation*. Mitchel was a very remarkable man, who had first shown his mettle when, at the age of twenty, he had eloped with the young daughter of his neighbour, Captain Verner. The young couple had run away to England, but they were pursued and discovered by the girl's irate father, and Mitchel had his first experience of prison as a result. When he was released he followed his Jenny back to Ireland. She was hidden in the country, but he found her place of concealment. He pleaded his cause to her custodians with such effect that they agreed to help him in spite of her parents, and a couple of months later they were pronounced man and wife by the Rev. David Decimus Babington, curate of Drumcree, Co. Armagh. Needless to say, they lived happily ever after—at least, in so far as Mitchel's political activities allowed. For the next ten years they lived peacefully in Banbridge.

Mitchell was the obvious choice for the chair which was so tragically vacant. Although his life so far had been that of a country lawyer, he had already attracted attention amongst the more literary Young Irelanders by his *Life of Hugh O'Neill*. A dynamic force was necessary to stimulate the movement so heavily stricken, and his was clearly the personality to supply it. Without hesitation, he came to Dublin and took up his new duties there.

It is interesting to compare Davis and Mitchel, the two great literary leaders of Young Ireland. One was a statesman in embryo, the other a revolutionary, as Washington and Jefferson were, or Mirabeau and Robespierre. It has been said that Davis was moved principally by love for Ireland, while Mitchel's chief inspiration was hatred for England. Had Davis not died young he might have led Young Ireland to constitutional power without bloodshed.

When Mitchel was given control of the *Nation* his fiery spirit took him in charge. Moved by passionate sincerity, he and his followers committed excesses which Davis would never have allowed. By ill-organized and over-hasty effort they placed themselves in an untenable position, fore-doomed to defeat because of the country's exhaustion. As Mitchel himself wrote of another: 'To take a man from the occupations and distractions of everyday life, to place him in a study where he cannot be disturbed, to drive him to mental exertion as a necessary pastime, to strengthen his intellect by discipline and constant application, and to steep his heart in gall and bitterness, and make it beat only for revenge, appears to be the maddest mode of checking dangerous opinions, or interfering with the most effective exertions of men.'

It must not be thought that Davis was not quite as sincere as

John Mitchel, aged 39

Mitchel. He was; but his fervour was tempered by wise judgement derived from scholarship.

In the field of literature, the scales balanced on the other side. Davis was a facile, and at times, brilliant ballad writer, but he was not a great poet. On the other hand, Mitchel's *Jail Journal* is amongst the prose classics of the English language. Seamus MacCall says: 'The style of his more literary work had much in common with his passion for rushing rivers and foaming torrents. Words tumbled from his pen like a pent-up river escaping from a rocky prison and foaming over and around all obstacles, or cascading down a mountain-side into some smooth and smiling valley below. As with Carlyle, this effect was realized in part by the cadence and rhythm of his phrasing, in part by his liberal use of adjectives and long compound sentences, and in part by the natural harmony of expression with the tumultous thoughts which set his words in motion. . . . He had a deep and intense love of wild nature, and his peculiar power of word-painting was at its best when this love was his inspiration.'

After Davis died, the national movement appeared to be paralyzed. O'Connell was discredited and broken, Dillon away in Madeira to recover his health. Mitchel's first duty was to bring the party together once more, and to infuse new life into it.

This he did in the same dingy editor's office where Davis had laboured a little while before. Here he encouraged the old associates, and gathered new ones. Gavan Duffy, Smith O'Brien, the unfortunate Mangan, Reilly, Darcy Magee, McNevin, and many others rallied round him. Soon the *Nation* was going full steam ahead once more.

II

Amongst the new contributions to the paper were a series of political articles signed 'John Fenshaw Ellis'. They were ably written, in a somewhat flowery style, and they at once awakened speculation as to the identity of their author. Gavan Duffy has told how he came to discover that John Fenshaw Ellis was really a woman. She was, in fact, none other than Jane Francesca Elgee, Wilde's future bride.

'I was greatly struck by the first contribution, and requested Mr. John Fenshaw Ellis to call at the *Nation* Office. Mr. Ellis pleaded that there were difficulties which rendered this course impracticable, and invited me to visit him in Leeson Street. I did so immediately, not without a secret suspicion of the transformation I was about to witness. A smiling parlour-maid, when I inquired for Mr. Ellis, showed me into a drawing-room, where I found only Mr. George Smith, publisher to the University. "What!" I cried; "my loyal friend, are you the new volcano of sedition?" Mr. Smith only answered by vanishing into a back drawing-room and returning with a tall girl on his arm, whose stately carriage and figure, flashing brown eyes, and features cast in an heroic mould, seemed fit for the genius of poetry, or the spirit of revolution. He presented me to Miss Jane Francesca Elgee, in lieu of Mr. John Fenshaw Ellis. Miss Elgee was the daughter of an archdeacon of the Establishment, and had probably heard nothing of Irish nationality among her ordinary associates, but, as the strong and generous are apt to do, had worked out convictions for herself . . . her little scented notes, sealed with wax of a delicate hue and dainty device, represented a substantial force in Irish politics, the vehement will of a woman of genius.'

Miss Elgee did not confine herself to prose, but soon came to be better known as Speranza, the poetess.

Jane Francesca Elgee was the daughter of Charles Elgee of Wexford. There is some mystery about the date of her birth, for Charles Elgee died in India in 1824, while it is generally understood that she was born at Wexford in 1826. This confusion probably results from an understatement of her age on her own part. In any case, when she was visited by Gavan Duffy at 34, Leeson Street she was not much more than twenty years of age. The Elgees were originally Italian, descended from the Algiati of Florence, the first member of the family to come to Ireland being Speranza's great-grandfather. Her grandfather, Archdeacon Elgee, rector of Wexford, played a remarkable part in the '98 rebellion, but remained unmolested by the rebels because of his great popularity and personality. Her mother was Sarah Kingsbury, whose father, Dr. Kingsbury, Commissioner in Bankruptcy, owned Lisle House in Dublin. Her uncle, Sir Thomas Ormsby, Bart., was a member of the last Irish Parliament. Dr. Robert McClure, the seeker of the North-West Passage, was her first cousin, and she was also related to the Rev. Charles Maturin, the famous novelist of the period. It is from one of Maturin's characters that Oscar Wilde got his last pseudonym, *Sebastian Melmoth*. Speranza's only brother, Judge Elgee, became a distinguished member of the American Bar.

From her childhood she was of a scholarly disposition. In her early years she acquired a sound knowledge of German, Italian and French literature, and she could read Æschylus for pleasure when her girlish associates were reading novels. She was brought up in an atmosphere of rigid Unionism. As we have seen, when the funeral of Thomas Davis passed her house in Leeson Street she did not know who he was. Her attention was attracted, she got hold of a copy of *The Spirit of the Nation* which fired her imagination, and soon she herself became one of the *Nation's* most prominent contributors.

Speranza's poems soon became famous. They were full of fire and spirit, seeking to arouse the furies of passion rather than to glorify the dead past. She often dwelt with savage indignation upon the horrors of the Famine.

They certainly had a great vogue in those troubled times, and continued to crop up in street ballads for many years, but now, like extinct volcanos, their day is done. Even the best of them, *Two Million a Decade* and *The Famine Year* are scarcely known to-day, although they are to be found in recently published editions of Speranza's work. Here is a verse from *The Famine Year* :

'Little child, tears are strange upon your infant face,
God meant you but to smile within your mother's soft embrace.
"Oh, we know not what is smiling, and we know not what
is dying,
But we're hungry, very hungry, and we cannot stop our
crying;
And some of us grow cold and white, we know not what
it means,
But as they lie beside us, we tremble in our dreams !"'

Sometimes she described her personal ambitions :

'For I can breathe no trumpet-call,
To make the slumb'ring Soul arise;
I only lift the funeral-pall
That so God's light might touch thine eyes,
And ring the silver prayer-bell clear
To rouse thee from thy trance of fear;
Yet, if thy mighty heart has stirred
Even with one pulse-throb at my word,
Then not in vain my woman's hand
Has struck thy gold harp while I stand
Waiting thy rise,
Loved Ireland !"

At times it was thought that she had aspirations to become a modern Joan of Arc—or as somebody said, "the Madame Roland of the Irish Gironde."

> 'Oh! that I stood upon some lofty tower,
>   Before the gathered people face to face
> That, like God's thunder, might my words of power
>   Roll down the cry of freedom to its base!
> Oh! that my voice, a storm above all storms,
>   Could cleave earth, air, and ocean, rend the sky
> With the fierce earthquake shout, "to arms! to arms!"
>   For truth, fame, freedom, vengeance, victory!'

'Her virile and sonorous songs broke on the public ear like the plash in later times of a great wave of thought in one of Swinburne's metres,' said Gavan Duffy, expressing the general view. Speranza's poems were undoubtedly overrated at the time of their first appearance. There is little of the music of true poetry in them, but they are redeemed by their fervid sincerity.

In spite of the masculine nature of her poems Speranza was a warm-hearted, romantic and generous girl. Perhaps her best characteristic was her capacity for loyalty, a quality which was to be tested many times in her troubled life.

She had other very feminine characteristics. One of them was her style of writing, which was florid and grandiloquent, in the habit of the period. She could not write an ordinary letter. Here is one she wrote to Gavan Duffy from 34, Leeson Street:

MY DEAR SIR,

I return with many thanks the volume of Cromwell which has been travelling about with me for the last four months, and shall feel obliged for the two others when you are quite at leisure, though not even Carlyle can make this soulless iconoclast interesting. It is the only work of Carlyle I have met with, in which my heart does not go along with his words.

I cannot forbear telling you, now the pen is in my hand, how deeply impressed I was with your lecture to your club, which was the sublimest teaching, and the style was simple from its very sublimity. It seemed as if truth passed directly from your heart to ours without the aid of a medium, at least, I felt that everywhere the thoughts struck you, nowhere the words, and this, in my opinion, is the perfection of composition, this soul speaking to soul. . . . Truly, one cannot despair when God sends us such teachers.

But you will wish me away for another four months, if I write you such long notes, so I shall conclude with kind compliments to Mrs. Duffy, and shall remain

Yours very sincerely,

FRANCESCA ELGEE.

At times Speranza's writings showed a lack of balanced judgement, or to put it more plainly, ordinary common sense. When somebody threw a stone at Smith O'Brien in Limerick, she wrote: 'What can be done for such idiots and savages? . . . This noble Smith O'Brien who has sacrificed all for the people, and who could gain nothing in return, for no position, however exalted, could add to his dignity, whose life has been a sacrifice to his country, a self-immolation—and this is the man who has to be guarded by English from Irish murderers! I cannnot endure to think of it. We are disgraced for ever before Europe, and justly so. Adieu!'

It is hard to imagine Europe being shaken by a stone thrown at Smith O'Brien in Limerick, although stranger things have happened, but Speranza viewed the transaction through her own magnifying glass.

Wilde met Speranza soon after she came to Dublin. He was immediately attracted to her. Of the many women in his life, she was probably the first whom he regarded as more or less his intellectual equal.

Although he respected her enthusiasms, he had sense enough not to be drawn into politics, preferring less spectacular work for humanity in his hospital and study. Nevertheless, he was no longer the uncompromising Unionist of his earlier years.

III

Meanwhile Mitchel and O'Connell continued their agitation for Repeal. About a month after Mitchel took over the *Nation* the *London Standard* published an article suggesting various repressive measures for dealing with the Repeal movement. In this the Government was reminded that should local rebellion occur the railways would bring every part of Ireland within easy reach of the troops from Dublin. To this Mitchel replied editorially. He said that nothing could be easier than to lift a section of track, or to fill a few perches of a cutting. The materials of the lines—'good hammered iron and wooden sleepers'—were capable of other uses than assisting locomotives; and further, troop trains might be ambushed in the cuttings. 'Imagine a few hundred men lying in wait at such a spot, with masses of rocks and trunks of trees ready to roll down: and a train or two advancing with a regiment of infantry, and the engine panting nearer and nearer till the polished studs of brass on its front are distinguishable, and its name may nearly be read: "Now, in the Name of the Father, and of the Son, and of the Holy Ghost! . . . Now!"'

This was frank sedition. Gavan Duffy, as proprietor of the *Nation* was charged with publishing a 'seditious libel'. Mitchel, profiting by his legal knowledge, instructed the defence. The jury disagreed, and Mitchel won his first political skirmish with the law.

He carried on the fight furiously, breathing hatred for England as well as love for his own country. 'The Irish people, always half-starved, are expecting absolute famine day by day; they know that they are destined to months of a weed diet next summer; that "hungry ruin has them in the wind"—and they ascribe it, unanimously, not so much to the wrath of Heaven as to the greedy and cruel policy of England. They believe that the seasons as they roll are but the ministers of English rapacity; that their starving children cannot sit down to their scanty meal but they see the harpy-claw of England in their dish. They behold their own wretched food melting in rottenness, off the face of the earth; and they see heavy laden ships freighted with the yellow corn their own hands have sown and reaped, spreading all sail *for England*; they see it, and with every grain of that corn there goes a heavy curse.'

This was about the time of the first Coercion Bill. O'Connell then made his alliance with the Whigs in return for certain proposed concessions in Ireland and, it must be added, a promise of the control of Irish patronage. This effort at compromise was distasteful to the Young Irelanders, who protested vigorously.

O'Connell was resentful, and framed a resolution calling for the expulsion of the 'juvenile members' at the next meeting at Conciliation Hall. In spite of vociferation and even eloquence the resolution was carried, and Mitchel, Meagher, Gavan Duffy, Devin Reilly and others were compelled to walk out.

Having left the Repeal Association, Mitchel and his fellows felt the need of a new platform and established the 'Irish Confederation'. It found a new and powerful ally in Fintan James Lalor, who had just become a contributor to the *Nation*. He was a clear-headed thinker, and the first Irishman to realize that the spiritual concept of nationhood is almost confined to city-dwellers, while the countryman thinks only of the patch of soil he owns.

But it was not only amongst Nationalists that converts were made. Gavan Duffy said 'of our opponents scarce one escaped its influence. Isaac Butt, who had been recently editor of the *University Magazine* and of the *Ulster Times* in Belfast, was still leader of the most extreme Orange party in the Dublin Corporation. His successor in the editorship of the magazine, Charles Lever, nursed a rage against O'Connell so preternatural that it overflowed into his novels. William Carleton, Joseph Le Fanu, William Wilde, and above all, Samuel Ferguson, were among the chief contributors. . . . Before half a dozen years had elapsed, Samuel Ferguson was chairman of a Protestant Repeal Association, declaring in prose and verse that he shared the principles of the Young Irelanders. Before a dozen more years Isaac Butt was leader of a National movement to establish a Parliament in Ireland, surrounded by professors of the exclusive University, clergymen of the Church of England, members of all the learned professions, the leaders of the Tory opposition in the Dublin Corporation, and his old colleagues, Dr. Wilde and Dr. Maunsell. At one of Butt's meetings Charles Lever advocated a Federal Parliament in Ireland. At an earlier date William Carleton declared himself a Nationalist and became a contributor to the *Nation*, and Joseph Le Fanu, who could not be seduced out of the tranquil field of literature, wrote books and poems which are still read by Irish Nationalists with affection and enthusiasm.'

The famine went yearly from bad to worse, and now the great tide of emigration began. Starving people, looking for a happier life across the ocean, were packed into fever-stricken emigration ships. 'Crowded and filthy, carrying double the legal number of passengers, and having no doctor on board, the holds were like the Black Hole of Calcutta, and deaths in myriads.'

O'Connell also left Ireland. He went to Italy in search of health, but was not to come back alive. With him perished the Repeal Association for all practical purposes.

Reports of the ghastly effects of the famine came in daily to the *Nation* offices, from the land, the workhouses and prisons. The scale of horror they described beggars description. They bred a savage resentment in Mitchel's heart, and made him throw caution to the winds. He saw in the Government assistance schemes nothing but a diabolical plan to break the people's spirit, to show them that they were an inferior, a pauper race; feeling that he could not look his own children in the face he resolved upon open defiance. 'Parliament Law' must be over-thrown, and he would show his people how it was to be done. 'Go to! The revolutionary Leveller is your only architect. Therefore take courage . . . stand upon your rights, and do your appointed work with all your strength, let the canting fed classes rave and shriek as they will.'

But the fire of Mitchel's fury was too formidable for his friends—so much so that it may have contributed to the ultimate rather ignominious failure of the movement. But divided counsel dogged it throughout, first between Young Ireland and O'Connell, later when Mitchel went too fast for his associates to follow him. The Protestant revolutionaries of Ireland have ever been firebrands.

Speranza continued to fan the flames with prose and verse. She translated stories of the first French Revolution from the history of the Girondins. Lamartine interested her, as was shown by another translation from the French, *The Wanderer and His Home*. To demonstrate her versatility she also translated *Sidonia the Sorceress* from the German in 1847. The latter work was re-published in an expensive folio edition by the Kelmscott Press in 1893. A third edition, with beautiful illustrations by Thomas Lowinsky, was published for the Julian Brothers by Ernest Benn as recently as 1926.

For a time Gavan Duffy and Smith O'Brien restrained Mitchel. Soon, however, his difference in policy was so marked that he felt compelled to resign from the *Nation* and from the Confederation. With Devin Reilly as his chief assistant he founded another paper, the *United Irishman*. Among its contributors were Mangan, John Martin, and Father Kenyon, a scholarly priest from Tipperary.

'The birth of the *United Irishman* was definitely the birth of a new era in Irish History,' says Seamus MacCall in his masterly biography of Mitchel. 'It was all that the *Nation* had been, and more besides. It did not merely preach patriotism; it elevated "sedition" into literature and made it holy. Its articles, written in masterly language, passionate and yet logical, and pointed with satire reminiscent of Swift, compelled the attention of friends and enemies. To the educated classes Mitchel's unshackled prose was an intellectual luxury; in the minds of the masses it was sparks of fire.'

'Mitchel,' said his modern disciple, Patrick Pearse, 'was of the stuff of which great prophets and ecstatics have been made. He did really hold converse with God; he did really deliver God's word to man, delivered it fiery-tongued.'

Week after week, the *United Irishman* preached Mitchel's gospel. Sales went up by leaps and bounds, and the Government became correspondingly alarmed. 'Things are in a very ticklish position,' said Sir Charles Napier.

And indeed so they were, in the year of grace 1848. Not only were they so in Ireland, but in England, and all over Europe. England had the Chartist movement to deal with, and in France the people, having got rid of Louis Philippe, had proclaimed 'a new era of liberty, and the brotherhood of all Europe.'

The success of the revolution in France had an electric effect in Ireland. The first repercussion was the conversion of the Confederation to the doctrine of physical force, and the return of Mitchel and his associates to the fold. Another was the first appearance of the green, white and orange tricolour, now the flag of Éire.

A public meeting was held to approve an address of congratulation to the French people. Smith O'Brien and Meagher went off to France to present the address to the French Republic. New branches of the Confederation sprang up like mushrooms overnight. Soon there was an Emmet Club, or a Sarsfield or Wolfe Tone Club in every village in Ireland.

New regiments were drafted into Ireland, and guns were

mounted on the roof of the Bank of Ireland, once the Parliament House. Hussars, lancers and dragoons galloped through the streets, and the infantry practised 'platoon firing' in the city squares. On the rebel side, the *Nation* and the *United Irishman* now spoke as one voice. The aim was no longer a home Parliament, but an independent Republic. Mitchel urged the people to drill and arm, and his red-headed assistant, Devin Reilly, went so far as to extol the virtues of vitriol as a weapon against the invader. 'Let the man among you who has no gun sell his garment and buy one,' wrote Mitchel.

IV

The Government could not stand this. It struck, swiftly, before any plans for rebellion had been properly organized. Soon all the Young Ireland leaders were arrested or scattered in concealment. Nobody was left to run the *Nation*.

Here Speranza and Miss Callan, Duffy's sister-in-law, stepped in. 'Two women of genius,' said Gavan Duffy. Miss Callan acted as editor, and Speranza produced a leading article 'suitable for the occasion'. This was the famous article, *Jacta alea est*, which appeared in the issue for July 29th, 1848. It was certainly a noteworthy production, "as lofty and passionate as one of Napoleon's bulletins after a great victory," said Gavan Duffy. He was hardly correct in this description, for it was less a pæan of victory than a straightforward incitement to rebellion:

'We must be free! In the name of your trampled, insulted, degraded country; in the name of all heroic virtues, of all that makes life illustrious or death divine; in the name of your starved, your exiled, your dead; by your martyrs in prison cells and felon chains; in the name of God and man; by the listening earth and the watching Heaven, lift up your right hand to heaven and swear by your undying soul, by your hopes of immortality, never to lay down your arms, never to cease hostilities, till you regenerate and save this fallen land!

'Oh! for a hundred thousand muskets glittering brightly in the light of heaven, and the monumental barricades stretching across each of our noble streets made desolate by England—circling round that doomed Castle, where the foreign tyrant has held his council of treason and iniquity against our people and our country for seven hundred years.

'... One bold, one decisive move. One instant to take breath, and then a rising; a rush, a charge from north, south, east and west upon the English garrison, and *the land is ours*. Do your eyes flash, do your hearts throb at the prospect of having a *country*? For you have had no country. You have never felt the pride, the dignity, the majesty of independence. You could never lift up your head to heaven and glory in the name of Irishmen, for all Europe read the brand of *slave* upon your brow.

'... To die for Ireland! Yes; have we not sworn it in a thousand passionate words by our poets and orators—in the grave resolves of councils, leagues, and confederations. Now is the moment to test whether you value most freedom or life. Now is the moment to strike; and by striking save, and the day after the victory it will be time enough to count your dead.

'... We must show to the world that we are fitted to govern ourselves; that we are, indeed, worthy to be a free nation; that the words union, liberty, country, have as sacred a meaning in our hearts and actions as they are holy on our lips; that patriotism means not merely the wild irresistible force that crushed tyranny, but reconstruction, regeneration, heroism, sacrifice, sublimity; that we have not alone to break the fetters of Ireland, but to raise her to a glorious elevation—defend her, liberate her, ennoble her, sanctify her.'

Jacta alea est was never published, for the whole issue was seized, and the paper suppressed. This, and another article, also by Speranza, *The Hour of Destiny*, which had appeared in the previous issue, were the chief points in the prosecution of Duffy, and laid him open to a charge of high treason. Isaac Butt, when making his speech for the defence of Gavan Duffy, said: 'I now hold in my hand a letter from the authoress of these articles, assuring me that Mr. Duffy never saw them before they were published, and that he was not present at the time. I would not be suffered to give pain to the highly-respectable connections of this lady and to herself, by placing her on the table, but I ask the Solicitor-General as a man of honour, and a man of honour I believe him to be—he knows the lady as well as I do—to contradict my statement if it is not true.'

No contradiction could be made. It must have brought

sorrow to Speranza's generous mind to know that her violent articles had done so much mischief to her friends.

Whether it did or not, whether she was right or wrong, Speranza was not one to hide her light under a bushel. When the Attorney-General was haranguing the jury, asking for a conviction, a female voice rang out in the body of the court: 'I am the culprit,' it said, 'I wrote the offending articles.' The voice was Speranza's. It had its effect, for the jury disagreed.

Nevertheless, this was virtually the end of Young Ireland. The movement which had promised so well, and had secured the almost unanimous support of the masses, fizzled out through the lack of concerted action by its leaders. Smith O'Brien and Dillon tried to raise a revolt in Munster, but it was a lamentable failure. There was no enthusiasm, for those of the peasantry who had survived the famine had scarcely the strength to hold a weapon. The only armed conflict took place at Ballingarry in Tipperary, between a police garrison and a few peasants led by Smith O'Brien. Soon O'Brien and the other leaders joined Duffy and Mitchel in jail. They were well-treated in prison, well fed and allowed to associate with each other. Wilde, Samuel Ferguson, and Father Mathew were amongst their many visitors. State trials followed in which several of them were condemned to death. The sentences were, however, commuted, and instead of being executed they spent some years in prison in Van Diemen's Land. On their release many of them continued to lead distinguished lives, and in some cases they reached high office under the British Crown.

The year 1848 is a key date in European history, and the events as a whole are typified by what happened in Ireland. It has been described as the turning-point in history at which Europe failed to turn. But in spite of the fact that the revolutions which occurred throughout Europe fizzled out ignominiously in most cases, they marked the beginning of a period of international unrest which was eventually to produce most important results. At home, the Young Ireland movement was followed by Fenianism, Sinn Fein, and eventually by the establishment of Éire; in Germany and Italy national unity was achieved; and France became a republic once more. But it was in the Austria that Wilde knew so well that the year 1848 was to produce the most important changes. Vienna then was still what Wilde had found it, an almost feudal city, from which the despotic Metternich ruled a vast conglomerate Empire for the Hapsburgs. Austria, Bohemia, Italy, and Hungary; Germans, Croats, Magyars, Hungarians, Poles, Slovaks, Rumanians, and Italians all came under their yoke. Nobody could hold this ramshackle Empire together.

First Sicily, then Vienna rose. Metternich was deposed, and forced to fly for refuge to the England which he hated. Next Milan and Venice rebelled, and in Hungary Kossuth proclaimed the doctrine of the fraternisation of free peoples.

All these movements failed for a time. Garibaldi was beaten in Italy, for he had not yet a united Italy behind him. Later, with the assistance of England and also of King Victor Emmanuel II of Sardinia, and Cavour, he was to establish Italy as we know it. In Austria, on December 2nd, 1848, the Emperor Francis Joseph began his reign, which was to last until 1916. In Bavaria Ludwig I lost his throne for his mistress, Lola Montez.

In the midst of all this turmoil, Wilde's friend Semmelweis quietly continued his great work for women.

CHAPTER XVIII   MARRIAGE

I

IN *SAUNDERS' NEWSLETTER* of 13th November, 1851, is the following bare announcement:

'Married on the 12th inst., at St. Peter's Church by the Reverend John M. Wilde, A.M., Incumbent of Trinity Church, Northwich, William R. Wilde, Esq., F.R.C.S., to Jane Francesca, youngest daughter of the late Charles Elgee, Esq., and grand-daughter of the late Archdeacon Elgee, of Wexford.'

The wedding went off very quietly, if we may judge by the absence of comment in the papers of the time. After three weeks Wilde brought his bride home to Westland Row. Where they had spent their honeymoon we do not know. They may have gone to London to see the great Exhibition in Hyde Park, or possibly they adventured farther afield and went travelling on the Continent. More likely Wilde visited none of these places, but took his bride instead to the West of Ireland.

Wherever they went, they must have looked an incongruous and strangely-matched pair. Wilde, at thirty-six, was small and slight, very upright, very active, rather untidy, with an open face whose best features were the large expressive eyes, quick to reflect every changing mood of his volatile mind. He still had masses of dark hair brushed back from a good forehead, which came down to mingle with a fuzz of black side-whisker and beard. His upper lip, like Abraham Lincoln's, remained clean-shaven to give full value to a wide, sensuous mouth. Speranza, by his side, towered above him, ten years younger, and as yet unaffected by the ravages of time and matrimony. She was undoubtedly the handsomer of the pair, for her features, if slightly coarse, were good, and her figure was still slender and willowy. She was darker than her husband, for her hair was blue-black as a raven's wing. Wide sleeves and heavily flounced skirts gave her a truly majestic appearance, but the small poke-bonnet of the period looked rather foolish on her Junoesque head. One cannot help sympathizing with large women on the millinery problem, and on the law of nature which makes them marry small men.

On the first of December they returned to Dublin to begin their married life in the mid-Victorian world of 1851. It was not a bad period in which to make a start, in spite of the troubled decade which had gone before. The great Exhibition had inaugurated a period of prosperity, and the railways had, as Disraeli predicted, made for a general levelling of the classes. There were still extremely nice social distinctions. Even the high standing of individual doctors in Dublin had not quite made their profession as a whole socially equal to the Church and the Services, whatever their personal position. The day of the merchant princes had not yet dawned, but it was not far off. The Exhibition heralded a golden age of great industrial and colonial expansion for England. Unfortunately for Ireland it marked the beginning of accentuated decline, but as yet this effect was not obvious.

To some eyes the mid-Victorian years are a period of execrable taste, when every art became a degenerate baroque which delighted to defeat its medium. Nevertheless, the bric-a-brac of stuffed birds and antimacassars notwithstanding, these rooms knew a solid and a comfortable leisure which many would envy to-day. Victorian residences may have looked forbidding and gloomy in the dim flickering of street-lights, but inside one was sure to find pleasant rooms with gas lamps hissing cheerfully. Warm turkey carpets and solid furniture of walnut and mahogany formed a comfortable background for large and happy families who depended upon their own devices for entertainment. There was no raucous telephone to interfere with one's privacy, and no motor-car to accelerate the *tempo* of work. A consultant's life was a gentlemanly one in those days, and if, as is probable, he saw only about half the number of patients attended by his modern successor, he had so much more time to think and write about them.

II

Among the regular visitors to Westland Row was another young married couple, for Samuel Ferguson had recently married a member of the Guinness family. Ferguson was an Ulsterman, and an old associate of Wilde's, with whom he had many interests in common. He had been called to the Bar in 1838, the year after Wilde qualified. Like Wilde, he had a passion for literature and archaeology, so great in his case that his profession soon came to take a secondary place. As well as being a first-rate scientific archaeologist, he was a good artist, capable of illustrating his researches with excellent pen-and-ink drawings. He was in sympathy with the Young Ireland movement, and in 1848 founded the Protestant Repeal Association to help it. Later he retired altogether from politics to devote himself entirely to poetry, in which his real interests lay. 'Your destiny,' said Speranza, 'is to become the Historic Bard of Ireland.' There was some truth in her statement. 'The author of these poems,' said W. B. Yeats, 'is the greatest poet Ireland has produced, because the most central and most Celtic . . . the one man of his time who wrote heroic poetry—one who among the somewhat sybaritic singers of his day, was like some aged sea-king sitting among the inland wheat and poppies —the savour of the sea about him and its strength.'

'What seems to me most noteworthy in your poems,' wrote Edward Dowden, 'is the union of culture with simplicity and strength. Their refinement is large and strong . . . they have spaces and movements which give one a feeling like the sea or the air on a headland.'

Ferguson was a man after Wilde's own heart, and they remained fast friends until the end. For years they worked and developed together, and had honours showered equally upon them. When Wilde fell from grace Ferguson did not desert him.

Lever had given up the editorship of the *Dublin University Magazine*, and returned to his continental wanderings, but Stokes, McGlashan, George Petrie, Butt, the crafty lawyer, and many other old friends, remained in the Wilde's intimate circle. New faces also appeared, amongst them the handsome features of a young archaeologist, John Gilbert. He was a Catholic, and a link with the poet, Denis Florence MacCarthy, with Gavan Duffy, and the great Newman, who was then in Dublin in connexion with the formation of the Catholic University. Gilbert owed something to Wilde, for he had been black-beaned when he first sought admission to the Royal Irish Academy, it was said because of his religion. It was Wilde who persuaded him to go up again, and who saw to it that his candidature was successful on the second occasion.

With the passing of the 'Hungry Forties' social tension eased, and entertaining became more common. Wilde's ready wit was much sought after. He was fortunate enough to be made a member of that select body known as the Friendly Brothers of St. Patrick, whose President a hundred years ago was Lord Gort, and he spent many pleasant leisure hours at their club-house in Sackville Street. Several cheerful dining clubs were formed about this time, amongst them the 'Mystics,' which he was also persuaded to join. John Pigot, a young barrister of the Nationalist group, seems to have looked upon this Society as too frivolous for a serious worker. He wrote to Gilbert: 'Ere this they have made a "Mystic" of you, and you have sacrificed to the Jupiter-Esculapius and Juno-Minerva of Westland Row. I wish you joy of the pleasant company you are likely to meet in your new courses, and of the pleasant anticipations of literary and historical eminence into which you are sure to rise in such company.'

Many amusements were offered to the carefree Dubliners in those days—'the car-drivingest, tay-drinking, say-bathingest people in the world', as Thackeray called them. To the pleasures of hunting, hacking in the Park, boat sailing and racing at Kingstown and Howth, was added the pageantry of official entertaining. 'The Dublin Castle business has, I cannot but think, a very high-life below-stairs look. There is no aristocracy in Dublin. Its magnates are tradesmen"—said Thackeray, without perhaps examining his own position very closely—'Sir Fiat Haustus, Sir Blacker Dosy, Mr. Serjeant Bluebag, or Mr. Counsellor O'Fee. Brass plates are their titles of honour, and they live by their boluses or briefs. What call have these worthy people to be dangling and grinning at Lord Lieutenant's levees, and playing sham aristocracy before a sham sovereign? Oh, that old humbug of a castle! It is the greatest sham of all the shams in Ireland.'

Well, perhaps Thackeray was right, but it was fun all the same, and Wilde continued to go to the Castle, and Speranza accompanied him, in spite of her political views.

There were numberless military reviews in the Phoenix Park, where they saw the garrison playing at warfare. Here were lumbering heavy dragoons charging in formation—aides-de-camp scampering about after the great ones in glittering accoutrements—here the Brazilian Ambassador in a glass coach, there the Commander-in-Chief in a great plumed hat, perhaps even the Lord Lieutenant himself. In the Fifteen Acres they may have seen Sir James Scarlett leading his men in the charge, as he was to do a year or so later at Balaclava. The military lent much colour to Dublin in those days.

Dublin Horse Police

There were also theatres, concerts, lottery sales and charity sermons by the score, and, of course, the inevitable tea-parties and receptions, in which Speranza delighted.

III

She did not, however, have much time to spare at the outset of her married life, for she had other preoccupations. Her first child was born the year after her marriage, and was christened William Charles Kingsbury Wills Wilde.

Two years later, on October 16th, 1854, another son was

born at 21, Westland Row. Destiny was in an impish mood that day, for this baby was Oscar Wilde.

He also was given a formidable complement of names. While Willie's was uncompromisingly Sassenach, Oscar's were equally Gaelic, and very alliterative, if not poetical. Oscar Fingal O'Flahertie Wills Wilde he was called in full.

Rowan Hamilton commented amusingly on the new baby and his string of names, incidentally furnishing a side-line on Speranza in the rôle of mother. 'A very odd and original lady,' he said, 'has lately had a baby; such things you know will happen, at least in Ireland; and at a party given by Colonel

and Mrs. Larcom in this neighbourhood, when I met her for the first time in my life, she told me of this "young pagan", as she called him; and she asked me to be a godfather, perhaps because I was so to a grandson of Wordsworth the Poet (who lately wrote to me an account of the death of his Aunt Dorothy), and because she is an admirer of Wordsworth. However, I declined. But it seems that I have not fallen entirely out of favour thereby, for she paid me, on Saturday last, a visit of three hours and a half, it being my *second* time of seeing her. You must observe, however, that I had made it a sort of open day, and had several other guests, including a troop of deaf and dumb boys. My visitress told me, as we drank a glass of wine to the health of her child, that he had been christened on the previous day, by a long baptismal name, or string of names, the two first of which are Oscar and Fingal! the third and fourth sounding to *me* as a tremendous descent, but I daresay she prefers them. You must know that I have been long acquainted with her husband, as a Member of the Royal Irish Academy, though he had not time to come with his wife on her long and entertaining visit of the other day. She is quite a genius, and thoroughly aware of it.

'One thing she said, as I was conducting her upstairs to the Dome, and while she was professing to admire the house (which she *hoped* was a *haunted* one) was: "Let a woman be as clever as she may, there is no prize like this for *her*!"'

Oscar was a very favourite name at this time, although later the acts and fate of this particular recipient killed its popularity for many a long day. Its vogue can be traced to the widespread popularity of Macpherson's translation of the old Celtic songs of Ossian, for Ossian had a son Oscar who was killed in single combat with King Cairbre at the battle of Gabhra.

It was usually accepted in Dublin, however, that this particular child was named after King Oscar I of Sweden, from whom Wilde soon afterwards received the order of the Polar Star. It is difficult to assess the truth of this story, for we do not know the nature of Wilde's connection with the King of Sweden, or even that he had met him at the time of Oscar's birth. It is quite possible that King Oscar was a patient of his, for Wilde was now internationally famous as an oculist.

It is easy to see Speranza's influence in the 'O'Flahertie', for did not the boy derive the Irish strain in his blood from the 'ferocious O'Flaherties' of Galway? Fingal is not quite so simple. It may derive, like Oscar, from the old Gaelic legend, or it may perhaps have a simpler explanation, for 'Fingal' in Irish means 'the fair-headed stranger', and it is possible that Oscar was fair at birth, in spite of having two dark-haired parents. The name Wills, shared by both the boys, was given to them in compliment to Wilde's relative, W. R. Wills of Castlerea House, from whom Wilde had received many favours.

It is said that Speranza had longed to have a daughter for her second child. She is supposed to have continued to dress Oscar as a girl long after his baby days had passed, and even to have hung jewels on him which made him 'look like a little Hindu idol'. This may or may not be true. We must remember that Victorian mothers dressed both boys and girls in skirts until they were six or seven; and the story is also unpleasantly reminiscent of the case histories of other unfortunate perverts.

IV

Life was now comfortable enough for well-to-do people, but the poor were not so lucky. One of Wilde's best characteristics was his sympathy for the poorer classes, and he was greatly moved by their sad condition in the post-famine years. The

Oscar, aged five

disaster had left an aftermath of bankrupt landlords, pauperizing poor-laws, grinding officials and decimating workhouses, which had uprooted many cherished traditions and shaken the foundations of social intercourse. In many cases, domestic life had been outraged, and the links which united the various classes of the community had been burst asunder. Religious ceremonial had been neglected, and sometimes even the rites of sepulture had been forgotten. The dead body had rotted where it lay, or was thrown into a ditch; sometimes to form a scanty meal for famished carrion dogs. No wonder the survivors, once strong and stalwart, were listless creatures, unable to shake off the lethargy of despair.

Wilde paid a visit to the west, his first for many years, and was shocked by what he saw. 'When now I inquire for the old farmer who conducted me, in former years, to the ruined Castle or Abbey, and told me the story of its early history and inhabitants, I hear that he died during the famine. On asking for the peasant who used to sit with me in the ancient Rath, and recite the Fairy legends of the locality, the answer is: "He is gone to America," and the old woman who took me to the Blessed Well, and gave me an account of its wondrous cures and charms—"Where is she?"—Living in the workhouse.'

It is small wonder the spirit of the people seemed to be broken, and their natural gaiety and fanciful spirit seemed gone for ever. 'Troth, sir,' said Darby Doolin, an old Connaughtman of his acquaintance, to Wilde, when conversing with him upon the subject of fairies, 'what betune them national boords, and Godless Colleges, and other sorts of larnin', and the loss of the pratey, and the sickness, and all the people that's goin' to 'Merica, and the crathurs that's forced to go into the work-house, or is dyin' off in the ditches, and the clargy settin' their faces agin them, and tellin' the people not to give *in* to the likes, sarra wan of the *Gintry* (cross about us!) 'ill be found in the counthry, nor a word about them or their doin's in no time.'

Darby's 'Gintry' were not, of course, the landlords, who in many cases had disappeared, to be replaced by new and more business-like English and Scotch proprietors, leaving the poor people in many cases with cause to regret them. He was referring instead to those who, though reputedly *lucky*, were scarcely ever known to frequent the gambling-table or the horse-race, but lived in 'pace and quietness at home, in the ould ancient habitations of the country', riding by night, up and down upon the moonbeams, changing their residences or localities with the whirlwind; creeping into the russet acorn shells; sleeping in summer in the purple pendent bells of the foxglove or the wild campanula; quaffing the dew from the gossamer threads of the early morning, and living a merry, social life, singing, dancing, and playing wild Æolian music, by the river's bank, or upon the green hill-side—in short to the 'fairies' whom the Irish country folk love to talk about, and about whom Wilde loved to talk with them. But the cottage people had little taste for fantasy now.

'True for you,' said Darby, 'they are going fast, that *gentle* race (the Lord be with them!) but sure you wouldn't have them that were always an *out-door* population wait to be taken by the scruff of the neck and sent by the guardians and commissioners just to try their feet on the flure of the poor-house, or be shot down like thrushes, as the boys at Ballingarry were. The *good people* are leaving us fast; nobody ever hears now the tic-tac of the *leprechaun,* or finds the cute little chap with his Frenchman's hat and yellow breeches, sated on a boochalaun bwee of a summer's morning, with lab-stone on knee, and hammer in hand, tick-tack, tick-tack, welting soles and lasting brogues for his elfin brethren.'

Wilde thought the native humour of the people was not as rich and racy as in days of yore: he missed the laughter of the people in the fields, and the jokes which used to pass from pedlar or bagman to the pig-driver as they trudged alongside each other to the fair. 'Well,' said he, 'honoured be the name of Theobald Mathew—but, after all, a power of fun went away with the whiskey'. The spirits of the people were not what they were when a man could get drunk for three halfpence, and find a sod on a sally-switch over the door of every second cabin in the parish to indicate 'good liquor within'. The pilgrimages formerly undertaken to holy wells and sacred shrines for cures and penances had been strenuously interdicted; the wells themselves were neglected, and the festival days of their saints had been forgotten; their legends, too, often of great interest to the topographer and historian, many of which were recounted by the bards and annalists of earlier times, remained untold. The very sites of many of these localities were in danger of being forgotten. 'The fairies, the whole pantheon of Irish demigods, are retiring, one by one, from the habitations of man to the distant islands where the wild waves of the Atlantic raise their foaming crests; or they have fled to the mountain passes, and have taken up their abodes in those wild romantic glens—lurking in the gorgeous yellow furze and purple heath, amidst the savage disruptured rocks, or creeping beneath the warrior's grave. . . .'

'Repeal is dead,' said Wilde. 'It's ghost was last seen in Ballingarry, but it vanished in smoke and a flash of fire; some say it is hid in a cave in Slievenamon; but I don't give in to that. O'Connellism was kilt by the Young Irelanders, who blew themselves up with the infernal machine with which they had arranged to shoot Dan and the sodjers.' Wilde was probably right, and he was also right in thinking that the events of the fateful year 1848 were more marked in Ireland than anywhere else in Europe. The decline in Ireland's fortunes which had set in with the passing of the Act of Union was undeniably hastened by the famine.

'The dynasties of Europe have been shaken; many of the most ancient governments overthrown; and the whole of the continent convulsed with internal strife, or shaken by sudden change as the late tempest of revolution swept along its plains and leaped over its mountain-tops. The very Pope himself, the head of the most widely-spread and numerous sect of Christians in the world, has been rudely driven from the seat of St. Peter, a wanderer and an exile, and in all probability his temporal power has been much abridged or even annihilated; but what are these revolutions to that which has been and is now affecting in Ireland by the failure of a single article of diet? All these countries will settle down, more or less, into the conditions in which they were before 1848. The German will twist his moustache, smoke, and live on his beer and sour-krout; and the Frenchman drink his wine at three sous a bottle, shrug his shoulders, and enjoy his fête as before. Not so the Irishman; all his habits and modes of life, his very nature, position and standing in the social scale of creation, will and must be altered by the loss of his potato. Ay, even more than if he was suddenly compelled to turn Mohammedan—changing all his chapels, churches, and meeting-houses into mosques—or had a parliament going round with the judge of assize, and sitting in every county town in Ireland twice-a-year.'

In this state of affairs, with emigration helping to produce the most tremendous depopulation, and with the spread of railroad communication and education in English, it was small wonder that the Irish language rapidly fell into disuse. Before the famine it was the vernacular for most of the peasantry and farmers in the western half of Ireland. Afterwards its use gradually diminished, until now it is the fireside language of but few.

Wilde, a fluent Irish speaker, deplored this decay of the Gaelic tongue, for in it 'most of our legends, romantic tales, ballads, and bardic annals, and the vestiges of Pagan rites were preserved.' These legends were the poetry of the people, and he determined to record them while he could.

The result was a small volume of folk-lore and personal reminiscence, *Irish Popular Superstitions*, much of which had previously been published in the *Dublin University Magazine*. Published by McGlashan the year after his marriage, it was dedicated simply 'To Speranza'. It was a very pleasant book, simply written in an easy style, without the tortuous construction and florid phraseology into which he was inclined to relapse in his earlier books. Many folk-lore books are dull as ditchwater, but Wilde's shrewd and humorous observation and ready expression place this little work high above the average. Speranza tried folk-lore in later life, but her *Ancient Legends of Ireland* is artistically a poor book beside her husband's. And yet *Ancient Legends* has been reprinted as recently as 1925, while *Irish Popular Superstitions* is apparently completely forgotten.

CHAPTER XIX

ST. MARK'S HOSPITAL

I

DARBY DOOLIN'S reference to the 'Godless Colleges' reminds us of all the fuss and argument there was at this time in connection with the establishment of a second university in Dublin. This was the forerunner of the present University College, Dublin, one of the constituent colleges of the National University of Ireland.

To us the importance of this new University lies in the fact that as a result of its establishment all the old private medical schools were abolished, amongst them the Park Street School. Wilde saw his opportunity, promptly bought the vacated premises, and transferred his hospital there.

From the first Wilde's hospital had been outstandingly successful, both at Frederick Lane and at Mark Street. The number attending was now so great that many patients were obliged to wait in the street until their turn came to be attended to. There were no proper sewers at Mark Street, and the hospital had no back premises whatever. On the other hand, the house in Park Street was just what he required. It was in a better neighbourhood, for Park Street, which had formerly had a most unsavoury reputation for haunts of vice, had recently been cleaned up, and to a large extent rebuilt. To complete the metamorphosis the street was renamed Lincoln Place about ten years later.

Structurally the house was large and roomy, for when it was being built Cusack, with typical caution, had insisted that it should be made on the lines of a Methodist Chapel, so that a ready sale should be found for the building should the medical school not be successful! Wilde was so taken with its possibilities that he bought it with his own money, and remodelled it at a total cost of about a thousand pounds. He then placed the building free of all rent at the disposal of his committee.

The new hospital had accommodation for twenty ordinary

patients, and three private rooms for pay patients. There was also 'a handsome operating theatre and lecture-room', a surgery, dispensary and a large waiting-room for out-patients. Living quarters were provided for a house-surgeon, but the 'nurse or nurses' were expected to sleep in the female ward.

The patients received a somewhat meagre diet—'such as can be supplied with little risk of either waste or peculation,' said Wilde. 'For an adult, twenty-four ounces of the best wheaten bread and one quart of the best sweet milk is supplied on six days of the week. On Sundays, sixteen ounces of bread, one pint of milk, and three half-pints of broth, with its meat, is given. The residue of the broth, with its meat, if any, is

divided amongst the patients on Monday. Extras, consisting of tea and sugar, fresh meat, and porter (when necessary) are allowed to some patients, and a portion of the ordinary diet abstracted from such persons.'

The 'nurse or nurses' received the same diet, with the addition of a quarter pound of tea and a half pound of sugar. She was expected to make good all breakages and damages done to the hospital furniture, and to assist the charwoman and female patients in washing floors and linen. If she was un-satisfactory—and we may be sure Wilde exacted a high standard —she would be punished by a fine 'varying from sixpence to a shilling', and she was liable at any time to be dismissed on a week's notice.

Wilde remained the only visiting surgeon to the hospital. Under his direction the good work carried out in the previous buildings continued and expanded, and soon became known throughout the world. Students and post-graduates flocked to it from all over Europe, England and America, and Wilde began to profit considerably from the fees they paid. For a long time it was the only hospital in the United Kingdom which provided teaching on diseases of the ear. Wilde, or his committee, showed much financial acumen in running the hospital, largely with money collected from private donors.

21, *Westland Row*

Patients came from every county in Ireland, and in his annual reports he was not slow in pointing out that from some of these districts no subscriptions had been received.

The success of the hospital affords a good example of the superior efficiency of a voluntary over a state-controlled hospital, and it also demonstrates clearly the value of one-man control, which has also been seen in the Rotunda Hospital since its foundation two centuries ago.

The old name of St. Mark's was still retained—'but why,' asked a contemporary, 'should it not be called Wilde's Hospital?'

Wilde was from henceforth to be numbered with Richard Steevens, Bartholomew Mosse, and other founders of hospitals in Dublin.

The hospital was transferred from Mark Street in 1850. A year or so before this Wilde himself had moved from No. 15, Westland Row to No. 21, a few doors further up the street. In this house Willie and Oscar Wilde were born.

On most Saturday afternoons during the winter Wilde was to be found at the meetings of the Pathological Society in the theatre of the medical school of Trinity College, just behind his house. This society had been founded mainly by the exertions of Stokes, in the year 1838, and has the distinction of being the first organization of its type in the United Kingdom. It numbered Colles, Cusack, Graves and Crampton amongst its past presidents. Dominick Corrigan was also an ardent supporter, while Stokes was still one of its secretaries. At the weekly meetings numbers of specimens were laid before large gatherings of doctors and students; they were fully described by the doctors who showed them, but no discussion was allowed. Numbers of students, as well as doctors, listened with breathless interest as the great ones told the stories of the illnesses which had furnished the relics of mortality displayed before them.

II

Wilde was already recognized as one of the leaders of the medical profession in Dublin, and indeed in Europe. His reputation was sealed by the publication of his *Aural Surgery* in 1853. This was the first textbook of importance on the subject, and is now a classic.

As was usual with Wilde's books, and others of the time, many parts of it had already appeared in the *Quarterly Journal* and other medical periodicals, some of them having been published in England and others on the Continent. It was, therefore, not a complete system, but rather a series of essays on the most common and urgent diseases of the ear.

Reading it to-day, one immediately recognizes the great advances the science of otology has made since it was published. Great attention was then given to classification of disease—nosology as it was called—for in the state of knowledge then existing the detailing of relationships was difficult. Wilde, as a statistician, naturally paid great attention to this matter. For the rest, infinitesimal detail is given of outward appearances, and a minute observation of superficialities appears to be the keynote. Many of the diseases described as incurable are now within the reach of surgery. In a world which seems to be slipping backwards into barbarism it makes encouraging reading, as one realizes the great extent of the strides we have made since Wilde's day. Nevertheless, *Aural Surgery* is far ahead of any book which had preceded it. It is indeed the first of the modern textbooks on the subject.

Like all pioneer books, it is stamped with the personality of its author.

'I have laboured, and I trust not in vain, to expose error and establish truth; to lay down just principles for an accurate diagnosis of Diseases of the Ear; to rescue their treatment from empiricism, and found it upon the well-established laws of modern pathology, practical surgery, and reasonable therapeutics. In dealing with my subject it was necessary to review the practice and opinions of others: yet, though on certain points a conscientious difference from other writers has been expressed, I have not failed to award merit where merit was due.'

These sentiments come naturally from a son of the great Dublin School of Medicine, a disciple of Colles and Graves. Wilde's knowledge was necessarily imperfect, and consequently his deductions were frequently erroneous, but he was working on the right lines, and therefore he did *not* labour in vain. Therein lies the secret of his greatness. 'The practitioner of Aural Surgery or Aurist ought to be a well-educated surgeon or physician who applies the recognized principles of medicine to diseases of the organ of hearing.'

His methods are a model for all. 'In an art but just emerging from the mists of quackery . . . it is of great importance to accumulate facts, and openly, fairly, and fearlessly to state the truth, even at the expense of what is termed popular reputation. I determined to make an accurate note of every case of disease of the ear among the patients who applied at the hospital for twelve months in succession. Each case, as it presented, was accurately investigated in the presence of a class of advanced students and young medical men, and a few remarks made upon the cause of the disease, its prognosis, and treatment. A shorthand writer, familiar with medical terms, who was always in attendance, recorded with accuracy what passed. These notes when reduced to writing I myself corrected, and frequently compared them with the appearances presented on the patient's next attendance. By this means a vast amount of information was collected. In most of these clinical cases a running comment is, as might be expected, mixed up with the description—a more colloquial, but perhaps not less useful, form of instruction than that commonly met with in medical books and periodicals.'

Wilde claimed, justifiably, that the statistics of St. Mark's Hospital since the year 1844–5 were the earliest and most complete records of ear diseases published in the British Isles. In support of this he gave a consecutive register of two hundred cases to illustrate his method of keeping records. In each patient the appearances of the ear and its deviations from normal were described with great exactness, and subjective symptoms were given with no less detail. The human side of the case did not escape observation.

Some of the type-cases were recorded more fully, to serve as a basis for discussion. They show Wilde's keen observation of psychology. 'A lady, aged between thirty and forty, applies for advice. She is very deaf, speaks in a loud, inharmonious voice, and has suffered from noise in her ears, of all descriptions, for several years. She usually prefaces the detail of her symptoms (which is generally very long and verbose) by stating that she does not think much can be done for her. She has a great objection either to be questioned or to have her ears examined until she has made a full statement of her case; and as she has had a great variety of opinions, and has used all manner of remedies, she is tediously accurate in her account. She also carries in her hand a formidable list of questions.'

Occasionally we get an insight on the workings of Wilde's own mind. 'A lady applied to me with her son, aged seven (one of those cross-grained, ill-reared bears of children, the very plague of doctors), and asked me if I could cure him of a "very bad deafness", with which he had been affected for the last five years. After much coaxing and some frightening, I was permitted to look into the ears . . .'

Teaching was the breath of life to Wilde: we can see this by his clear-cut method of marshalling facts, and by the emphatic way in which he states his opinions; for a good teacher is nearly always dogmatic. 'The clinical case reports with which Wilde supports his observations are models of clear reporting' says Dr. Douglas Guthrie of Edinburgh; 'in reading them one is almost transported to the bedside of the patient, and one feels that something has been lost in these hurried modern days which necessitate a telegraphic method of case-taking.'

Many of the points which Wilde makes in his book seem to us almost self-evident. That they were not considered so in his day is clear from the way in which he labours them. 'So long as otorrhoea (discharge from the ear) is present, we never can tell how, when or where it will end, or what it may lead to.' This is now well recognized, except amongst the poorer classes, and no insurance company will now accept a person with a chronically discharging ear, yet in Wilde's day many doctors thought such cases were best left alone. He fulminated against this doctrine, in which he saw the influence of quackery and the 'modern French school'. He was one of the first to hold that brain abscess was often the result of direct extension from an abscess in the ear. In brain-abscess cases with a running ear the ear discharge was, therefore, the primary condition, and not, as some thought, the result of an abscess which, starting in the brain, found an outlet through the ear.

In controversy Wilde was a bonny fighter. Kramer, the Berlin ear surgeon, was an old enemy, the more so since he had the temerity to enter the field of statistics, which Wilde considered his own. 'Some of these tables,' said Wilde, 'are more curious than valuable; thus No. VIII shows the fatherland or country of his different patients from all parts of Europe and from America.' This from Wilde, who, for ethnological interest, tabulated the colour of his patients' eyes and hair! Later he insinuates that Kramer did not know what a normal ear-drum looked like; that his material had been loosely collected, and that his figures were unreliable! 'Statistical calculations remind one of the Kaleidoscope, which, when turned or shaken, presents new and beautiful combinations of figure and colour, irrespective of the objects which produced such being crooked pins and glass beads or spangles and diamonds.'

Wilde also crossed swords with James Yearsley, the London aurist who had founded the *Medical Circular*. In this instance, the argument was about the removal of the tonsils, a subject which has been a perennial source of controversy since

Hippocrates first scratched out his patients' tonsils with his finger-nails. Yearsley advocated excision of the tonsils for deafness; Wilde disagreed. He applied to Dr. Mayne and Dr. Kirkpatrick, who were in charge of the Dublin workhouses, for their opinion. They told him that enlarged tonsils were almost unknown amongst the poorer classes; and they attributed their more frequent occurrence amongst more well-to-do people to 'high-feeding'. Wilde, however, gave Yearsley full credit for his discovery of the use of the artificial ear-drum, although he claimed to have made a similar discovery himself some years previously.

During the preparation of *Aural Surgery* Wilde suffered an almost personal bereavement. 'It is with heartfelt sorrow I have now to speak and write of Dr. Graves in the past tense. Since my previous notice of this distinguished physician, the science of medicine at large, and the Irish nation in particular, have experienced a loss which is not likely to be replaced in the lifetime of the present generation; and the author has been deprived by death of one of his earliest, firmest and best of friends.'

Aural Surgery had an immediate success. An American edition was brought out in New York by Dr. Addinel Hewson, who had been a pupil of Wilde's at St. Mark's. It was translated into German by Dr. von Haselberg of Stralsund. For many years it remained a standard textbook, not only in the English-speaking world, but also in Austria and Germany.

In the year of its publication Wilde received his first public honour when he was appointed Surgeon Oculist in Ordinary to the Queen in Ireland. This was the first appointment of the kind made in Ireland. It was a notable distinction for a young man of thirty-eight, and Wilde did not hesitate to return thanks by dedicating his book, with permission, to the Lord Lieutenant, the Earl of St. Germains, 'as a mark of respect for his public character, and of personal gratitude'. What Speranza thought of this transaction we do not know.

III

Aural Surgery had the field to itself until seven years later when Joseph Toynbee published his *Diseases of the Ear*; a quite distinctive and equally brilliant book.

While Wilde was working on otology in Dublin, Toynbee in London had been attacking its problems from a different angle, with equal or even greater success. Wilde and he are now generally recognized as the greatest English-speaking pioneers in the science of otology.

Wilde and Toynbee were born in the same year. In each case their medical work formed but a part of their mental activity. Wilde, as we have seen, was a great archaeologist, so great indeed that until the present day his fame in this respect was greater than his reputation as an aurist. Toynbee was a man of great charm of manner, a connoisseur of the arts, and a keen social reformer, who devoted much time to philanthropic work. Like Wilde, he was the father of a brilliant son, for Arnold Toynbee, before he died at the age of twenty-six, had already made his name as a brilliant social worker. His name is perpetuated in Toynbee Hall.

Toynbee's approach to otology was different from Wilde's, for Wilde made his deductions in the manner of the Dublin School by painstaking bedside observations and investigations. Toynbee, the anatomist, took the line of dissecting healthy ears and making post-mortem examinations of diseased ones. Some idea of the extent of his researches is given by the fact that he dissected about two thousand ears. These preparations now form the Toynbee Collection of the Museum of the Royal College of Surgeons of England, and are a fitting memorial to his lifework. He died at the age of fifty-one, as the result of an experiment he made upon himself. Believing that head noises might be alleviated by the inhalation of the vapours of prussic acid and chloroform he submitted himself to the test. He was found lying dead on a couch in his consulting-room, with his notes and the fatal bottles by his side.

The work of Wilde and Toynbee was equally important and mutually complementary. Wilde was essentially a clinician, Toynbee a morbid anatomist. Each recognized the other's worth, and each gave full recognition to the other. Wilde disagreed with Toynbee at times but never let himself go in whole-hearted abuse of him as he did with others, while Toynbee, who had the pleasanter personality, never spoke anything but praise of Wilde.

The far-reaching and intricate operations which modern aurists perform were beyond the scope of Wilde and Toynbee, for their development was not possible without the help of anæsthetics and aseptic surgery. None the less, to them, and to Wilde in particular, we owe the credit for originating mastoid surgery. Inflammation of the mastoid process, the bony mass behind the ear, is a complication of middle-ear abscess. When this abscess spreads into the mastoid, it is a serious matter for the patient. Not only will the ear not heal until the mastoid does, but inflammation in the latter position may spread inwards to the brain or its linings, causing brain abscess, meningitis, or septicæmia. These conditions were not amenable to the methods of treatment known to Wilde and his contemporaries.

If, however, the abscess in the mastoid bone bursts outwards, it is more accessible, and it can then be drained by a simple cut through the skin, as Wilde pointed out. 'Should the mastoid process become engorged, or even an indistinct sense of fluctuation be discovered,' said Wilde, 'we should not hesitate to make a free incision at least an inch in length. The head should be firmly secured against some unyielding substance, and the blade of a stout scalpel inserted steadily till the point reaches the bone. . . . From the swollen state of the parts, we are sometimes obliged to introduce the instrument to the depth of nearly an inch. Immediate ease follows the operation, even though we fail to discover the existence of pus.' This operation is still called 'Wilde's incision', and it is still done in selected cases.

It was not new. It probably had been performed many times before. A French surgeon had anticipated Wilde in the early eighteenth century, but his work attracted little notice and was soon forgotten. Wilde, however, rediscovered the operation and gave it a rational basis, so that it became the first step in modern mastoid surgery.

Toynbee, writing, it must be remembered, some years later, suggested the advisability of carrying things a step further. 'Perforation of the mastoid process (to reach the abscess before it bursts out of the bone) suggests itself in serious cases likely to terminate in death. I have never performed the operation, but should not scruple to do so when the life of the patient was threatened. It seems to me that the best plan of operating would be to use a trephine over the middle and posterior part of the process, and to remove a piece of bone three-quarters of an inch in diameter.'

Toynbee may never have performed this operation himself, but his assistant, Hinton, certainly did so, and was perhaps the first surgeon in these islands to open the mastoid process. He first performed Wilde's Incision, but 'if the division of the periosteum over the mastoid process leaves the symptoms unchecked, the perforation of the mastoid cells should not be delayed more than a day or two. . . . A gouge or drill may be used; I employ a drill with a movable guard so that the bone may be penetrated to any desired extent.' We must remember that Hinton wrote when the art of anæsthesia was well established; Wilde about the date of its introduction.

Toynbee was lucky to be followed by such a man as James Hinton, who was his lifelong friend and associate. He was far from being a mere satellite, and made many original observations and discoveries in otology. Nevertheless, his heart was not wholly in medicine, and he is now remembered chiefly for his philosophic and metaphysical works. His book, *The Mystery of Pain*, is still widely read. It is, as Guthrie remarks, a beautiful piece of writing, although 'the help we get from it is in its quality and not in the argument'.

The simple mastoid operation, as it is now practised, was described by Schwartze in 1873. These three men, Wilde, Toynbee, and Hinton, are the pioneers who made it possible, and we may justly be proud of them.

CHAPTER XX

SUMMER
LIGHTNING

' Tis an old maxim in the schools
That Flattery is the food of fools;
Yet now and then your man of wit
Will condescend to take a bit.'

SWIFT.

I

WILDE'S POPULARITY as a doctor was now at its zenith. Although not yet forty, his hours of work were only limited by his own disposition of them. He turned patients away daily to gain more time for statistical and antiquarian researches, and was nevertheless able to afford summer residences in the mountains and at the seaside for his wife and young family.

It must be confessed that at this stage of his career he appeared at times to be overconscious of his own importance. In extenuation it must be remembered that he had already a very considerable achievement behind him. At the age of forty he was an internationally famous doctor, who had founded and now successfully controlled his own hospital. He had been editor of one of the foremost medical journals of the day, and his work on the Census Commission was unequalled. He had written several most successful books, was an acknowledged antiquarian authority, and had a large and lucrative practice. All this he had done by his own unaided efforts, without the assistance of high birth or hereditary influence. It is no cause for wonder if his success had gone to his head. After all, he had been constantly before the public for fifteen years, and had not yet suffered a serious reverse.

It was true that stories were beginning to spread about his private life; and particularly about his relationships with women. In the month of July, 1854, a dark, attractive girl of nineteen came to consult him, accompanied by her mother and bearing a letter of introduction from Stokes. A few years later Wilde was to rue the day he first met her.

II

For the present, however, his skies were cloudless. His conceit showed itself in various eccentricities of dress and entertainment, in which he was aided and abetted by Speranza, whose stock stood as high as her husband's. She was thought to be a woman of warm feelings, high aspirations, and real

genius, and she consorted on equal terms with the most eminent men of the day.

Many curious rumours began to pass around amongst Dublin's countless gossips. It was said, quite untruly, that Wilde owned the *Dublin Quarterly Review*, a paper of Nationalist leanings. Denis Florence McCarthy, who does not appear to have liked Wilde, wrote to Gilbert: 'When you told me that the new number of the *Irish Quarterly Review* contained some strictures on our friend, Dr. Wilde, I little thought that the castigation was inflicted by the fair hand of your reviewer. You have, of course, seen the announcement (in *Saunders' News-Letter*) that the *Irish Quarterly Review* is the property of Dr. Wilde, that he is also the editor, and that the leading articles *are all written*

by him and his gifted wife, Speranza! Now, as I suppose that
even doctors perform painful operations on themselves but very
rarely, I must conclude that the critical scalpel was in this instance
wielded by the editor's gifted partner, Speranza. What a
touching tableau this would make! What a sublime picture
of private feeling sacrificed on the altar of critical justice! Talk
of Brutus, and his sons, the Warden of Galway and young
Lynch, or any other tragedy of ancient or modern times! What
are they all to the idea of Speranza, terrible and beautiful as an
Amazon, with one hand brandishing an enormous steel pen
dripping with the avenging fluid, and then dashing it in the
face of the pallid and collapsed Wilde, who lies drooping and
subdued across the other arm of the heroine!

'Oh! for the pencil of Cruikshank or Doyle, or better still,
Leech (typical of the profession of the victim), to depict such
a group!'

III

Speranza's acquaintance with Rowan Hamilton soon ripened
into close friendship. They corresponded at length, principally
on the subject of poetry, for Hamilton also wrote verse, but also
on more intimate and personal matters. Hamilton obviously
had a high regard for Speranza's character, and was very interested
in her mentality. He introduced her to another poet, his friend
Aubrey de Vere. Religious feelings ran high in those days,
and he felt compelled to apologize for the fact that de Vere
had been converted to Roman Catholicism.

'Can I better, or more pleasantly, commemorate our first
meeting, which occurred exactly three years ago, on the 13th of
April, 1855, at the hospitable house of Colonel and Mrs. Larcom,
than by introducing to you my old and dear (I regret that I am
obliged to add my Popish) friend, Aubrey de Vere, the poet and
prose-writer, with some of whose principal works in prose you
are already acquainted?'

The meeting seems to have been a distinct success. De Vere
said that he would never forget the pleasant day the three spent
together: the merry dinner, followed by rambles in green fields;
and the 'poetical recitations' all three indulged in. From this
time on de Vere was numbered amongst Speranza's intimates.

He may perhaps have influenced her by his religious beliefs,
for it seems that the mystic in Speranza was attracted by Roman

Catholicism. It has often been said that Oscar Wilde was baptized a Catholic at the age of eight or nine, and the source of the rumour has been traced to a letter written by the Rev. Father Lawrence C. P. Fox, published in 1905 in *Donahoe's Magazine*, at Boston, Massachusetts. Father Fox related how Speranza used to take lodgings every summer for herself and her family at a farmhouse in the valley of Glencree in the Dublin mountains. Father Fox was then stationed at the near-by reformatory. Speranza asked permission for herself and her children to attend Mass, and the request was granted. After a few weeks Speranza asked Father Fox to instruct the two children, and soon afterwards he baptized them. At Speranza's request Father Fox called upon Wilde to acquaint him with what had been done, for Speranza apparently did not care to do this herself. However, Wilde's only comment was that he hoped they would become as good as their mother.

This is Father Fox's story, and it is not for us to contradict it: on the contrary it seems quite in keeping with Speranza's character. However, in May 1937, the secretary to the Roman Catholic Archbishop of Dublin stated that 'inquiries have been made and that there is no record or tradition in Glencree or district that Oscar Wilde was baptized a Catholic there'.

IV

Wilde, for his part, seems to have drawn somewhat away from Speranza, and become immersed in his other preoccupations.

Although he was best known to the public as an oculist, his chief interest was in ear surgery. Otherwise he could not have failed to appreciate a development which completely revolutionized the science of ophthalmology. This was the invention of the ophthalmoscope by Helmholtz in 1850, which first made it possible to inspect the interior of the living eye.

From the time of Pliny, many writers had expressed curiosity as to why certain animals' eyes were luminous in semi-darkness. The answer did not come until the eighteenth century, when Mery performed an experiment which would certainly have got him into trouble with the N.S.P.C.A., had that body existed in his time. He held an unfortunate cat under water to show that the luminosity of the eyes was still visible, and he noted that the back of the eye became visible as well. This showed that an optical problem underlay the phenomenon, and pointed the way to others who wished to look at the back of the eye during life. Kussmaul tried to do so by applying a plano-convex lens to the eye, but failed to see anything because he could not appreciate the necessity for illuminating the eye. He acted as though his own eye would supply the light which was necessary, as if it were an electric torch. In England, Babbage almost solved the problem, but unfortunately he was discouraged by Wharton Jones.

The solution came in December, 1850, when Helmholtz announced the invention of an 'eye-mirror'. In its final form it was very simple, merely a mirror with a central hole. The observer looks through the hole, his line of vision being parallel to the light rays which illuminate the interior of the eye. Simple as the device was, it required a genius to discover it. From that day dates the modern science of ophthalmology.

From the ophthalmoscope is derived the circular, slightly concave, perforated mirror which the ear, nose and throat surgeon carries on his forehead all day long. Every layman to-day is familiar with it. He probably remembers it from his childhood days, when his parents brought him to a darkened room where strange instruments glittered, and introduced him to a suave gentleman who wore one of these mirrors. He may remember the mesmeric awe with which the mirror inspired him, and his own resentment at the liberties which were sub-sequently taken with his person, if that gentleman was not one of those who understand the minds of little people. In later life it may have lost some of its terrors for him, and having lost the curiosity of childhood, he contents himself with a vague dislike of the discomforts it implies, and a mild curiosity as to how it works. In fact, its principle is exactly the same as that of the ophthalmoscope. The mirror is held in front of the doctor's eye, and a strong light is focussed upon it from behind the patient. This light is reflected and shone upon the patient's throat, ear or nose. The doctor, looking through the hole in the same direction as the rays, can never get in his own light. Equally important, he can see down deep cavities without his vision being impeded by shadows thrown from their walls, as would be the case if the light were thrown obliquely by a lamp beside his head. The head mirror is even more important to the aurist and laryngologist than the ophthalmoscope is to the oculist. If the general surgeon took the trouble to learn the trick of using it he also would find it very useful in many spheres. But after all, the principal reason why general surgeons leave the cavities of the body to specialists is because they have not mastered the art of illuminating them.

The early efforts of throat surgeons and aurists to see what they were doing were very similar to those of the oculists. They first invented the instruments which made it possible to see the cavities of the ear and throat, but largely failed because they could not illuminate them. Manuel Garcia, the music master, is generally given the credit for first seeing the vocal cords with a small mirror placed at the back of the palate, which reflected

sunlight down the throat. Czermak, the physiologist of Leipzig, who developed the idea, said that it would have been still-born had he not used the head-mirror to illuminate the throat. This is quite true, for Babington, whose ancestors came from Derry, had in 1829 described a laryngeal mirror almost exactly the same as that of Garcia, and Liston had suggested the use of a dental mirror for the same purpose. But, for want of light, both these men were defeated, and their instruments were still-born.

v

The statistical side of Wilde's Census work gripped and fascinated him, for he was possessed by a burning curiosity about his fellow-creatures and their complexities, deviations and variety, alike in health and disease. In his professional work he studied each case in minute detail, noting every tiny abnormal blood vessel, almost every flake or scratch on the skin surface. In his census tabulations he found a complementary collective experience which gave him a wide view of each subject in the aggregate. His mental equipment made him especially suited for work of this kind, for he could comprehend multitudinous detail without losing the essential broad grasp, and he was possessed of tireless enthusiasm.

Vital Statistics was then a new science, analysing and keeping pace with the rapid development of medical knowledge which was taking place at the time. It is not, however, an exact science, any more than medicine is. The variety and frailty of human nature ensures this. For instance, there are at each Census more women who return their ages as between twenty and twenty-five than there were girls between the ages of ten and fifteen ten years before. It is, therefore, very necessary to be able to take the wide view in assessing the value of the returns, and in this Wilde excelled.

He had already made his name by his part in the analysis of the census of 1841. The reputation he had then achieved was greatly enhanced on the publication of his medical report on the census of 1851.

Here opportunity had played into his hands, for the preceding decade was one which will never be forgotten by the social historians of Ireland. Every circumstance connected with the famine and its attending pestilences was of the greatest public interest, and he discussed it in full detail. He delved deep into history, collecting material from every library in the country to add to the figures given by the census returns themselves. The result is one of the most striking compilations which has ever been published, one which involved an amount of labour and research which would have deterred anybody else from making the attempt. It was published in 1854, the year after *Aural Surgery* came out, in the form of a Parliamentary bluebook, extending to almost six hundred folio pages. A bluebook of this size written by a single individual must be almost unique.

When making this return Wilde took the opportunity of compiling what is really a complete story of medicine in Ireland from the earliest times. In order to make this history suitable for its vehicle, he assembled it in tabular form—the 'Table of

Cosmical Phenomena, Epizootics, Famines and Pestilences in Ireland.' This device takes nothing from its interest to those who have the leisure to read such chronicles in these hurried times. Here is a small part of one of the first few pages:

DATE.	EVENT AND CIRCUMSTANCE.	AUTHORITY.	CONTEMPORANEOUS EPIDEMICS.
A.D. 734	'There was (the appearance of) a dragon, this harvest, seen (in the sky), and a great thunder heard after him in the firmament. This year Venerable Beda died in the 88th year of his age, and was called "The Sage of All England." This entry is repeated in the Ulster Annals.'	Colgan's *Acta Sanctorum.*	'Two most glorious jewels Brigitto and Maura, daughters of the King of the Scots, were born on the same day, at whose birth famine and pestilence which had long devastated that whole land of Scotia are said to have ceased.'
A.D. 735	'Faylan O'Brayn, King of Leinster, died of a sudaine immature death little thought of before.'	Annals of Clonmac-noise.	732. Numbers perished from pestilential disease in Norwich in England and in Syria.
A.D. 739	An earthquake in Ireland, on the second of the Ides of April. 'Fergus Glut, King of Cobha, died; it was he that used to spit out much saliva from his mouth: and this caused his death.' O'Connor translates the foregoing 'poisoned saliva.'	Annals of Ulster.	The Sun eclipsed and in 734 the moon appeared as if stained with spots of blood and by the same omen Fatume and Beda departed this life. Ethelward's Chronicle.

In this form Wilde gives us a completely documented consecutive history, starting with the legendary Parthalonians, who died in thousands from some sudden epidemic 'in the year of the world 2820, according to the long chronology of the Septuagint', as recorded in the Annals of the Four Masters. This particular table extends to almost two hundred pages of the folio; the early part of which is concerned with the distant past when such pleasant things were wont to happen as 'the shower of pure silver, shower of wheat, and shower of honey', which fell at Inishowen in A.D. 759–63. Unfortunately, the later, and greater, part of the table, is sombre and unrelieved, dealing with the fearful ordeal of famine and disease, from which Ireland had just emerged. Here the ancient Irish annals are replaced by newspaper accounts and reports of the proceedings of societies and parliament. Every aspect of the famine time was dealt with, and this part of the Census return is now a standard reference on the subject.

VI

Wilde's self-inflation showed itself by an increasing sharpness in controversy, and he made enemies in this way. He was never one to suffer fools gladly, and he could be extremely cantankerous and cross-grained at times. About 1853, for some reason, he resigned his membership of the Academy. The Council, not to be bullied, accepted his resignation without comment, and he was glad enough to be reinstated in a similar laconic fashion the following year. Next year he was placed upon the Committee for Antiquities, and in 1856 he was made Secretary for Foreign Correspondence. His knowledge of languages made him particularly well fitted for the latter post, for, like Speranza, he had more than a superficial knowledge of most European tongues. He signalized his return to Academic grace by two excellent papers, one about the old Dublin Bills of Mortality as described in a manuscript written by a Dublin physician, Willoughby, in 1690, the other on the subject of *The Food of the Irish*. He had already published the latter paper in popular form in the *Dublin University Magazine*.

This was the height of the great period of the Academy. The leading figures on the scientific side were Hamilton, Haughton,

McCullagh and Lloyd. Sir William Rowan Hamilton still stands in the very front rank of mathematicians, by virtue of his calculus of quaternions, and his deductive anticipation of the phenomenon of conical refraction. McCullagh was restricted to the field of pure geometry, but the beauty of his methods and results are most attractive. He is chiefly remembered by his work on Fresnel's wave, and on the surfaces of the second order. The Rev. Humphrey Lloyd worked on meteorology, magnetism, and on the experimental verification of conical refraction. The Rev. Samuel Haughton was a versatile genius, whose interests ranged from geology and tidal variations to calculating how a judicial hanging should be carried out in a proper scientific fashion, with particular reference to the length of the drop. When he was about the age of forty and already a Fellow of Trinity College, he noted that the Medical School was not progressing satisfactorily. He, therefore, entered as a first-year student, not so much in order to qualify as a doctor, but to ascertain why the School was not prospering. Not until he qualified five years later did he report to the Board on the state of education in the School. As a result of his report three incompetent teachers were dismissed, and he himself was appointed Registrar, or Dean, of the Faculty. He retained this position for fifteen years and soon had the satisfaction of almost doubling the number of students. This expansion necessitated new buildings, and one consequence of having a Registrar who was also Professor of Geology is that these buildings were built of flawless granite. When the Registrar came to College in the mornings he 'blue-pencilled' any block of granite which did not meet with his approval, and if it had already been put in a wall it came out again forthwith.

These were some of the principal scientists of the Royal Irish Academy at the time. The antiquarians were no less eminent. Petrie, their doyen, had, as we have seen, dispelled the dreams of Vallancey and Ledwich, and founded an era of inductive research in archaeology. Todd, O'Donovan and O'Curry in Irish history and philology, Larcom in topography and local history, and Wilde in his own line, all took equal part in the cultural flowering of the time.

And now Wilde's protégé, John Gilbert, appeared unexpectedly as a new star which shone as brightly as the rest of the galaxy, for when, at the age of twenty-five, he published his *History of Dublin* he gained immediate and lasting fame. He received many congratulatory letters, but one from Speranza was anything but pleasant.

'In the *History of the Philosophical Society*,' she said, 'you scarcely appreciated my husband's labours. From the passage one might think he had only compiled a catalogue, whereas he *first* was the one who wrote the History and told the world all that is known on the subject. . . . Besides, posterity in ten or twenty years will certainly think W. R. Wilde was a poor wretch of a clerk who copied catalogues for a livelihood. There is nothing to identify him as a man who has done something in his generation, both for literature and humanity . . . when vapid commonplaces are thought worthy of immortality in Mr. Gilbert's *History of Dublin*.'

Poor Speranza! The quality of her genius may not be as high as was thought in those days, but she was nothing if not loyal.

VII

The compilation of the catalogue she refers to was another notable achievement on Wilde's part. In the late fifties all scientific Dublin was agog with excited anticipation of the visit of the British Association which was to take place in 1857. It was felt that the meeting should be made a memorable one, as befitted the greatest school of archaeological research in western Europe. In particular, the great wealth of antiquities in the museum of the Royal Irish Academy should be properly displayed and explained, but how was this to be done in the absence of a proper descriptive catalogue? Obviously the want had to be supplied.

A committee was, therefore, appointed for this purpose, with Petrie at its head. High hopes were at first entertained. In 1853 'Several very successful experiments had been made on the possibility of applying the newly discovered photographic processes to the object of the Pictorial Catalogue,' by the Rev. Dr. Graves and Mr. Tenison. 'A photographic apparatus' had been purchased, and the Council felt that they would soon be able, at a very trifling cost, to distribute pictures of Irish antiquities to the archaeologists of other countries.

Unfortunately, the work was held up for various reasons.

The Collection was lent to the Dublin Exhibition of 1851, and when it came back to the Academy's house many of the numbers on the articles had come off owing to the dampness of the new rooms set apart for them. The photographs also were not forthcoming, because of the want of 'a suitable glass chamber for conducting the practical operations of the photographic processes'.

Time dragged on, and no progress was made. In 1856 the Council had to announce, with regret, that little or no progress had been made, and that the glass cases for the reception of the objects were not yet ready.

Wilde watched this incompetent bungling with undisguised impatience. He felt that it would be a disgrace if the catalogue were not prepared in time for the visit of the Association. Impatience grew to exasperation. Finally, he offered to take on the whole undertaking himself.

The Council of the Academy thankfully accepted his offer. They took the work out of the hands of Petrie and his committee, and entrusted it to Wilde, together with £250 for his expenses.

Wilde was faced by a task whose magnitude had defeated an able committee working for four years. He was expected to catalogue, describe, and in many cases illustrate a rich store containing about ten thousand articles, and he had not four years, but four months, to do it in.

He attacked his task with his usual tremendous vigour. The muddled work of his predecessors was completely scrapped. He adopted a new basis of classification, that of the nature and use of the objects, irrespective of their age. This was an eminently sensible arrangement. It facilitated rapid expansion of the catalogue, and on the other hand the ignorance which existed of the exact age of objects would not matter as far as the catalogue was concerned.

Petrie and his coadjutors, as might perhaps be expected, did not take this view. They considered that it was extremely important to arrange the articles in correct order of chronological succession; and in this way a controversy was started which eventually hampered Wilde's work so greatly as to bring it to a standstill, to the lasting detriment of Irish archaeology. It is fortunate that Wilde was able to do much valuable work before their objections gained much support.

Photography was still a clumsy process, and in any case it was

an art which never appealed to Wilde. He thought, as many
of us do still, that a bad photograph was worse than a bad
drawing, and a good photograph no better than a good drawing,
if as good. He, therefore, employed Wakeman and Du Noyer
to draw the articles for him, and had them engraved on wood
by O'Hanlon and Oldham.

He had many difficulties to contend with. The Academy
house was being painted and decorated for the forthcoming visit
of the British Association; glass cases were still being erected,
and workmen were constantly in and out of the premises.
Wilde's energy always generated heat. His temper was thin,
he had many clashes and bickerings with the staff and his fellow
members. Not even the President and Council escaped his
castigations. The only colleague with whom he appeared to
work peacefully was young Gilbert.

Slipshod work was impossible for him, and it soon became
obvious that he could not complete the catalogue in the time
at his disposal. He, therefore, concentrated upon the articles
of stone, earthenware, and vegetable materials, leaving the objects
of gold, animal materials, and bronze to be completed at a later
date. There remained a description of the silver and iron objects,
and the coins and other miscellanea which, unfortunately for
posterity, he was never able to publish.

Part I. of the *Catalogue* was laid upon the table at an
extraordinary meeting of the Academy on 24th August, 1857,
two days before the British Association assembled. It was at
once seen that Wilde had achieved a great feat in compiling such
a work in the short time which had elapsed since he had begun
it in March, for it must be remembered that this was no mere
list of objects with numbered references, but a detailed description
of every article, together with its history and provenance, with
a wide background of historical allusion and references. It is
probably safe to say that no other member of the Academy,
before or since, could have compiled it in the time, for the task
demanded not only a minute knowledge of the subject, but a
positively encyclopaedic memory for details and references.
Wilde had done the first part of his task most admirably. It
had been made easier for him by the fact that he himself had
first described many of the objects. When Parts II and III of
the *Catalogue* appeared, they attained an equally high standard
—so high indeed, as to paralyse all similar efforts ever since.

Wilde's *Catalogue* is quoted in every serious work on Irish archaeology which has been published since it appeared. The Council of the Academy rewarded him by their thanks, by presenting him with a hundred copies of the *Catalogue*, which cost them £20, and by electing him a Vice-President.

The publication of the first part of the *Catalogue* marks the end of the great productive period of Wilde's life. During the twenty years which had elapsed since he had qualified he had worked with immense energy. Now it was time for him to relax somewhat, and enjoy the fruits of his labours in the little leisure time that his ever-increasing practice left to him.

After this he made no more discoveries in medicine, laid down no fresh principles in surgery and treatment, although in his teaching and lesser writings he continued to elaborate those he had already outlined. It was the same with his archæological work. We must not think the less of his work if, in the words of Herman Melville, his achievement was left 'unfinished, even as the great Cathedral of Cologne was left, with the crane still standing on the top of the uncompleted tower. For small erections may be finished by their first architects; grand ones, true ones, ever leave the copestone to posterity. . . . Oh, Time, Strength, Cash and Patience!'

CHAPTER XXI

FLOOD TIDE

I

THE POKY little house in Westland Row was now hardly imposing enough for the Wildes, who were very conscious of their position as leaders of scientific and literary society in Dublin. Stimulated by the approaching visit of the British Association, they looked around for a new abode, and finally chose No. 1, Merrion Square, which has ever since been known to Dubliners, quite erroneously, as 'the house where Oscar Wilde was born'.

No. 1, Merrion Square, which stands at the corner of Merrion Square North, and Lower Merrion Street, is a splendid specimen of Georgian Dublin. It stands on the main road which goes on to skirt Dublin Bay through Booterstown, Blackrock, and

Dun Laoghaire, forming the first of the terrace of thirty or more fine houses which form the north side of Merrion Square. From his drawing-room window Wilde could look out over an extensive grassy square—now, alas, desecrated by air-raid shelters. Three sides of the Square were occupied by houses such as his. On the west side was Leinster House, and beside it the National Gallery was soon in course of erection.

Wilde's new house was amongst the best professional residences in the city. It stood at the beginning of a particularly favourite row. Stokes lived in No. 5 and Lord Justice Fitzgibbon in No. 10. Other houses in the terrace were occupied by Sir Philip Crampton, Sir Henry Marsh, Sir Dominick Corrigan, Evory Kennedy, Maurice Colles, and other leaders of the medical profession. There were also half a dozen lawyers and two peers.

These are fine houses, spacious and well-proportioned, comfortable in the winter and bathed in sunshine in the summer. They have not deteriorated as so many of Dublin's best houses have. One likes to think of them in the piping days of pros-

H. Marsh

perity when they were first built of new and sharp-edged brick-work. Then they were mainly occupied by peers and members of parliament. Later judges came to predominate in them, and then the medical profession, so the occupations of their owners in Wilde's time gives their history in epitome. More recently the doctors have to a large extent moved to the neighbouring Fitzwilliam Square, and Merrion Square has been invaded by Government offices and blocks of flats, but it still retains much of its ancient glory. Wilde's side of the Square has always been the favourite, because of its sunny aspect. 'The footway on the north side,' wrote Whiteway in 1812, 'is on summer evenings the resort of all that is elegant and fashionable in this vicinity.'

For our present purpose we must think of Merrion Square as occupied by hirsute mid-Victorian doctors and lawyers, in frock coats, peg-top trousers and paletots; by Victorian mamas in crinolines and poke bonnets, and be-ribboned children in stiff muslin dresses. In the afternoon patients from all over Ireland descended from carriages to consult Stokes, or Wilde, or Marsh next door. For them, perhaps, it was the portals of death itself they entered, but for the gossiping coachmen, or for little Willie and Oscar as they peered through the railings of the square opposite, it was merely another week-day afternoon which would shortly be crowned by the grand Victorian tea-table. Sundays were another matter, for then bearded, fussy Papa Wilde, enormous, languid Mama Wilde, the two little boys, and later, for a time, a little girl, all dressed up in their best finery and went off to church together. Sometimes Papa

Wilde and Stokes, 1854

could not go—he had gone off to see his patients, or to look at old stones, or on other mysterious errands, and then, of course, the rest of the family must go without him.

II

This drawing is made from a photograph which is interesting in many ways. For one thing, it was taken in the late fifties of last century, and therefore must be one of the earliest 'conversation-pieces' in photography. It was taken by Lord Justice Fitzgibbon, who was one of the great men of the time. And what an insight it gives us into the men—Wilde with his bright quizzical eye, full of humour—surely he must have been a most pleasant companion when he was so minded. Stokes looks down upon him indulgently, for to him Wilde's good points out-weighed the bad. Both subjects are what Americans call 'photogenic'. Stokes, in the photograph, looks quite handsome, and Wilde himself not unprepossessing. This is an early disproof of the ridiculous statement that 'the camera cannot lie', for the story is still told of the merriment caused, sometime about this date, when Wilde, Stokes, and 'another ugly man' acted in charades as 'The Three Graces'.

There was much entertaining in various ways about this time. An event of some note, in which Wilde was directly interested, took place in 1856. This was the revival of the old Medico-Philosophical Society. It had been founded exactly a hundred years previously, when it had had a more serious mien, for the seven members after dining in each other's houses had read original papers, many of which were of scientific importance. These are now in the Library of the Royal Irish Academy, and in the Library of the Royal College of Physicians in Ireland, some contained in the minutes of the Society and some in a book called the Repository. The original society lapsed in 1831.

As now revived, the Society consisted of fourteen members, amongst whom were Sir Henry Marsh, Cusack, Stokes, Adams, Rynd, who first invented the hypodermic needle, Joliffe Tufnell of Tufnell's diet, Sir Philip Crampton, and, of course, Wilde. They were still a distinguished gathering, but the new meetings were conducted in a much more light-hearted vein than formerly. In the ordinary way dinners were held at the members' houses in rotation, but 'any member who attained a position of honour or considerable emolument was allowed the privilege of giving an extra dinner to the Society'. Instead of the discussion of learned topics, the evenings were spent in arguing on the merits of boned turkey, how to serve snipe, or how a saddle of mutton should be carved. On one occasion a most heated argument arose between Stokes and Irvine—'The great picture case which had originated at the former meeting of the Society came on for decision, Mr. Irvine having wagered with Dr. Stokes a dinner for the Society that his (Mr. Irvine's) great-grandfather was a handsomer man than Dr. Stokes' great-grandfather. The gentlemen both produced miniature pictures of their respective progenitors. The greatest care was taken to have an impartial judgement from the members of the Society, and after a very solemn inspection of the portraits a ballot was taken when nine votes appeared for the ancestor of Dr. Stokes and three for Mr. Irvine's. The latter member accordingly lost the wager.'

The Medico-Phils are still full of whimsicalities to-day. They are now the oldest medical dining club in existence. Dr. Nugent in 1862 presented an album to hold portraits of the members, which is still kept up to date. It is passed around with the port, for the benefit of visitors. Then the minutes of the last meeting are read, followed by the minutes of fifty years ago. Soon it will be the minutes of a hundred years ago.

In addition to the Medico-Phils, Wilde took a prominent part in the dining club of the Royal Irish Academy, which happily is also still in existence. In those days it met at Macken's Hotel in Dawson Street, an old-fashioned place, with a reputation for good cookery and old port. For years two ravens lived in a public-house opposite, to the great interest of the diners, who watched them with interest as they hopped around the busy street. The club now meets at the Gresham Hotel, in O'Connell Street, and its members have an even more curious ornithological wonder to look at, for in front of the hotel are three plane trees crowded every winter with hundreds of pied wagtails. They fly away in the daytime and return to roost at night, undisturbed by the glare of electric light and the clatter of trams and buses.

III

Wilde took a prominent part in the activities connected with the meeting of the British Association. The visit was a great success, from both the scientific and the social points of view. Wilde's particular interest was the Ethnological Section, of which he was President. On the conclusion of the meeting, when the debates and festivities were over, he organized an excursion of his Section to the islands of Aran off the coast of Galway.

The success of this excursion marked the climax of a memorable meeting. No fewer than seventy members took part in it, including Ferguson, Petrie, Stokes, Burton, O'Curry and O'Donovan, Gilbert and others, under the presidency of the Rev. Dr. McDonnell, Provost of Trinity College. Amongst the distinguished foreign visitors were Professor Simpson of Edinburgh, a noted Celtic scholar, C. C. Babington, F.R.S. of St. John's College, Cambridge, who later published an account of the trip, and Norton Shaw of London. The party left Dublin for Galway early on the 3rd of September, 1857. There they were taken on board the Trinity House Yacht *Vesta*, which after a run of thirty miles disembarked its freight of antiquaries near the little village of Killeany, on Aranmore, or Inishmore, the largest island.

The Aran Islands must for ever remain one of Ireland's most treasured possessions, for it is impossible to think they can ever be spoilt. They are fairly easy to reach, but not easy enough for casual trippers, and while one can put up comfortably enough, luxury is not to be had. Nor is the land valuable enough to draw covetous settlers from the mainland. On the contrary, the Aran Islands are one of the most barren spots in Europe, and they must surely hold the record for the number of stones which lie upon their surface. Stones are everywhere —lying in the fields, built up to form loose boundary walls, built into cottages. In many places the ground beneath one's feet gives place to acres of naked fissured limestone, with here and there a granite boulder deposited by glacial action in ages past.

From time immemorial the islands of Aran have given sanctuary to those who were persecuted or defeated in battle, and in consequence they are full of the most interesting antiquities of both Christian and prehistoric times. Wilde could not have brought his guests to a richer feast of antiquarian lore. Dolmens, clochans, round towers, crosses, castles and churches abound in bewildering variety.

The party got down to business quickly enough, for immediately on landing they examined the Elizabethan castle of Arkin. This seems to be a very noteworthy castle, for it goes directly contrary to tradition in that it was actually *enlarged* by Cromwell. The same evening they examined the stump of the round tower, which Petrie discoursed upon. He said that it had been considerably reduced in height since he had last seen it twenty-five years before, and told his listeners that at that time he had met an old islander who remembered it when it was eighty feet high. However, old men such as this are inevitable, and it is at least comforting to know that the tower has not appreciably diminished since the ethnologists saw it more than eighty years ago.

Next day the party wandered in easy stages along the nine-mile axis of Inishmore. They made many digressions, to examine here a Pagan stone fort or burial, there a Christian settlement, at each of which Petrie or Wilde held forth for the benefit of the visitors. Wilde was able to show them the collected fragments of a beautifully sculptured cross, which he had gathered amongst the ruins of the 'Seven Churches' situated six miles north of Kilronan. When visiting Aran some years before he had gathered the pieces together and laid them on the threshing floor of Martin O'Flaherty (almost everybody in Aran is an O'Flaherty), and had constituted Martin the guardian of the ruins. Wilde was delighted to meet his Aran friend again, and to find that he had done his duty well, even to the extent of building a low stone wall around the cross.

On the right-hand side of the party as they wandered to the westward end of the island the sea broke gently on sandy shores. On their left the land rose evenly but rapidly, to terminate abruptly at the western end in sheer undercut cliffs. On the top of the highest part of these cliffs they saw the great fort of Dun Ængus, black against the evening sky.

The stone forts on Aran are perhaps the most interesting of the archaeological remains on the islands. They are all dry-built without mortar. Dun Ængus is semicircular, open only on the seaward side, where the great cliffs render attack impossible. There are three concentric semicircular walls, the innermost, that of the citadel, being eighteen feet high, and from twelve to eight feet thick. On the inner side of the citadel wall is a platform-walk for the defenders. Between the two outer walls is a *chevaux-de-frise* made of large stones set irregularly in the ground, for all the world like a prehistoric tank-trap. The masonry throughout is of the most skilful workmanship, as indeed it must be to have survived the hazards of two thousand years. The labour involved in building this fort must have been immense. Some idea of its extent is given by the size of the outside wall, which is about 1,900 feet long.

The cliff face which bounds the fort on the south and east sides measures some 1,500 feet. It was well that the ancients made Dun Ængus strong, for if the enemy breached the citadel there was nothing left for the defenders but to be driven headlong into the sea.

Dun Ængus has been described as 'the most magnificent barbaric monument extant in Europe'. Whether this claim is true or not, it must surely carry off the palm for the beauty of its situation, for the lonely grandeur of the scene is beyond description. North and west lies the limitless Atlantic. To the south the dark cliffs of Clare are dimly seen through silvery

mist, while on the eastern side the sense of solitude is accentuated by a dreary waste of barren limestone.

On the evening of the second day the party of archaeologists slowly wended their way to this Pagan fortress

<blockquote>
'upon a rock
Environ'd with a wilderness of sea.'
</blockquote>

The day had been long, and many of them were not a little exhausted by the rapid survey of multitudinous antiquities, and by the hard going over the rocky island. When they reached the citadel they must have felt as the children of Israel did when the manna descended from on high, for there, upon the velvet turf, a plentiful repast lay spread before them.

And there in the gathering dusk, while increasing shadows clustered around the gloomy walls of Dun Ængus, the party of old-time antiquaries feasted themselves, no doubt both liberally and well, as the roaring breakers of the Atlantic broke three hundred feet below them. The scene must have been a strange one, and it is a great pity we can only see it in imagination. The proceedings had naturally attracted a crowd of peasantry, who, no doubt, thought their visitors slightly insane to set a banquet in such surroundings. They wanted to see all they could of these curious people, and so they sat watching them, sitting here and there amongst the ruined walls of the fortress, or standing unobtrusively at a distance. It must have been a picturesque sight, the men in light-coloured tweeds and pampooties, the women and children in red with purple cloaks and gay head-dresses, contrasting with the black frock-coats, tweed trousers and top-hats of the city dwellers.

There were speeches, of course. Petrie proposed the principal toast, which was the health of the resident magistrate of the island, Mr. O'Flaherty. Then came various other toasts, including that of Wilde. It was unanimously resolved that a book should be published by the expedition, to describe the antiquities of Aran, and at the same time to 'serve as a lasting memorial of our appreciation of the services of Mr. Wilde, as director of the expedition'. Wilde rejoined suitably to this proposal, which, most unfortunately, never fully materialized. Finally, he addressed the people of Aran in Irish, exhorting them to preserve the monuments from dilapidation. O'Donovan and O'Curry also spoke on the same subject in the native tongue, and finally one of the Aran men replied in Irish at considerable length.

This concluded the dinner, for the sun had long since sunk into the western sea.

The next day most of the party returned to Galway after visiting Inishmaan and skirting the cliffs of Moher in the *Vesta*. Wilde went with them, but Petrie, Stokes, Ferguson, O'Curry and Burton remained behind. They passed a most enjoyable fortnight on Inishmore, Burton painting the people and their children while Margaret Stokes and Ferguson sketched the antiquities. They chartered a hooker and sailed from island to island, taking with them all those of the locals who 'had music'. In the evenings they went to the cottages, Petrie with his music manuscript and violin, and always accompanied by O'Curry. The singer—an old woman perhaps, or a girl or young man— would sit on a stool in the chimney corner, while Petrie and O'Curry sat opposite. The first time a song was sung, O'Curry would write down the Irish words. Then it would be repeated slowly, for Petrie to record the music. When he had it perfectly, the violin was produced, and the air played upon it as only Petrie could.

Many of the villagers of Kilronan crowded into the cottages on these occasions, while those who could not get in stood outside to listen. The light of a blazing turf fire playing on the faces and richly coloured dresses of the throng gave a vivid and varied effect of chiaroscuro such as only Rembrandt could paint. When the music stopped, a soft acclaiming murmur in Irish began, which continued until the next song was started.

It must have gone to Wilde's heart to miss this pleasant holiday in the west, amongst the people he loved so well, but a successful doctor's life is a busy one, and he had his work to do.

CHAPTER XXII

SATURNIA
REGNA

I

THERE WAS now no immediate necessity for haste in compiling the rest of the *Catalogue*, and before resuming the work Wilde decided to take a holiday in the north of Europe, partly in order to study the contents and arrangement of the principal museums. Accordingly, he visited for this purpose Berlin, Copenhagen, Lund, Stockholm, and Christiania. The antiquarian school of Scandinavia rivalled the Irish, and the megalithic culture was almost as interesting. As an ethnologist he was enthralled, for he was going to the home of the Nordic race.

His reputation had gone before him, and the visit was a triumphant progress. Everywhere he was received with honours and great attentions. The medical men of Stockholm gave him a public dinner. He was given an honorary degree by the ancient University of Uppsala, and entertained publicly by the Viceroy, Baron von Kramer. Next day he drained a horn of mead at the great mounds of Thor, Odin, and Freya at *Gamle Uppsala*, where he might have fancied himself back once more on the Boyne, from the striking similarity of the scene and the monuments which adorned it.

He examined the prehistoric remains closely, to correlate them with those which are strewn so thickly on the soil of Ireland. In the museums he studied the ancient tools, ornaments, and weapons, so that he could better understand the purpose of those of his native land.

In Sweden particularly he was received with the greatest kindness. Oscar Montelius, Gustaf Retzius, Sven Nilsson and the rest treated him as their equal in their own sphere. '*Quant à moi,*' wrote Nilsson to Gilbert, '*je connais un seul vrai et impartial Archéologue en Irlande, et vous le connaissez aussi, son nom est* William Wilde. *Dans son livre sous le titre de* Beauties of the

Boyne *j'ai recueilli beaucoup de renseignements précieux; car son auteur a vu d'autres parties du monde qu'Irlande, et il sait faire des comparaisons ingénieuses de ce qu'il a vu. Il ne veut balayer les traditions populaires, mais il les examine avec sagacité, et il en prend des résultats profitables pour la science.'*

It is small wonder that Wilde was still pleased with himself on his return to Ireland. His personal prestige had been greatly raised, and many new facts were pigeon-holed in his retentive memory. It came as a rude shock when, after all his labours, the Academy decided to stop all work on the *Catalogue*.

This was a bitter blow to Wilde, for the first part of the *Catalogue*, his greatest effort in pure archaeology, and the only one published in book form, had been a great success. It had been termed 'the only scientific Museum Catalogue in the British Isles'. Since it appeared he had received an almost overwhelming congratulatory correspondence from home and abroad. Now he had returned from Scandinavia with his knowledge filled in and enlarged, only to find the work was to be stopped. 'Had I known the amount of physical and mental labour I was to go through when I undertook the *Catalogue*, I would not have considered it just to myself to have done it; for I may fairly say, it has been done at the risk of my life.' Many of his friends sympathized with him. Martin Haverty, author of a *History of Ireland* and other works, wrote to Gilbert: 'When last in town I saw Dr. Wilde. He seemed a good deal annoyed about the proceedings in the Academy, and I think justly. He has been badly treated.' Wilde seems to have reacted strongly, for in a later letter Haverty remarked: 'I am afraid that our friend, Dr. Wilde, has been too hasty with the Academy. His nature is too impulsive, if it could be helped.'

It does not seem to have occurred to Wilde that he could easily have put up the money himself, as he was now more than comfortably off. Instead a subscription was started amongst the Academy members, in spite of strong opposition from some of them. In this way funds sufficient for Parts II and III were eventually collected, and the work on the *Catalogue* went on once more, but not without rancour. Part II of the *Catalogue*, which described the articles of animal materials, copper and bronze, was published in 1860. Part III, dealing with the wonderful collection of prehistoric gold, appeared in 1862. It is on these three parts of the *Catalogue* that Wilde's fame as an archaeologist now principally rests.

II

While the work on Part III of the *Catalogue* was proceeding Irish archaeology suffered a severe blow when O'Donovan and O'Curry died within six months of each other. Although they were not amongst his closer intimates, Wilde mourned their loss in an almost personal manner, for he had long been associated with them in the Celtic and Archaeological Societies, as well as in the Royal Irish Academy.

Many famous people came to visit Wilde, and study his museum. M. Boucher de Perthes came from Abbéville to investigate the markings on the Irish megaliths. His theory was that they were portraits in profile of the early inhabitants; Speranza thought the idea 'strange and peculiar', but it may not have been far wrong, for they may represent human figures in some cases. Nilsson came from Lund, and the Emperor Napoleon, who had projected a magnificent work on Celtic antiquities, sent over a special Commissioner to interview Wilde. The Abbé Domenech also came, with the Empress Charlotte and the ill-fated Maximilian, while on their way to Mexico.

A year or so later Wilde was presented to one greater than any of these. This was the Prince of Wales, who, as Edward VII, was to become one of England's most successful rulers. At this time there was a move in political circles in England to make him Viceroy of Ireland, thus providing a truly royal vice-regent for the country instead of one who was really a military governor. Unfortunately, Victoria, who never liked the Irish, refused to allow the appointment. She did not even like to hear of her son visiting the country, but changed her mind when Disraeli pointed out that, in two hundred years, English rulers had only passed twenty-one days in Ireland altogether.

Wilde conducted the Prince over the Museum, and was surprised to find that he possessed a sound knowledge of Celtic antiquities, which he had acquired in Copenhagen from a mutual friend, Professor Christian Jürgensen Thomsen.

All this intercourse with notabilities went to fan Wilde's self-importance. 'Wilde, Waller, McGlashan and the rest are are all gone clean mad with mutual puffery and praising,' said poor Lever, thinking himself neglected while on one of his periodic visits to Dublin from the Continent. A couple of years later Wilde's self-esteem was still further raised when, in 1862, King Charles XV of Sweden bestowed upon him the order of the Polar Star.

We learn this from a notice in the *Dublin University Magazine*, which states that the King of Sweden 'conferred on him the honour of knighthood, and presented him with a decoration of the Order of the Polar Star, which made him Chevalier of the Kingdom of Sweden.'

There must be some doubt as to whether Wilde received two honours, both that of knighthood, and that of membership of the Order of the Polar Star. He certainly received the latter, but this did not confer knighthood nor the title of Chevalier upon him. In fact, no Swedish Order carries title rights, and therefore Wilde was not entitled to call himself 'Chevalier' on account of the award of the Order. It must, however, be remembered that Roslin, who was, of course, a Swede, used to call himself 'le Chevalier Roslin' while in France, after he had received the Order of Vasa, which is inferior to the Order of the Polar Star.

If Wilde had been knighted, as *well* as given the Polar Star Order, he would, of course, have been fully entitled to call himself Chevalier. Unfortunately, it has proved impossible to find any evidence that he was ever knighted by the King of Sweden, and in these anxious times the Swedish Foreign Office has more to do than to answer foolish questions about the matter. For this very good reason they have also postponed examination of the Archives of the Order, which alone can tell us why Wilde received his decoration, or rather how he was eulogized when receiving it.

The possibilities of this latest distinction did not escape the notice of the wits of the Medico-Phils. In the minute for April 2nd, 1862, it is stated: 'Mr. Wilde having submitted to the President a letter conferring upon him (Mr. Wilde) the Order of the North Star of Sweden, and having also exhibited to the Society the very handsome decoration of the Order, it was resolved that the congratulations of the Society be offered to Mr. Wilde on the acquirement of this very distinguished honour and that henceforward at every meeting of the Society he shall be addressed as Chevalier Wilde.'

And thus he was, in fact, referred to by the members of the Society until the day of his death, and after. On the occasion of the next meeting but one we learn that 'Chevalier Wilde having failed to produce his likeness it was moved by Dr. Stokes and seconded by Dr. Nugent that they two along with the Secretary shall be a committee to arrange the Chevalier in a proper and becoming position, and have his photograph taken.'

III

Wilde was now in prosperous circumstances, and he was able to escape frequently from Dublin to various country residences. At first he contented himself by taking his wife

1863

and young family to the seaside, at Sandymount or Bray. But the west still called him, and he was happiest in the highlands of Connemara. He built his first holiday house in Connemara amid wild mountain scenery on the far western sea-board, on a wooded peninsula on Lough Fee which bears the lovely name of Illaunroe. A few hundred yards of tumbling river connect the lake with the Little Killary, a deep inlet of the sea, which, with the Great Killary, forms the nearest approach to a Norwegian fjord to be found on our coasts. Lough Fee looks as though it should afford excellent white-trout and salmon fishing, and this is no doubt what attracted Wilde to it in the first instance.

A little later he acquired part of the ancestral estates of his maternal ancestors, the Fynnes of Ballymagibbon. John Fynne, the tyrannical Dipper, had died, and the property had passed to Wilde's aunt, Miss Fynne. Miss Fynne's mind was never very well-balanced. Soon it became completely unhinged, and she was certified a lunatic, partly through Wilde's intervention. The Ballymagibbon estate came up for sale in the Landed Estates Court, and Wilde seized his opportunity and bought part of it.

The land he acquired lay some ten miles inland from Illaunroe at Moytura, near Cong, in the neck of land which separates the Corrib from Lough Mask. Here he found a wretched tenantry, far too numerous to wrest a decent living from the land at their disposal. He went tactfully to work, enlisted the sympathy

Moytura House

of the neighbouring Catholic clergy, and was eventually able to remove a number of them 'without the sacrifice of any large sums of money'. The remainder he put into comfortable cottages, and gave a generous measure of tenant rights. He then built himself a house upon a commanding position on the shores of Corrib, and here he spent his holidays for the remaining thirteen years of his life. It is a small house, but beautifully proportioned, although built at a bad architectural period. He supervised its building closely, and did much work with his own hands.

Soon after Moytura was built, Wilde asked the Medico-Phils

R

to come down and see it. They were not slow to accept his invitation, and the visit proved to be one of the most memorable events in the history of the Society.

IV

The household at No. 1, Merrion Square soon welcomed a new-comer, for Speranza had her wish in the shape of a little girl. This was Isola Francesca, the little sister of whom Oscar said he was so fond. There were children's parties, at which a favourite amusement amongst the guests was to ask Oscar what his name was. 'Oscar Fingal O'Flahertie Wills Wilde,' he would reply, repeating the whole rigmarole with the greatest solemnity.

Wilde's hospitable invitations were many. 'To-morrow is Oscar's birthday, and you are such a favourite of his you must come.' Or, 'Billy has passed his examination, and you will join us in drinking his health.' Grown-up parties were equally numerous—'My dear Mary—du Chaillu is to be with us to-morrow evening, and we are to have a shilloo for him. . . . I hope you will come in. . . .'

Any stranger or foreigner of intellectual or artistic distinction was certain of an invitation to the Wildes' assemblies. Speranza dressed in long flowing robes of Irish poplin and Limerick lace, and adorned herself with gold chains and brooches, modelled on the ornaments of Éire's ancient queens. She was undoubtedly becoming more and more eccentric, and she now spent half her days in bed. Wilde's peculiarities were equally noted. He was becoming untidy, even dirty. Many witticisms floated around Dublin at the expense of the pair. 'Why are Dr. Wilde's nails black?' 'Because he scratches himself.'

Rumours began to spread about other aspects of the menage —of a strange female sitting in Wilde's hall, and invading Speranza's bedroom, of Wilde escorting a lady from a Castle function on foot, while Speranza followed, watching them jealously from her carriage.

V

In his medical practice Wilde had now the assistance of his son, Henry Wilson, who had studied medicine at the Royal College of Surgeons, and at the Royal City of Dublin Hospital. He qualified in 1858, at the age of about twenty, later taking the Fellowship of the College. Wilde put him through his paces as house-surgeon at St. Mark's and afterwards made him his assistant in private practice. Before doing so he sent him to work abroad as he himself had done, at Vienna, Heidelberg, Berlin and Paris.

Wilde was now very busy indeed, and was glad to be able to send the overflow of his work to Wilson, including those cases which he wished to have examined with the ophthalmoscope. Wilson soon had a good practice of his own, for many patients preferred his charming suavity of manner to the abrupt rudeness which Wilde could often show.

The Census for 1861 was published in 1864. It was not as remarkable as the return for the previous decade, if only because it had not such a harrowing tale to tell, but it was a very creditable production.

Honours continued to be showered upon Wilde. He was made an honorary member of the Antiquarian Society of Berlin, and he received a Diploma from the Royal Society at Uppsala. In 1864 he received the degree of M.D., *honoris causa*, from Dublin University. This was his first official connection with Trinity. His crowning distinction came in the spring of 1864 when he had the honour of knighthood conferred upon him by the Lord Lieutenant, Lord Carlisle. The ceremony was performed in the magnificent public rooms of Dublin Castle, which are the envy and admiration of foreign diplomatists stationed in Dublin. The Knights of St. Patrick had held a chapter for the installation of new Knights to their illustrious order. On the retirement of the Knights his Excellency, still seated upon the throne, bade Wilde come forward, and said:

'Mr. Wilde, I propose to confer upon you the honour of knighthood, not so much in recognition of your high professional reputation, which is European, and has been recognized by many countries in Europe, but to mark my sense of the services you have rendered to Statistical Science, especially in connection with the Irish Census.'

His knighthood marks the climax of Wilde's career. As a reward for his labours in many fields it was not more than sufficient. He might reasonably have been expected to go farther, but this was not to be.

His many friends joined with each other in congratulating him on his latest distinction. The Medico-Phils allowed him to entertain them to dinner, at other parties he was the guest of honour. *Saunders' Newsletter* published an 'Epigram on a Recent Dubbing in Dublin'.

'The news of thy knighthood was welcomed with cheers;
Oh! eminent aurist, 'twas good for our ears.
The *Gazette* that records it, wherever it flies,
To thy friends through the world, will be good for their eyes;
Thus Carlisle, judiciously dubbing thee, Will,
In honouring thy merit hath rivalled thy skill.
SAMUEL LOVER.'

The first indication that all was not well was given by a letter to the author of this epigram, which appeared in a later copy of the same newspaper:

'To Samuel Lover, Esq., My dear Sam—Apropos of the memorable event which you have chronicled in the above lines, I beg to send you the following bit of a doggrel; and if you do not at once procure its insertion in the paper in which your epigram appeared, I shall be coerced, when we next meet, to confer upon yourself the signal (dis) honor of a sound d(r)ubbing.—Ever yours, fraternally,
SAM WELLER.'

CHAPTER XXIII   PERSECUTION

I

'SAM WELLER'S' letter was accompanied by a scurrilous rhyme:

'*The Late Dubbing in Dublin Castle.*'

The other day, with great surprise,
I saw it in the paper,
Great W. W. rose a knight
By touch of Carlisle's rapier.
The doctors have it their own way,
Though neither wise nor witty,
Not long ago 'Gray' got his *tip*
For watering our city.
Then why should not another man
'Gainst fickle fortune fight, sir,
And try by art of surgery
To be a belted knight, sir,
For deeds of blood and slaughter?
But now a man may win a name
By bottles of eye water.
The deaf can hear—the blind can see,
These are his triumphs great, sir.
The only wonder really is
They were discovered so late, sir,
Backed by our honest *Dublin Press*
By friendly *puff* and *pars*, sir.
Publicity he sought and found—
Oh! don't he bless his stars, sir?
For, perched upon a niche of fame,
Dame Fortune opes her store, sir,
And all with admiration gaze
On him for evermore, sir.—S. W.'

Nobody knew who 'Sam Weller' was, beyond the fact that it was obviously somebody who did not like Wilde. But Wilde had many enemies, as would anybody who was so completely devoid of the quality of *suaviter in modo*. Dubliners chuckled a little, the tongues of the gossips wagged awhile, and the whole affair would soon have been forgotten but for incidents which occurred a couple of months later.

The scene was the Metropolitan Hall, and the occasion a public lecture by Sir William Wilde. It was to be one of a series given by distinguished men under the auspices of the Young Men's Christian Association. He had chosen as his subject: '*Ireland: Past and Present: the Land and the People.*' Wilde's reputation was such as to make people expect something good, and indeed so it proved, for it was much the best of the series.

Fashionable Dublin thronged to the lecture; Abbey Street was crowded with carriages setting down their cargoes of notabilities, and there was the usual mob of sight-seers. Amongst this crowd ran a small boy ringing a handbell, while four or five others sold copies of a pamphlet, entitled *Florence Boyle Price: or a Warning*, by 'Speranza'. They also distributed broadcast a fly-sheet on which were printed letters of a very private nature which had been written by Wilde. 'Sir William Wilde's letters, Sir William Wilde's letters!" they cried, thrusting them into the hands of all and sundry. Soon commotion was added to sensation, for some of Wilde's friends bought pamphlets, and seeing their real nature, attempted to seize the rest.

In a carriage drawn a little way apart, a 'woman scorned' sat gloating with green eyes upon her handiwork, for she, and not Lady Wilde, whose pen-name she had assumed, was the author of the pamphlet. She had arrived early and remained feasting her deranged senses for a full hour.

II

The pamphlet told a tale in parable, the tale of Wilde and his paramour. It was a diffuse, long-winded production, even when the major irrelevancies are excised.

The story told was that of a high-spirited girl who was basely seduced by a doctor in his consulting-room, while she was under the influence of chloroform. The girl was called 'Florence Boyle Price', and the doctor, who was easily recognizable as Wilde, was referred to as 'Dr. Quilp'. The authoress represents herself as meeting Quilp when walking with Florence. 'Had the introduction taken place in the dark, or with my eyes blindfolded, I should unhesitatingly have pronounced him to be an amiable man, the tone of his voice was so sweet and attractive. After parting from him, I remarked to Florence how little physiognomy or facial development can be relied on, as indicating character; for her friend, the doctor, struck me as having a decidedly animal and sinister expression about his mouth, which was coarse and vulgar in the extreme, while his under-lip hung and protruded most unpleasantly. The upper part of his face did not redeem the lower part; his eyes were round and small—tbey were mean and prying; and, above all, they struck me as being deficient in an expression I expected to find gracing the doctor's countenance—I mean candour: there was lack of candour. My severe remarks called forth from my friend some indignant rejoinders, which I contrived to laugh off, little suspecting how soon and how terribly her feelings on this subject should be changed. I think it is as well to observe here that Mrs. Quilp was an odd sort of undomestic woman. She spent the greater portion of her life in bed, and except on state occasions, she was never visible to visitors. Therefore, whenever she gave an entertainment, it was perfectly understood by her circle that a card, left by her guests on the hall-table, was all she required of those who had enjoyed her hospitality.'

The pamphlet proceeds: 'The scene is changed to a doctor's study. The patients have been seen, prescribed for, and dismissed—all, save one, an intimate friend, whose throat requires to be touched with caustic. The trifling operation has been performed—another is deemed advisable—an appointment is made for her to come the following day—she rises to say good-bye, but she is detained! The doctor asks her is she "afraid" of him. She answers—"No; why should I be afraid of you?" "You look pale," he says: "here," and he places a handsome scent-bottle close to her face—she grasps it, and, pouring out some of the liquid, says: "I will put it to my temples." He snatches the bottle from her excitedly, and roughly asks her why she did that? No answer was needed. The bottle con-

tained a strong solution of chloroform; the vapour filled the
room rapidly; and the handkerchief on which the liquid had
fallen was snatched violently, and flung into the fire by the
medical man, whom we may now call Quilp. The scene was
enacted in a shorter space of time that I have taken to write it.
Florence—for it is she—rushes to the door, but is interrupted
by the detected Quilp, who, flinging himself on his knees,
attempts a passionate outburst of love, despair and remorse;
but the horror-stricken Florence implores to be released from
this dangerous place. She dreads to give an alarm, knowing
the irreparable disgrace, the everlasting ruin it will entail. . . .
Some days later a letter from Quilp arrived, which read as
follows—"Forgive—I am miserable and very ill—utterly sleep-
less. Remorse and illness are doing their work. For God's
sake see me, and say you forgive before I die!' Florence knew
that Quilp was sometimes at death's door with asthmatic and
gouty attacks, and she could not help feeling concern for the
unhappy man, now that he was stricken down in pain of both
body and mind. . . . She thought it too much sternness for her
to refuse a death-bed request. She went; she hastened, as she
thought, to the dying man; she was ushered into the study
where she was surprised to find Quilp seated. He threw an
agonized look at her as she entered. Neither spoke for a
moment. Florence stood at the table by his side. He spoke
first—"See my drawn features—my sunken eyes—my haggard
face. Florence, have pity; oh, forgive and forget." "I forgive,"
she replied. "You do not say that from your heart," he said.
"You hate me! I always knew it, but I——" "Hush," she
said, "or I leave you. I forgive, I must forget—forget I ever
knew you. I esteemed you above all others; here our acquaintance ends. Farewell for ever!" She left the house, as she
thought and intended, never to enter it again. Little she dreamed
she would again enter it, and again leave it, under very different
auspices. . . . Quilp's study again. Florence, with flashing
eyes and scornful tone, indignantly flings a book on the table.
"How dare you, sir," she says, "tell me you want my 'intellect
strengthened by reading' when it is such a book as that you
presume to offer me. Better far say you wish my heart to be
corrupted! Think you I have never heard of Goethe's *Elective
Affinities*? Yes, too often have I heard it condemned by competent judges to be ignorant of its immoral tendency. Impious

unbeliever, I now leave you to the mercy of the God you say does not exist except in man's intellect. Never approach me again. I am no longer the credulous simpleton of old; your subterfuges will not mislead me, attempt them not again; disguise your handwriting, put false addresses on your letters to me, to deceive me into opening them if you will; 'forewarned is forearmed.' You tried all this before, it will not succeed again. I never will recognize you on this earth; we are strangers from this hour, my ——" "Florence, Florence," exclaimed Quilp, "I am no longer a suppliant for mercy from the passionless, unnatural woman that I have loved for years in silence, because I dared not strive to win her, but whom I determined to conquer. Florence, you would give your life to do me a service—do not repel me; you are true as the magnet, notwithstanding all your threats; you will never divulge what has occurred." Florence thunders to him to open the door or she will raise an alarm, but Quilp says: "I will turn the tables on you now—you are now in my power. If you breathe a syllable of the chloroform, you blast yourself by revealing it, for you should never have entered my doors after the attempt—my cleverness got you back. I am not in your power quite so much as you think, but if the devotion of a life-time can——" The crisis had come; the hypocrite unmasked himself, and there was no longer to be a spark of compassion for him. Florence recovered her presence of mind in a moment. She left the house and wrote the following note: "Miss Price's compliments to Mrs. Quilp, and requests she will make it her convenience to be at her town residence as soon as possible. Miss Price considers it necessary to inform Mrs. Quilp, in her husband's presence, of the immorality and brutality to which she has been subjected by Dr. Quilp, in his own house." This letter was duly posted and delivered, but Quilp found means to intercept it before it could reach his wife. After some days Florence learned that her letter had never reached its destination. About the same time a rumour reached her that Quilp was artfully circulating a report that she was mad, and had suddenly and unaccountably taken a dislike to him, and indeed that he feared she would become dangerous. Here was a master-stroke of the too clever Quilp! Mrs. Quilp returned to town, when Florence called and sent up her card, requesting to see Mrs. Quilp. Quilp (who was in the hall when she entered) darted up stairs to his

wife. The result need scarcely be told; Mrs. Quilp refused to
see her visitor. Florence was thoroughly roused at this indignity,
her blood boiled at the audacious affront; but this was not all
she had to endure upon that memorable day. Mr. Quilp came
racing down the stairs, proclaiming to Florence, in exulting
tones: "Mrs. Quilp will not see you; she does not want your
acquaintance; you may write to her if you wish!" "For you
to intercept the letter," thought Florence. . . . Over the scene
that ensued, I draw a temporary veil; suffice to say, that the
false-hearted coward Quilp so far forgot himself in the presence
of others as to exhibit himself in his true character of ruffian
and bully!! The foregoing is merely an outline of events that
took place many years ago; the details, many of which are
painful, but important, are reserved for future publication. . . .
"Hope" being the English of Speranza, I have assumed that
name for its appropriateness, hoping this "warning" will be
of use to more than

'SPERANZA.'

It was clear to everybody that Wilde was the person referred
to as "Quilp" in this effusion, which formed the major part
of the pamphlet. With it were also included a number of
letters written by Wilde, and the following explanatory statement
which put the meaning of the story beyond all doubt:
"If Mr. W. R. Wilde, 1, Merrion-Square, North, had not
been guilty of gross misconduct to a lady, in his own house,
why did he not take legal proceedings against the person, or
persons who had dared to tamper with his moral character? . . .
Should he be able to prove that my statements are untrue, he
has a remedy which I have not attempted to evade—his
explanations must be public to be effective. To be quite above
board, and to prevent misconstruction or misapprehension, I
print and publish this contradiction of Mr. W'.s unjustifiable
slanders. Should any persons wish to inquire further into the
matter they can see the original letters addressed by Mr. Wilde
to the lady in question on applying to "Ignotus", 20, Fownes's-
street, Dublin. . . . A lady cannot chastise the canine creature,
and since those who ought stand in the way of those who are
willing to inflict the chastisement due, there is no alternative
but to print and publish this contradiction to Mr. W.'s disgusting
statement.'

III

This production provided the gossips of Dublin with the best tit-bit they have had perhaps before or since.

Eight or nine dozen copies of this pamphlet were sold for a penny each. Next day a letter appeared in *Saunders' Newsletter*, inquiring as to the nature of the tumult which had occurred outside the Metropolitan Hall, and suggesting that, if there had been no provocation for it, 'the Knight' ought to take action against the offender.

This letter was, of course, written by the author of the pamphlet, with whom we have already had a fleeting acquaintance, for she was the girl of nineteen who had been sent by Stokes to consult Wilde some ten years previously. Her name was Mary Josephine Travers, and she was the daughter of Dr. Robert Travers, Professor of Medical Jurisprudence in Trinity College, and sub-Librarian of Marsh's Library.

There can be no doubt that Wilde and she had consorted regularly for some years after their first meeting. In her youth she is said to have been beautiful, and Wilde was also, no doubt, interested in her because she had some literary pretensions. He had taken her to the meetings of the British Association, and in 1859 had given her a season ticket for the Exhibition. He had corresponded with her the same year while on his tour of the Northern capitals, and on his return to Dublin their intimacy was renewed. He introduced her to his household, took her to see his hospital, and brought her round the museum.

One day Speranza entered Wilde's bedroom and opened a little box in which was an antique ring which he intended to present to the Royal Irish Academy. In it she also found a more modern ornament. ''Pon my word, I have seen this in Miss Travers's bonnet.' She saw what was going on, and decided to take a hand. Walking one day into her husband's study, she found the two of them there, and a photograph of Miss Travers on the mantelpiece. 'Do you want to take my husband from me?' she said. The direct attack was ever Speranza's method. With that she gave her enemy 'a good pinch'. It was said that this was done in 'half joke, half earnest', but we may suspect that the joke was considerably the lesser half.

Miss Travers was by no means thin-skinned, and did not take this too seriously, for soon after she announced her intention of calling to take the Wilde children to church. Speranza, however, forestalled her, and brought the children to the Chapel Royal herself. Even still Miss Travers—'Ernest Moll', as Wilde called her—was undaunted, but finally the inevitable happened. She came uninvited into Speranza's bedroom after a party. There was a glorious row, Speranza threw her out, and from that day there was no equivocation in their animosity.

Wilde himself had already begun to tire of her. He realized she was an impossible woman, and he was probably genuinely fond of Speranza, although she also was probably a very difficult woman to live with. In any case, he was painfully anxious to avoid a scandal, for he, who had fought so hard when right was on his side, found his courage had completely evaporated when he was in the wrong. He was undoubtedly in a very tight corner, for he had no ordinary woman to deal with now.

From the day 'Ernest Moll' realized she was to be discarded, the trouble really started. Wilde cajoled and implored her, gave her tickets for the ball, money for 'panjams and warm clothes'. He tried to persuade her to go to Australia, where her brothers were. He presented her with her passage money, and even offered to accompany her as far as Liverpool, no doubt for the pleasure of seeing her safely on the boat. She actually got as far as Liverpool on two occasions, but unfortunately for Wilde returned each time.

For a time the thought of her own personal disgrace acted as a brake on her desire to get her own back on Wilde, and she contented herself with squeezing money out of him, which must have pained him considerably, and generally making his life a misery. This phase soon passed. She threw all discretion to the four winds of Heaven, and determined to get vengeance, cost what it might. Speranza's repeated snubs had aroused in her a hatred equal to that she had for Wilde. The best way she could make Speranza suffer was by publishing the whole sordid business. She might not come out of it very well herself, but she did not care.

She laid her plans accordingly. She would drive Wilde to take action against her in self-defence, and then it would all come out in the law courts. One effort was to drop a venomous

rhyme into his letter-box enclosed in an envelope closed only
by a pin—

> 'Your progeny is quite a pest
>   To those who hate such "critters";
> Some sport I'll have, or I'm blest
> I'll fry the Wilde breed in the West;
>   Then you can call them Fritters.
> The name is not equivocal,
> They dare not by their mother call,
> Nor by their father, though he's Sir,
> A gouty knight, a mangy cur;
> He does not dare to call them Frits—
> How much he'd wish that I'd say Quits.

For next week's Handbills—The Miss Fritters!!! with most
affectionate regards. Please show this to her ladyship at the
dessert!!!'

The allusion is quite obvious. The rhyme refers to Wilde's
numerous illegitimate children. As she said herself later: 'The
meaning is that Sir William Wilde was so very sore on the
subject of any person alluding to his children, or, as he called
them, his "breed", that I wrote this for the purpose of making
him think that he would be exposed, and that he might try
to prevent my taking any legal means or get the interference
of my family to prevent me from annoying him, because I wanted
to give my explanation of all that had gone on in his house
during my intercourse with him'; 'Show it to her ladyship
at the dessert' refers to the fact that Wilde had told his tormentor
that he would, in future, show all her letters to Speranza.

This was not Miss Travers's first attempt, for previously she
had sent him a rhyme which was merely abusive:

> 'The oculist cured,
>   I give you my word
> With his own bottle, too, I have dosed him.
> I have sent him a drink,
>   That will set him to think,
> Until his own blushes will roast him.'

Wilde fled to Cong to escape her; to annoy him she sent on

a printed scrap of paper announcing her death—'Suddenly at the residence of her father, Mary Josephine Travers, eldest daughter of Robert Travers, Esq.' Speranza, who was at Bray, also received one of these communications, with the addition of a roughly drawn sketch of a coffin at its foot.

On Wilde's return Miss Travers made several efforts to see Speranza, but failed. Finally she secured an entrance into Wilde's hall and sat with folded arms on a marble-topped side table. She retained this chilly perch for two hours, until finally Speranza came downstairs followed by the two boys. She spoke to Willie, whose mother immediately enjoined him not to reply. This improving scene was watched by young Mr. Hogan, son of the famous sculptor, who was also present on the occasion of the bedroom scene. Speranza packed the children into her carriage, and went straight to Bray.

Having failed to bolt her quarry by these crudities, Miss Travers rose to greater literary heights, and composed *Florence Boyle Price: or the Warning*. Now the fun started in real earnest. This was in October, 1863, about six months before the episode at the Metropolitan Hall. The pamphlets came by post, at first singly, later in numbers. They were sent to patients, brought in by busy friends, and were scattered all round Dublin from Rathmines to Inchicore. The Wildes were simply deluged with them.

Wilde's knighthood fanned the flames of Miss Travers's hatred. She sent the rhyme on *The Late Dubbing in Dublin Castle* to *Saunders' Newsletter*, but still she felt *Florence Boyle Price* and its fly sheet, the parable and the explanation, was her best weapon. She saw an opportunity on the occasion of Wilde's lecture, and she certainly made the best of it.

After the lecture Speranza, in despair, took her children to the house on the sea front at Bray. But even there she was not to remain unmolested, for three days after the lecture a grimy urchin brought the wretched pamphlet to her house. The servant laid it on her tea-table; Speranza in wrath went out and found the newsboy. He told her he had got the pamphlets from 'a lady who had desired him to cry it out on the esplanade'. Speranza lectured the lad, who went away; but then, just as some callers arrived, another and cheekier urchin arrived, with four more tracts for sale.

Speranza's patience was exhausted. She tried to buy the

tracts, but the boy refused to sell them all, saying that one was enough for her. Whereupon Speranza threw him out, keeping the pamphlet in her possession, but unfortunately did not pay for it.

Next morning, little Isola came to her mother while she was still in bed, saying that there was a wretched boy in the hall selling things about 'Speranza' and 'Lady Wilde', and wishing to know what they were about. This was the last straw. Speranza exploded with rage, and in her heat she made a fatal mistake, for she sat down and wrote a furious letter to Dr. Travers about his daughter's conduct. Wilde was at this time in Dublin, and knew nothing about this letter until considerably later.

At first 'Ernest Moll' knew nothing about it either, but she was determined on litigation, come what might. The best she could do for the moment was to summon Sir William and Lady Wilde for illegally retaining the pamphlet and placard offered her for sale. It was, of course, illegal to retain them without payment. The case was heard at the Petty Sessions at Bray on the 14th May. Speranza must have regretted the fact that she had not given the boy his penny.

Worse, much worse, was to come. Robert Travers, 'Ernest Moll's' father, seems to have been an insignificant woolly-minded creature. He lived apart from his wife, but one cannot blame him for this if she was anything like her eldest daughter. He was apparently quite incapable of controlling his family, and seems to have given up Mary as a bad job. When he received the letter he threw it into a cupboard in his room, where it remained unanswered for three or four weeks.

At the end of this time it was found by Miss Travers. She opened it, and read as follows:

Tower, Bray, May 6.
Sir—You may not be aware of the disreputable conduct of your daughter at Bray, where she consorts with all the low newspaper boys in the place, employing them to disseminate offensive placards, in which my name is given, and also tracts, in which she makes it appear that she has had an intrigue with Sir William Wilde. If she chooses to disgrace herself that is not my affair; but as her object in insulting me is in the hope of extorting money, for which she has several times applied

to Sir William Wilde, with threats of more annoyance if not given, I think it right to inform you that no threat or additional insult shall ever extort money for her from our hands. The wages of disgrace she has so loosely treated for and demanded shall never be given her.

JANE F. WILDE.

To Dr. Travers.

Moll Travers trembled with joy as she read this letter. Her hour of triumph was come. Her object would soon be gained, for here at last was her opportunity. The next thing Speranza knew was that she was served with a writ for libel.

CHAPTER XXIV

THE TRIAL

I

MANY PEOPLE in Dublin had now read the *Florence Boyle Price* rigmarole, and knew that Wilde was Dr. Quilp, and Miss Travers the injured girl. When they heard that she was taking proceedings against him, they naturally thought action would be taken against him for criminal assault, rape or seduction. The case did not, however, take this form. It was a civil action for libel based on Speranza's letter, claiming £2,000 damages.

The summons and plaint charged that this letter was a libel reflecting on Miss Travers's chastity. Wilde, as husband of the lady who wrote the letter, was merely joined in the action for conformity, although it was obvious that it was he who was the real defendant. His advisors pleaded in his defence, first, that there was 'No libel', secondly, that the letter did not bear the defamatory sense alleged by the plaint, thirdly, a denial of publication, and fourthly, a plea of justification. The final plea was evidently the real defence, and was based on the facts of the persecution which had led Speranza to write the letter.

The case came up for hearing on Monday, December 12th, 1864, before Mr. Justice Monahan and a special city jury. The leading counsel at the Irish bar were briefed for both sides. Sergeant Armstrong led for Miss Travers, with Wilde's old associate, Isaac Butt, who had done much political trimming since the early days of the *Dublin University Magazine*. There was another senior counsel in Mr. Heron, Q.C.; and two juniors, Mr. Hamill and Mr. Quinn. Wilde was represented by Sergeant Sullivan, Mr. Sidney, Q.C., and Mr. Morris, Q.C., with Mr. John Curran and Mr. Purcell.

Curiosity-mongers crowded the old Four Courts to the walls, for the suit 'shook Dublin society like a thunderclap'. Wilde's great reputation was well-known, and had been emphasized by his recent knighthood. Speranza was still idolized by the populace for her passionate labours for *Young Ireland*. With such a scandalous story, and such prominent people involved,

s

it is not surprising that the case proved one of the greatest *causes célébres* of Victorian times. Fashionable crowds thronged the courts on each day's hearing, intent upon their Roman holiday. Learned counsel, conveniently forgetting the fat fees they were getting, and the equally valuable publicity, shed the usual crocodile tears. Nothing, they said, but their strong sense of public duty would permit them to appear in such a case. The jury settled themselves comfortably in the box, and the case began.

Sergeant Armstrong opened for Miss Travers. After assuring the jury that it was no language of affectation he used when he declared that he would have been glad to have been relieved of any responsibility in the case, he proceeded to outline the sequence of events which has already been recounted. In his hands the attack was direct and deadly. He told how Miss Travers had been sent to Wilde by Stokes ten years before, for the treatment of deafness. Wilde cured her, but would accept no fee, as she was the daughter of a doctor. The friendship continued after he had made her well, and the pair exchanged a voluminous correspondence. Wilde had sent her books and tickets for entertainments; he had accompanied her to dances and theatres, and had given her money. He had even expressed dissatisfaction with her methods of dressing, and had bought clothes and bonnets for her. For some five or six years, Sergeant Armstrong said, the friendship had continued in a platonic, if sentimental, manner, but then a subtle change had appeared in Wilde's behaviour.

Miss Travers, it seemed, had a scar on her neck resulting from a burn which she sustained in childhood. Wilde began to take an entirely unnecessary interest in this scar, which he examined from time to time, and to do so it was usual for him to make her kneel on a cushion while he sat at his chair—surely a curious position in which to inspect a scar on the neck. About the same time Miss Travers complained of a corn on the sole of her foot, which Wilde excised for her. The sergeant appeared to think that these were questionable, if not risky, practices. 'There are men of such temperament,' he said, 'that it would be dangerous to have such a manipulation going on.'

He then came to the denouement of the charge, the accusation that Wilde had criminally assaulted Miss Travers. There was one point of difference from the account given by Miss Travers in the pamphlet. In it 'Dr. Quilp' was accused of seducing 'Florence Boyle Price' while she was under the action of chloroform. Miss Travers now, by her counsel, stated that he had overcome her, not by chloroform, but by partially choking her. In the words of Sergeant Armstrong, 'She called upon him on Thursday, and he received her in his study. She was there at half-past one o'clock. He all at once expressed great concern about the burn across her throat, and said he was anxious to see how it was going on. The strings of her bonnet were untied for the purpose of allowing him to make the examination; she was in the habit of wearing a circlet of black velvet around her neck to conceal the mark, and the strings of her bonnet being untied, he suddenly put his hand between her throat and the band, pressing his knuckles against her throat. He pressed against her very forcibly at that place, and she, as well as she could under the circumstances, said: "You are suffocating me." "I will," said he, "I will suffocate you—I can't help it." He (Sergeant Armstrong) would leave it to the plaintiff to tell what followed. He would only say that "she went in a maid— that out a maid never departed more."

II

Next day Miss Travers, a slender, dark girl with good features and fanatical eyes, went into the box to substantiate this highly improbable story. Under Mr. Butt's guidance she unfolded her story. She told how she had often borrowed money from Wilde, even taking her passage money for the journey to Australia, but impressing the fact that she had always paid him back. She went on to relate how on one day when she had assumed her customary kneeling position before Wilde, he had taken her in his arms and embraced her, declaring that he would not let her go until she called him William. She had been grossly offended by this action, and for a time had dropped Wilde's acquaintance: however, his penitence and pressing attentions had eventually brought about a reconciliation.

She then came to the seduction incident, which she alleged had occurred when Lady Wilde and the children were away at Bray, and Wilde was consequently alone in the house at Merrion Square. Miss Travers had called, and had been shown into his study.

Mr. Butt: 'Do you recollect paying him a visit in October?'

'Yes.'

'Did he examine your throat?'

'He did; I had a ribbon tied round my throat.'

'Tell me what occurred."

'He came over to look at it, and took off my bonnet; he then passed his hand over it, as he had often done before, and in so doing he fastened his hand somewhat roughly between the ribbon that was on my neck and my throat; I suppose I resisted it.'

'I believe I said: "Oh, you are suffocating me," and he said: "Yes, I will; I can't help it," and then I do not recollect anything more until he was dashing water over my face.'

Mr. Butt: 'Did you at any time during that interview lose consciousness?'

'Yes, I did, before the water was flung on my face.'

Miss Travers said that when she had partly recovered her senses Wilde took her upstairs to a bedroom, and made her lie down, giving her some wine to drink. After some time she left the house, but she could not say whether Wilde accompanied her to the door or not, for she was too dazed to know what she or anybody else was doing.

Mr. Butt: 'Are you now able to state whether in that interval of unconsciousness you have described, your person was violated?"

'Yes.'

'Was it?'

'Yes.'

And with this the case was adjourned until the third day.

Miss Travers admitted that this unsavoury incident did not end her association with Wilde. On the contrary, she continued to borrow from him. However, a new element began to colour her behaviour, for she was now determined to annoy him in every possible way, even, it seemed, to the extent of attempting to commit suicide. Much to the delight of the crowd in court she told how they quarrelled after she had extorted some money from him, and how she had taken opium before his eyes in his study.

He had asked what she would do if he gave her the money she asked for. 'You will fling it into the hall,' he said, 'as you did before.'

'What was his manner?" asked Mr. Butt.

'Excited and sarcastic; he felt convinced I was going to do something; he said he would rather I would stab him, and that he knew I would take his life yet.'

'Were you calm in that interview, or were you excited?"

'I was excited; I went away and took a long walk to try and reduce the irritable feelings that I had; I went back to his house and had a second interview with him; I went to his house three times that day; before going back I bought four penny-worth of laudanum at Ray's, in George's Street; when I went back the second time I told him that I considered he spoke in an unbecoming and ruffianly manner to me; he said "No": and he spoke in a very excited, tormenting manner; I then went away.'

'Was it then you bought the laudanum?"

'Yes; I brought it back with me, and took it in his study; I poured it into a wine glass and drank it off.'

'What did he say then?"

'Flung himself on the floor, and shouted out: "Revenge! revenge!—you will have your revenge, for every one will say I poisoned you; but I will have in the police." He kept screaming out revenge in the most frantic manner, and suddenly he said: "Go at once and get an antidote!" He told me to be sure to say that it was a dose of laudanum I had taken accidentally, for "every one will say I have poisoned you, then you will have your revenge."'

'Did you go out of his house then?"

'I did; he told me to go to the first apothecary's for an antidote; but I did not go to the first; I went to Dr. Walshe's, in Westland Row; in about ten minutes Dr. Wilde came into Walshe's; first he gave a very wicked look at me, and then said to Dr. Walshe was not this terrible; the emetic was being prepared, and he appeared very uneasy lest it should not be in time; he asked Dr. Walshe had I got the emetic; there was a long argument as to the propriety of my going home; Dr. Wilde was opposed to my going home; Dr. Walshe wished me to go in a cab, but Dr. Wilde objected, and said if I was to go home I should walk.'

Miss Travers seemed to think that this was very heartless behaviour on Wilde's part, but he was right, for, as every first-aider knows, one of the best ways of getting rid of the effects of opium is to walk it off. Wilde's solicitude was probably unnecessary, as it later came out in evidence that she was in the habit of taking laudanum, and was, therefore, probably much more tolerant of its effects than the normal person.

It also appeared that Wilde had greatly annoyed Miss Travers by saying that she was mad. 'Everybody that looked in my eye would know I was mad—he had seen fire in my eye repeatedly. I was mad and eccentric and absurd—no one but a person that was mad would wear such a bonnet.'

Poor Wilde! He was only too correct.

III

Sergeant Sullivan, in cross-examination, brought out a long series of discrepancies and contradictions in Miss Travers' evidence. She could not remember the date of the alleged assault; she even said the incident had been repeated, although she quickly withdrew this statement when questioned more closely about it. He succeeded in shaking her story very severely. In particular, he made it very clear that everything she had done was activated by an almost fantastic animus against Wilde—in fact, that her whole behaviour was that of a discarded mistress rather than of an innocent creature who had been wronged. She made no bones about the steps she took—her 'acts of vengeance', as she called them. She admitted that the publication of the pamphlet was by no means the first 'act of vengeance', for before this she had administered garlic to him in a handkerchief, and had also put garlic in the soap-tray in his consulting-room. At first she said she had done this 'to cure an asthmatic man', but later she admitted that she used the word 'cure' ironically. Her next 'act of vengeance' was to publish a review of Lady Wilde's book, *The First Temptation*.

It was later suggested by the defence that it was a passage in this book, which Speranza had translated from the German, which had inspired Miss Travers to claim that she had been forcibly violated.

Miss Travers alleged that the occasion of the seduction was the only time when anything of the kind had occurred. Nevertheless, she had borne a child to Wilde. This appears from a letter she wrote to him in the July before the trial:

'9th July, 1864.'

'Sir W. Wilde—The return I offer to make for the loan of your money is to remove myself from under the obligation by taking up from you my son as quickly as I possibly can, so as to avoid "injury or exposure" to myself, and annoyance to others. With regard to the application you persist in stating I made to you for the loan of £3 lately, I again negative that statement of yours, as I did in my former letter to you.

'M. J. TRAVERS.'

This is the only reference during the proceedings, to the birth of an infant, but its meaning is clear.

Questioned as to why she had written the rhyme about the 'Wilde breed in the West', Miss Travers made no bones about it. She said she had done so because Wilde was so sensitive about his illegitimate offspring, or, as he called them, his 'breed', that she wrote it in order to make him think that he would be exposed. She said that she had often heard him alluding to them in this way.

On Thursday morning Sergeant Sullivan addressed the jury on behalf of the defendants. It must be confessed he made the best of a pretty bad job. He made the usual legal quibbles, and drew the usual red-herrings across the trail. He had a few knocks at his opposite number: 'Sergeant Armstrong, in a very defiant speech, said "I defy them to show that this woman ever applied for money to this man." "I defy them," said he, with the voice of a Stentor, and a manner somewhat sarcastic.' Sergeant Sullivan added no facts to what was already known, but he painted Moll Travers, not as the prosecution did, a picture of sweet injured innocence, but as the crazy, vindictive, drug-addict she really was.

His chief witness was Speranza, now aged thirty-eight, still handsome, but a little battle-scarred after ten years of marriage. Her usual ornate finery was not in evidence. Instead she was swathed in black, for her brother, a judge in New Orleans, had just died.

She was closely cross-examined on the letter she wrote to Dr. Travers, the immediate cause of the action. She denied that she had intended to convey immoral relations by the statement that Miss Travers 'consorted' with all the 'low newsboys' in Bray. Loyal as ever, she denied that she had any idea that

Wilde ever had illicit intercourse with Miss Travers. She maintained stoutly that even in the light of all that had transpired, she still did not believe it. She also said, what was probably true, that Wilde had no idea she had written the offending letter until he was served with the writ for libel.

Speranza kept her end up very well, in a grilling duel with the opposing counsel. In the end they were gentlemanly enough to throw her a bouquet for her knowledge of German.

IV

When the case was resumed next day there was a fresh sensation. The Chief Justice said that he had received an anonymous letter about the case that morning. He said he had thrown it immediately in the fire; that such letters had no effect on him, but least of all the effect desired by their author. After he had delivered himself of this contradiction in terms, Mr. Sidney, for the Wildes, said that their side had received about twenty such letters. This was obviously Miss Travers' form, and everybody looked her way, but Sergeant Armstrong announced that Miss Travers was present and ready to deny all knowledge of the matter.

Wilde was now faced with a most difficult decision. Should he go into the box, or not? There was no compulsion on him to give evidence, for he was only joined as defendant for conformity, but it was clear that if he did not do so it would create a very bad impression. It would be tantamount to a confession of illicit relations with Miss Travers, although the story of the seduction was pretty obviously nonsense. If, on the other hand, he did come forward, he would certainly be riddled with questions about the various melodramatic incidents Miss Travers had sworn to.

He decided, wisely, not to run the gauntlet. It was the best course, but infallibly led to the accusation that he was sheltering under his wife's wing.

Mulrenin, the artist, and Hogan, the sculptor's son, gave evidence, and then Mr. Sidney did his best to whitewash the whole nasty business, without much success. He was on a very tricky wicket, and had such a difficult task that at times he appeared to be arguing for the prosecution.

Then came the trial's high-light of oratory. The brilliant Mr. Butt, summing up for Miss Travers, loosed a creaming flood of forensic eloquence. He said it was the most painful duty he had ever been called upon to perform. He might well say so indeed. He 'was aware of the ties that influence the heart when a man like Sir William Wilde was brought into court— they were not, perhaps, unknown to himself personally. Nevertheless, it was a sacred obligation on him to see that these things did not influence the jury's verdict'—and so on and forth.

He did not fail to point out that Wilde, and not Speranza, was the real defendant in the case. 'In this solemn case, between Sir William Wilde and the plaintiff here, in which two human

Isaac Butt

beings seek for justice, you will decide, without respect to persons, if this lady's story be true. I ask you, therefore, to give me your attention while I argue this case, to follow me where your judgement approves; but by your love of justice forget the rank of the defendant—forget the estimation in which you have ever held him, and judge this case between him and the woman who was his victim as you would deal between two parties of whom you have never heard before—I say, between Sir William Wilde and this woman. "Oh," says my learned friends, "this is not an action against him; it is not an action against Sir William Wilde; he is only joined by conformity." Gentlemen, it is he who will pay the damages.'

He did not fail to make full use of Wilde's failure to enter the witness-box. Where, he asked, was Sir William Wilde? 'Why was he not there? He owed it to the jury, if the woman's story was not true, to leave no doubt on their minds if his denial on oath could have cleared up the case. He owed it to the noble profession of which he was an honoured member to come forward and say he had not violated the sacred confidence which that profession carried with it. He owed it to the lady whom he sent the previous day to represent him to calm the horrible suspicions that must agitate her mind; every motive that could sway the mind of man called on Sir William Wilde to come forward if the story was false. He owed it to morality, he owed it to public justice, that his oath should be pledged that the story was untrue. He would even say that if the story was true, the temptation was almost too strong for Sir William Wilde not to have denied it upon his oath, if the evil spirit had so far got the mastery of him as to let him do that act.'

He went through the story once more, 'this miserable story of woman's weakness and man's sin,' from the day he first saw her. He paid a nice compliment to Stokes—'that man whom everybody who knows, loves.'

All this was simple stuff to Butt, and he played his part with the ease of a master. He hadn't apparently read his brief very carefully, for he was wrong in his facts more than once, but he was none the less very impressive. 'If my client is entitled to your verdict, I tell you, on your souls, you can do no more terrible wrong than drive that bleeding, broken-hearted woman disgraced and dishonoured from this court, and it will be a crime for which most assuredly her cries will be heard in Heaven. If you believe that she has fabricated this story, and perjured herself for the purpose of extracting money, no words can express her degradation, and God forbid I should ask you for a verdict; but, oh, before you condemn her, remember that the man who asks you to say by your verdict that she has committed perjury, has shrunk from coming before you to deny her story. If you believe her story, then her case is true, and I implore of you by all that is sacred in domestic life, in the name of the noble profession to which Sir William Wilde belongs, as you value the purity of your own children, by the solemn oaths you have taken, in the sacred name of justice, I ask you to give ample reparation from this man to the woman he has wronged and outraged.'

This concluded Butt's speech. He sat down, and was applauded loud and long.

We may be sure that Wilde and Speranza passed a very uncomfortable week-end. To a man of Wilde's temperament it must have been torture. Many a time he must have wished he had paid without question the £2,000 damages Miss Travers had asked for, but he realized it was not money but his public disgrace she looked for. If he had paid the damages this time, she would find another pretext for another law-case later.

On the Monday morning the Chief Justice's summing-up came as somewhat of a cold douche after Mr. Butt's righteous eloquence. It was hardly credible, he said, that a woman could be forcibly outraged as Miss Travers alleged she had been, with servants and patients passing to and fro in the hall beyond the door of the consulting-room. Surely, if she had struggled

at all, somebody *must* have come to her rescue. He pointed out that a woman who is forcibly violated normally tells her story at once, and immediately discontinues all relationships with the man concerned. In this case Miss Travers had not said anything about the matter until a considerable period of time had elapsed, and on her own showing had continued to have dealings with her alleged assailant for a long time. If the action had been taken for rape or criminal assault she would not have had a leg to stand on. But was there a seduction? He went over the whole story yet again, and finally directed the jury on the various counts of the prosecution, and the question of damages.

The jury must have been composed of supermen, for some

of the technicalities of the case, as reported, seem beyond·the comprehension of the ordinary layman. Sergeant Armstrong objected to some of the judge's statements. 'Yes,' said the Chief Justice, 'you may be right. At the end of my charge I said the letter was the only thing they were to consider, and the jury and the counsel for the plaintiff might understand from that, that they were to consider nothing else. I will call out the jury.'

The jury had already retired. They were called out, and this knotty point explained. They retired again.

After an hour and a quarter they called for coals for their fire, but before the coals were brought they came into court with their verdict.

Chief Justice: 'Well, gentlemen, have you agreed?'

Foreman: 'Yes, my lord. We find for the plaintiff with one farthing's damages.'

V

The verdict reminds us of the story of another case, probably apocryphal. This was also a trial for seduction. At its conclusion, the jury announced that they had assessed damages at the same amount, one farthing.

The defendant approached the plaintiff. He produced a penny from his pocket, slapped it down upon a desk, and cried: 'There's the price of your virtue. Now give me the change!'

IT IS pleasant to be able to record that in the hour of his disgrace, Wilde had the sympathy and support of most of his fellow doctors. There was, however, one notable exception. The *Dublin Medical Press* made full use of the opportunity to kick him when he was down. In a leading article the following pronouncement appeared:

'If there is one unanimous opinion which pervades all minds, it is that Sir William Wilde has not satisfactorily refuted the charge of which he stands accused, of having taken advantage of that confidence which ought to be sacred for an immoral purpose. True it is that the nature of the legal process did not render legal denial absolutely essential to the defence . . . but, nevertheless, there were demands on Sir Wm. Wilde for a denial or a refutation of the accusation of having outraged his patient, as binding as any legal necessity could make them. He owed it to his profession, which must now endure the onus of the disgrace—he owed it to the public, who have confided, and are still expected to confide themselves to his honour—he owed it to Her Majesty's Representative, who had conferred an unusual mark of distinction on him, to purge himself of the suspicion which this moment lies heavy on his name.'

. . . 'It is little to the point to recriminate upon the plaintiff, Miss Travers, to whom the public has not pledged itself, and with whom little sympathy exists.'

These remarks were written by Wilde's rival, Arthur Jacob, the owner and editor of the journal. Although, as we have seen, he was a great oculist and anatomist, he was apparently not above indulging his professional jealousy. This was not the first time he had publicly tilted at Wilde, for he had some years previously accused him of 'puffery' and self-advertisement.

On this occasion his attack was received with considerable disfavour, and led to public protests and some loss in the circulation of his journal.

The *Lancet* was more soothing, if a little specious in its comment:

'Sir Wm. Wilde has to congratulate himself that he has passed through a trying ordeal supported by the sympathies of the entire mass of his professional brethren in this city; that he has been acquitted of a charge as disgraceful as it was unexpected, without even having to stoop to the painful necessity of contradicting it upon oath in the witness-box, by the expressed opinion of one of the ablest of our judges, by the verdict of a most intelligent special jury, by the unanimous opinion of his fellow citizens, and by, what I am sure he will not value least, that of every member of his own profession.'

The Medical Times and Gazette was much more convincing— 'Genius has its penalties as well as its privileges; and its necessarily

Arthur Jacob

more erratic and irregular walk must subject it to collisions unknown in the humdrum existence of commonplace mortals. Persons whose imagination is of great development, are, as is well known, liable to form friendships of a most enthusiastic and exaggerated cast; and if the parties be of opposite sex, it is perfectly possible that either of them may put too warm an interpretation on what really are outpourings of genius, through indiscreet and unconventional friendship. To any one who knows the hysteric temperament, there is not only no evidence for, but plenty of it against, the probability of the plaintiff's story.'

Jacob was stung by these remarks and forced to defend his views in another leader, this time perhaps a little apologetic in tone. He also published a letter in Wilde's defence from 'A Constant Reader and Lover of Fair Play', perhaps to show that he also could appreciate the latter quality. It was not a particularly notable composition, being merely a repetition of the principal arguments for the defence.

And so the wordy battle continued in the papers. *Old Times* dealt a shrewd blow in reply to the statement about 'the penalties of genius' in *The Medical Times and Gazette*. 'If "collisions" such as these are the necessary accompaniment of genius in a physician, I think most of your readers would prefer to remain the patients of the undistinguished crowd of "commonplace mortals".'

Another anonymous correspondent struck a note of disgusted disappointment:

'MY DEAR SIR,

When the prolific writer, Charles Lever, blown up with success, asked his former master, Dr. Cusack, 'Was there anything he could do for him?', what was the reply. 'Will you do one thing for me, Lever.' 'Oh, yes, I am so proud.' 'Well, let me alone.' 'Save me from my friends,' should be Sir W. Wilde's prayer. One suggests a demonstration of his brethren, as if we could sympathize with conduct which has at least been miserably indiscreet and lowering (in public estimation) to all his brethren, whether humble or exalted; another declares that Sir William Wilde has to congratulate himself on having 'passed through a trying ordeal', supported by the sympathies of his medical brethren in this city. Let a meeting be called and the opinion of the profession elicited before the promulgation of such an assertion that we could countenance even imputed immorality without requiring a full and searching investigation to disprove it, more especially when the accusation fell on one of whom we were so justly proud. Surely Sir Wm. Wilde should have been the first to demand that he should have been permitted *on oath* indignantly to deny, and leave the test to twelve of his fellow-citizens. Let every friend of Sir Wm. Wilde's drop the subject is the advice of

December 28, 1864.'   ONE OF HIS BRETHREN.

The *Lancet* correspondent came out as Wilde's principal protagonist, much to Jacob's annoyance. 'The Dublin Correspondent of the *Lancet* appears to have worn his veracious pen to the stump in a wordy defence of the version of this case, which he has ventured to put forward for the information of the profession in England, and we must confess he has so far out-generalled us to have taken us completely by surprise. Will it be believed when we announce that "Our Own Correspondent" has cooled down within one short fortnight from his hissing-hot rhodomontade about the "universal sympathies of the profession", "the unanimous acquittal", and all the rest of it, to a rather watery attack on *The Medical Press*, spiced here and there with italics and an occasional safe because unproveable innuendo. . . .

'"Our Own Correspondent" may credit himself personally with having chosen the pleasant paths of journalism—good cheer, generous wine, warm greetings, and perhaps even an occasional professional reciprocation, are easily earned by statements, from the responsibility of which, if they are a *leetle* incompatible with facts, the author is secured by the friendly wing of an editor; while misrepresentations, imputation of motives, and the pretentious parade peculiar to flunkeyism are the lot of him who is betrayed into an unpleasant truth. Yet would we rather have done the worst of which we have been accused than be suspected of deliberately penning the statements which "Our Own Correspondent" had the effrontery to lay before the profession as a truth.'

The medical journalists were now engaged in attacking each other instead of Wilde, and the matter soon wss dropped, but the Travers-Wilde trial has never been quite forgotten in Dublin.

CHAPTER XXVI   M O Y T U R A

'Now with the coming in of the spring the days will stretch a bit,
And after the feast of Brigid I shall hoist my flag and go,
For since the thought got into my head I can neither stand or sit
Until I find myself in the middle of the county of Mayo.
        James Stephens (from the Irish of Raftery).

'There are accidents in Life that are inevitable and must be sub-
mitted to, and Tattle by the help of Discretion will wear off.'
        Swift (in a letter to Vanessa).

I

MISS TRAVERS, in her spite, had dealt Wilde a terrible
blow; one from which he never really recovered.   At the time
of the trial he was not quite fifty, and still in the full power
and pride of intellect.   From that date forward he seems to have
degenerated.   His originality disappeared.   He lost interest in
his profession, became dirtier, uglier, more abrupt and intolerant
of others.   He was not the same physically upright, energetic
man he had been.   He appears to have burnt himself out, to
have shrunk, mentally and physically.   Temporary flashes of the
old fire only served to heighten the contrast.

His first escaping instinct was to seek temporary sanctuary in
Connemara.   He had always loved his native Connaught, and
now in his trouble he found his first comfort there, amongst the
simple peasants he knew so well.   In Dublin he was shunned
and stared at, but here the natural good manners of the people
helped to restore his self-esteem.   Rumours of his disgrace may
have reached them, but if they knew of it they gave no sign.
To them he was still *an docteur mor*, the great doctor who would
willingly cross bog and mountain to go to their aid, who could
restore the blessed light to their blinded eyes.

His mental refuge was deeper pre-occupation with the distant
past.   For the moment he had had enough of society.   Social

T

and professional success had proved to be Dead Sea fruit, and he turned with relief to the ancient manuscripts and prehistoric remains of Connemara.

Fortunately, he was in comfortable circumstances financially, and he was able to take things easily, and spend more time at his country home.

Moytura House stands upon an elevation a mile or so outside the village of Cong. Looking at it from the hill of Tonelegee opposite, its beautiful situation is apparent. In front are the waters of Corrib, in the background the Moycullen hills, rising gradually into the great peaks of the Western highlands. The steep slopes of Benlevi, the most southerly mountain of the Partry range, rise behind it. Towards the north may be seen the great quartzite dome of Nephin. Far off, above the deep blue range of Partry, rises the conical top of Croagh Patrick.

Looking westward one gets glimpses of Maamturk, and the Twelve Bens beyond, steeped in dark purple, and draped with gold-fringed clouds. On clear days Mweelrea, 'the bald King', can be seen from the upper lake, guarding the Killaries by the Atlantic. Connemara should be seen in spring or autumn, when the sunshine, playing on projecting crags of schist and gneiss, produces colours of surpassing beauty. Scotland and Wales may have more grandeur in their natural features, but the colour of their scenery is hot and sharp compared with the cool atmospheric brilliance of Connemara's blues and greens.

East of Moytura House the country is sharply different. Here are no longer the old metamorphic rocks which form the mountains and wild bogland of the highlands. Instead, there is the flat limestone plain which forms the centre of Ireland. The edge of this great plain fringes the eastern margin of the chain of great lakes which runs almost north and south—Corrib, Mask, Lough Carra, and Lough Conn. Seven or eight miles from Moytura the plain is relieved by a single elevation, the wooded hill of Knockma. It is of no great height, but it is a very remarkable hill none the less, for standing as it does in a very flat terrain, it commands most extensive views in all directions. The beautiful abbey of Knockmoy, the towers and city of Galway, 'the Ford of the Kings', Connemara and Achill, Slieve Bloom and the Clare Mountains, may all be seen on a fine day. But Knockma has other claims to fame. On its summit is a great cairn in which one of Ireland's earliest colonists, and a lady at that, is reported to be buried. She was Ceasair, who led her Fomorian tribe to Ireland from across the Spanish Main. Tradition has invested Knockma with a wealth of fairy legend: for here Finvarra, the Oberon of Irish sylvan mythology, holds his court. To add to the curiosity of the place, a modern has added a remarkable castellated 'antiquity' of his own design some distance to the west of Ceasair's tomb. It does not interfere in any way with the cairn, but Wilde thought that another tumulus lay beneath it. It is marked as 'Finvarra's Castle' on the Ordnance Survey map.

Cong itself is a very curious place, and so is the country surrounding it. The name itself—in Irish, *Cunga*, a neck, or narrow place—is derived from its situation on the isthmus which separates Lough Corrib from Lough Mask. In Wilde's time the village consisted of some ninety houses, with less than five hundred inhabitants, nearly every one of whom spoke Irish. It is a market town, and once possessed extensive mills. There is water everywhere—gliding rapidly past in the river, gushing from the surrounding rocks, bubbling up in great pools to supply the mills; oozing through stones; rising up in the interior of caverns; —in fact going everywhere except where it is wanted to go.

Lough Mask has no visible outlet, for the surplus water drains through to Lough Corrib by subterranean rivers and rocky, sunken channels, under the few miles of land which separate the two lakes. Near the village this water rises in considerable volume to form the river of Cong.

Shortly before Wilde built Moytura House, the Board of Works had carried out extensive drainage operations, as a result of which many miles of good pasture had been redeemed from

Lough Corrib. They had also made the Corrib navigable, and had made a ship-canal to connect it with the sea. Then they thought they would connect the Corrib with Lough Mask by another canal. They cut the canal, and in due course admitted the water. Unfortunately, they had not reckoned with the nature of the country. The bottom of the canal was as pervious as a colander, the water rushed in for a couple of hundred yards, and then sank straight into the earth. The canal is there to this day, dry as a bone.

The vagaries of the water in these parts are unlimited. On the eastern side of Corrib are two fine specimens of turloughs, which are lakes with a hole in their bottom through which the water can drain, so that they are often completely dry in summer.

Nymphsfield Stone Circle

In the winter they give excellent wild-fowling, in the summer they form grassy basins with a 'swallow-hole' set among a few rocks in the middle. Sometimes one may see a stream crossing the dry bed of the lake, rising in a spring and disappearing again in one of these swallow-holes.

When he came to Moytura Wilde retained possession of Illaunroe, no doubt for the fishing. It was, of course, the antiquities which had attracted him to Cong. From time immemorial down to early Christian times the great plain to the north-west was thickly populated. The early inhabitants have left remains which are amongst the most remarkable in the

British Isles. The Annals of Cong might begin with the battle
of Moytura, which the bards say was fought in the year of the
world 3303. Souterrains, or 'caves', abound all over the plain
of Moytura, from Knockma to Benlevi, in many cases surrounded by cahirs or forts. They take the form of roofed
trenches sunk in the ground, ten to twelve feet deep and twelve
to fourteen feet wide. They are from thirty to forty feet long,
and sometimes turn at an angle midway. The walls are formed
of stones, and are about two feet thick. The roof, which is about
two feet below the surface, is formed of large flags. At the
distant end the cave may open into a large oval chamber with
a small aperture in the roof.

The Moytura caves have a peculiarity in that they are divided
by a sort of D-trap into two compartments. This is apparently
a device for concealment. Wilde discovered a particularly good
example at Kildun, near the road leading to the village of Cross
from The Neale. He was exploring a cahir when he found an
aperture leading into a gradually widening chamber, twenty-two
feet long. At the far end of this chamber he found a horizontal
passage six feet long, and three feet square. At the end of this
a perpendicular shaft arose. Climbing up this, he was faced
with another, but shorter, horizontal passage. Scrambling
through he found himself in a large chamber, twenty-four feet
long by six wide and seven high, whose roof was formed of
immense flags which spanned the top. It must be an excellent
specimen of its type, but unfortunately it cannot now be
examined as the mouth has once more fallen in.

Caves such as this abound in every townland in the district.
Sometimes the primitive builders saved labour by adapting
natural caves to their purpose, as they did the cave to the west
of the hill of Carn, where a long artificial passage leads into a
large natural cave, with stalactites hanging from the roof.
Caves of every type are a feature of Cong, almost as much as
water. Sometimes the two are combined, as in the Pigeon
Hole, in the Ashford estate. Here one descends a steep flight
of steps fifty or sixty feet into the bowels of the earth, to find
in summer a dry river-bed of boulders, in winter perhaps a
rushing torrent. It is a weird place, dark, with the daylight
filtering weakly through ferns and ivy tendrils above one's head,
and the river disappearing into Stygian gloom on either side.
There are several other caves of this type in the locality—one of

them known in Wilde's time as 'the Horse Discovery', because
it was first found when a horse fell into it!

Cong is rich also in Christian art and antiquities. It does
not appear that St. Patrick himself ever visited Cong, although
his nephew, Lugnaedon, is said to be buried in a little graveyard
on the island of Inchangoill, in near-by Corrib, beside two of the
most interesting little churches in Ireland. If, like many others,
you doubt that Lugnaedon lies there, they will refute you by
showing you his headstone, carved with crosses and lettering
in Latin uncial characters. It does not matter that Wilde thought
that this was originally a corbel stone from one of the churches,
and that the inscription was still 'susceptible of further elucida-
tion'. He himself had no doubt that the mortal remains of St.
Lugnaedon lie below it, and to-day those who disagree with him
are wise if they keep their doubts to themselves, for otherwise
they will only succeed in making themselves unpopular.

Nobody should leave Inchangoill without examining the two
churches. One, the church of St. Patrick, is very early and
primitive, built in the Cyclopean style of masonry, with a narrow
square-headed doorway with inclined jambs. Near-by is the
Teampull na Neave, which Wilde first described to the archaeological world, and of which he presented a restored model to
the Kensington Museum. The western doorway of this church
is a splendid example of Hiberno-Romanesque, with its highly
decorated semicircular arch and clusters of pillars. The pilasters
are crowned by human-face capitals, from which springs the
arch, the middle portion of which is formed of deeply carved
horizontally projecting chevrons above which is a row of faces,
each different from the others. They may have been portraits,
and there are ten of them, not twelve, as might be expected.

If St. Patrick himself did not visit Cong, he had a worthy
disciple, St. Fechin of Fore, who came and blessed the place in
the seventh century. His traditions remain, but his churches are
gone, for they were burnt, along with several other ecclesiastical
establishments, in the year 1114. From the ashes arose a splendid
abbey and monastery for the Canons Regular of the Order of
St. Augustine, whose splendid possessions extended throughout
Connaught, and into the south and east of Ireland. They too
have gone from Cong. The bells have tolled their last peal, the
altar lights are extinguished, and Cong Abbey is a ruin, but they
have left behind them the grandest piece of metal work of its

age now extant in Europe—the famous processional Cross of Cong.

II

Wilde had sent Willie to Portora Royal School, Enniskillen, in 1863, and Oscar followed him there the following year, at the tender age of ten. Portora was, and is, an excellent school of the conservative type, and Wilde could not have chosen better for his sons. Nevertheless, there must have been a strong contrast between the home influence at Merrion Square and Moytura, and the atmosphere at Portora, where Speranza's outpourings of twenty years before would hardly be considered with favour. It is probable that Wilde was always at heart a supporter of the

British connection, in spite of his waverings at the time of the Young Ireland movement. Speranza herself was no longer so anxious to 'burn the Castle' or to 'starve the English Garrison', since she had received so many favours at their hands.

Both boys were doing well at school. Willie was perhaps quicker, more engaging and popular, but Oscar, although a clumsy, lumpy boy, and no athlete, commanded respect by his conversational powers. Both boys could tell a story well, and Oscar entertained the other lads by his faculty of making comic contortions with his limbs. He had his father's long arms; and, like him, he could twist his limbs into weird attitudes; imitations of saints in stained-glass windows, and so on. As he developed he became overgrown and awkward, and soon displayed a doubtless hereditary objection to the use of soap and water. His only exercise was rowing, in which he was not as proficient as he should have been, for at Moytura he had every opportunity of becoming a good waterman.

The three children spent most of their school holidays at Moytura, studying the ways of birds and beasts and wild flowers, wandering about the countryside free as larks, or accompanying their father on his excursions. They helped him with his excavations, and Willie, who had a moderate talent for drawing, made sketches of various of the antiquities for him. At other times, the boys pulled a boat across Lough Mask to visit another youth who, like Oscar, was destined to become a famous writer. This was George Moore, whose father, George Henry Moore, was a friend of Wilde's, and a frequent visitor both at Moytura and Merrion Square. Another lad whom they may have met in the west was young Edward Carson, whose path in life was to cross Oscar's so tragically. At this time, Carson was a frequent visitor to his mother's people in Galway, the Lamberts of Castle Ellen.

Wilde himself was very happy at Cong. He spent much time rummaging around the ruins of Cong Abbey, restoring where he could, and exhorting the villagers to care for their heritage. One relic which he did not replace in its proper position was the base of an old sandstone cross, beautifully decorated with Celtic scrolls, which stood in his garden at Moytura. It had been removed from the Abbey either by Mr. Fynne, the previous owner of Moytura, or by Father Prendergast. Wilde promised that he would return it when the shaft of the market cross, then in the Abbey, was replaced in the base which still stood in its original position. The shaft has been replaced, but there is now no trace of the sandstone cross, either in the Abbey or at Moytura.

III

An ancient cahir stood on an elevation a little to the north of Wilde's new house. In the centre was a tower, surmounted by a flag-staff. On top of this tower he sat on many summer evenings, surveying the site of the ancient battlefield, and studying the accounts of the conflict given by the annalists. His principal source of information was a manuscript transcribed by Cormac O'Cuirnin in the fifteenth century. With O'Donovan's translation in his hand, he sat there many times until the evening light was gone, and the sun had long sunk into the sea over the western hills. In his absorption he lost himself in time, until Fir Bolg and de Danaan ranged Moytura's plain before him, and raised great monuments of stone in memory of their dead. Spears were shivered and green-edged swords of bronze were dyed with blood, while bards sang the exploits of the warriors.

By day he returned to the planes of reality. He wandered far afield over meadow and bog, using his expert knowledge to identify the places mentioned in O'Cuirnin's text, digging, preserving, and recording.

The battle of Moytura was not, perhaps, such a very terrible affair when judged by modern standards. It began by a trial of skill between champions, which is still a common practice amongst savage warring tribes. In this case twenty-seven warriors from each side engaged in a hurling-match. It must have been even more energetic than most modern hurley matches, for all the de Danaan team were killed. The game took place in a smooth valley near a hazel-wood, where now a haunted castle stands, a castle which is often seen afire on summer nights, when the fairies hold revel after their hurling game. The twenty-seven de Danaan youths were buried in a cairn which Wilde identified—the *Carn-an-Cluithe*, or 'monument of the game.'

Another tumulus which Wilde identified was the *Carn-in-enfhir*, 'the cairn of the one man.' According to Wilde, it covered the remains of the Fir Bolg youth who single-handed slew three de Danaans who had taken a most unfair advantage of King Eochy, whom they cornered when he had gone down a deep well to perform his morning ablutions. Unfortunately, the Fir Bolg youth was mortally wounded when rescuing his king. Wilde identified the well as that which is locally known as the *Mean Uisge*, which has on its immediate south-east a cairn surrounded by a circle of standing stones.

With O'Cuirnin's manuscript in his hand Wilde directed the excavation of this cairn, promising the workmen that they would find the remains of the Fir Bolg hero. They soon came down to the cist, in which, after removing the cover-stone, they found a beautiful urn which contained his incinerated remains. The urn is a very good specimen of about five and a half inches high, and six inches wide in the mouth, tapering gracefully to the bottom, which is only two inches in diameter. It is now in the Collection of the Royal Irish Academy.

King Eochy and his men fought valiantly, but the magic of the de Danaans was too much for them. The King made his last stand on the shores of Lough Mask, and there he died fighting. His cairn is to be seen to-day on the great grassy hill of Killower, a mile from the lake. Like most of these monuments, it forms a conspicuous landmark. It is the most extensive and remarkable cairn in the West of Ireland, and we cannot contradict Wilde's statement that it was erected in memory of Eochy Mac Erc, the last of the Fir Bolg Kings of Erin.

This was the end of the battle. The dispirited Fir Bolgs withdrew to their camp on Corrib's shore, the de Danaans to their mountain fortress. Both sides took stock and burned their dead. The Fir Bolgs held council, and finally challenged the enemy to single conflict, man to man. This was refused, and finally a peace was concluded, by which the Fir Bolgs retained only the province of Connaught. Some of their hardier warriors fled to the islands of Aran, where they erected Dun Ængus, Dun Conor, and other magnificent fortifications.

IV

It was time for Wilde to return to Dublin, to the cares of practice and the stares of the people. Before doing so he prepared an account of the battle, in which he correlated the results of his excavations with the incidents described in the manuscript. The result was a most interesting paper which he presented to the Royal Irish Academy in 1866, some time after his return to town.

Another important work came from Wilde's pen this year, on the subject of some Scandinavian antiquities which had been found on an ancient Danish battle-field at Islandbridge, near Dublin. He also was still working on the fourth part of his Catalogue. 'Trinity College has long fought shy of depositing its Irish antiquities with us, chiefly because most of our officials were on the board of Trinity College or expected to be there,' he wrote to Gilbert. 'Now, however, I think it is high time to make a stir in the matter, and, at all events, give them the option of refusal. . . .

'I am off by the mail train, and heartily wish you could be with me, as I expect to take a survey of the plain of Moytura Conga, from the Firbolg monument on the top of Knockma, at 12 o'clock to-morrow morning.' Obviously, he had not altogether lost his relish of life, in spite of his troubles.

Unfortunately, his health broke down in the autumn of 1866. As soon as he was fit to travel he went down to Moytura to recuperate. 'Many thanks for your letter,' he wrote, once more to Gilbert, 'I am better, and able to oversee workmen and take short antiquarian journeys, but nothing more. Either the sword hilt is a lie, or a loss' (refering to his work on the Catalogue). 'Which is it? How I wish you could come down to us for even a day. Did you hear that part of New Grange has fallen in?'

In 1866 George Petrie died. Wilde felt his loss severely. From their first disagreement over the excavations at Lagore a quarter of a century previously, down to the controversy over the Catalogue, they had quarrelled many times, but with Petrie Wilde's malice was always short-lived. He recognized the qualities of his diverse genius, and had always gone out of his way to give the older man full credit for his achievements, for Wilde, when he saw fit, could give lavish praise as well as crushing condemnation. He mentioned Petrie many times in his writings, and never once spoke ill of him.

A few months later, in the spring of 1867, he lost his beloved little daughter, Isola. She died at the Glebe, Edgeworthstown, where Wilde's brother-in-law, the Rev. Mr. Noble, was then the rector. Isola was then in her tenth year. Her loss was felt keenly by Oscar, who was then, according to the doctor in attendance, a gentle, retiring, dreamy boy 'whose lonely and inconsolable grief found its outward expression in long and frequent visits to his sister's grave in the village cemetery'. His father also was inconsolable at the loss of this gay and happy child—'embodied sunshine' he called her—but Speranza was calm. She thought it was, perhaps, all for the best, and she may have been right.

CHAPTER XXVII

LOUGH CORRIB

I

THE BRITISH MEDICAL ASSOCIATION met in Dublin in August, 1867, when Joseph Lister read a paper 'On the Antiseptic Principle in the Practice of Surgery'. If Wilde was amongst those who listened, languishing in the summer heat, he certainly does not appear to have appreciated its tremendous importance. Instead, he was probably thinking dreamily of the excursion of the Association's members which he was about to conduct around the antiquities of the Boyne Valley; and calling up memories of past days, of the original immediate success of the *Beauties of the Boyne*, and of how he had brought the great Macaulay to the scenes he was now about to re-visit.

He seems to have lost all interest in medicine after the trial. His *Aural Surgery* was still a standard textbook, not only in the United Kingdom, but also on the Continent and in America. A new edition was urgently called for, but none appeared. In the three years which had elapsed since the débâcle he had regained much of his practice, but he himself had done little enough to get it back. He wrote nothing, he snubbed his colleagues, and he was rough with his patients. At St. Mark's he contented himself by superintending the work which was now carried on principally by Wilson. One day a little boy who had some eye trouble was brought to see him by his mother. Wishing to put some lotion in his eye, he looked around for an eye dropper. Finding none, he seized a pen from his desk, dipped it in the lotion and flicked some drops of the liquid into the eye. Unfortunately, he cut the eye badly in doing so, and the patient, who is now an old gentleman, still bears the scar he gave him.

In spite of all this, his name as an oculist remained a legend for many a long day. For years 'Wilde's Eye Ointment' was sold by Dublin chemists as a panacea for all eye ailments. It was probably harmless enough, but for the public the label was as good as the contents.

In politics, too, he had lost interest. Isaac Butt, the quondam Unionist, was now busy defending the Fenians after their abortive armed rising in '67, and was shortly to go to Westminster at the head of the first Home Rule party. The politics of the time were interesting enough, but Wilde no longer took any part in public affairs. The truth was, that although always a keen advocate of social reform, he was at heart a lukewarm politician, as every medical man should be. There had, of course, been a short period when Speranza had wooed him from the broad path of tolerance, but this phase had passed twenty years before. His political allegiance was described quaintly, but in all seriousness, in a contemporary journal, which stated that he was 'a Liberal-Unionist, with Nationalist proclivities'.

What was the cause of this decline? It was not altogether the trial and its attendant disgrace, for he had many sympathizers and supporters for whom his genius enamelled and excused the rougher facets of his character. Like Oscar, he had a magnetic charm of personality, which could make people forget his faults. Unlike Oscar, his vices were natural, and therefore more readily forgiven. His friends realized that he had been really and truly most unfortunate to have run foul of a half-cracked monomaniac like Moll Travers.

It has been suggested in some of Oscar's biographies that his father was addicted to alcohol. We might think, therefore, that at this stage of his career he gave way to drink, and in this way explain his decline, but of this view there is no confirmation whatever. His photograph does not look in the least like that of a toper. He still, it is true, enjoyed his dining-clubs and dinner-parties. Speranza, more theatrical than ever, held increasingly numerous *salons* for the intelligentsia and celebrities, and there were many Bohemian suppers at Merrion Square which ended in the small hours of the morning. These were, to be sure, by no means teetotal parties, but there is no reason to think that Wilde ever drank to excess. He was no stranger to the mellowing effect of alcohol, and nobody appreciated good wine better, but he was by no means intemperate.

It is more likely that the slowing of his *tempo* was due to physical causes. He had worked hard and played hard all his life, had never spared himself, and now he was paying the price.

To use a mechanical metaphor, his engine had proved too big for his body, and was now beginning to shake it to pieces. Those who believe in 'glands' will say that his personality resulted from over-activity of the pituitary and adrenal glands, and in this way explain his great energy and early maturity, his sexual activity and his short life. This view may be correct, for these are two of the most important of the ductless glands which the moderns say control our mental and physical development and behaviour. The subject is one which is still very much *sub judice*, but it is none the less fascinating. It is impossible to resist considering it in more detail, but Speranza and Oscar are equally interesting characters, and we shall therefore postpone doing so until later. In the present instance, it is more fitting

that it should be a post-mortem examination, and we shall make it so.

II

The waning of Wilde's powers was probably not noticed at first, even by his friends. Shortly after the British Medical Association's meeting of 1867, he published his most popular work, *Lough Corrib*. It is a delightful book, and now, with the *Boyne and Blackwater* the most sought after of his writings; and the only one which has run to a third edition. In the preface he tells us that he wrote it 'as a pleasing occupation during leisure hours.' It is easy to believe this, for it is written in an easy effortless style. It is so easy indeed, that, as Lynn Doyle points out, he begins all unconsciously in verse

'WESTWARD HO! Let us rise with the sun,
and be off to the land of the West.'

Nevertheless, it does not alter our opinion that the creative phase of his life had passed, for Wilde could produce material like this from the rich storehouse of his memory without the least difficulty.

In saying this, it is not intended to disparage the book in any way. It is one of the best books which have ever been

written on Irish topography. Wilde makes full use of his capacity for appetizing antiquities to the layman—no small feat, for nothing is duller to the uninitiated than archæology. He had a talent born of enthusiasm, which enabled him to teach without boring.

The plan he followed in the *Lough Corrib* was somewhat similar to that of the *Boyne*. He gave his readers an itinerary to follow, by rail, long car, and steamer, (for there was a regular service of steamers on the Corrib in those days) and as they went he described the natural features and sights of the neighbourhood, with a great deal of local history and archaeology thrown in. He wrote for English as well as Irish readers, and it is perhaps surprising to find that in those days one could travel by rail and boat from London to Galway in a very short time. It was possible to 'leave London by the night mail, and at a very trifling expense, and with little wear and tear, reach Galway at 1.45 p.m. the next day.' It is even more surprising to learn that the cost of the whole round trip to London and back, first class, including long cars and steamers on the lake, was about six pounds.

Corrib and its shores and islands are a panorama of ever-changing beauty, of which Wilde proved an adequate painter. Whether one finds sunshine and glorious colour, or dark cloud-armies sweeping over sodden bogland and grey rocks, there is always pleasure for the wanderer in Connemara. With Wilde's book in his pocket his appreciation is multiplied. He will find many changes since Wilde's day—some old castles now ruined, some ancient monuments restored. He will be surprised by the accuracy of Wilde's descriptions and stimulated by his keenness. 'The man who takes you by the hand in this book is an enthusiast,' says Lynn Doyle. 'He pulls you along; his eyes are bright; and he is talking vehemently as he goes.'

The *Lough Corrib* was very well received, and did much to restore its author in the public's confidence. A second edition was published in 1872, and a third, in which Wilde's prefaces are omitted, as recently as 1936.

The last edition is not an exact reprint, for the editor takes legitimate exception to the place-names used by Wilde, the spelling of which he says in many cases agrees neither with the Ordnance Map, nor with the suggested Gaelic version. There is truth in this criticism, for Wilde was not a great Irish scholar. He could speak the language fluently, but was inclined to spell it as he felt disposed. The editor has endeavoured to reform this by giving an intelligent Irish rendering of each name, with variants in an index. 'God grant," he says, 'that I have not made confusion worse confounded.' The change in terminology will undoubtedly make the book more interesting for the younger generation of Irishmen and women who are more familiar with their native language than their fathers were, but for them it would have been still more interesting had the whole book been translated into Irish. For those of us who have not had their education, and for visitors from abroad, the new version has its difficulties. 'Galway to Annaghdown' becomes 'Gaillimh to Eanach Duin', for instance—and these are difficult spellings to reconcile when reading a map, especially as the Ordnance Maps are not yet printed in Irish. The difficulty becomes more pronounced when we find the old and the new spellings used indifferently in the text—as, for instance, Knockma and Cnoc Meadha, Moytura and Magh Tuire. One must not be too critical in a matter such as this, for intelligent reform in the spellings of Irish place names is needed, but is it fitting that this particular book should be chosen to make 'one protest for one district'? Surely the trouble should first be attacked at its source in the maps themselves?

Several of the drawings which illustrate all three editions have an added interest for us, for they were made by Willie Wilde. It was the chance discovery of some twenty of the original woodblocks which prompted the recent third edition. The editor, before taking the course finally adopted, considered first an exact reprint of the original, and secondly a revised and modernized edition, corrected 'according to the modern view of history and archaeology'. He wisely decided against the latter course, realizing that by doing so he would lose much of the Mid-Victorian flavour of the original. We suggest that should he contemplate a fourth edition, he should give us an exact reprint, with a postscript to each chapter, in which time's changes in theory and structure are described, and the correct place-names given.

Ross-Errily

CHAPTER XXVIII

DECLINE

I

IN THE early '70's a sad ceremony was enacted near what is now the border between the North and South of Ireland. The place was a tiny country churchyard; the occasion the funeral of two young girls, who were both natural daughters of Sir William Wilde.

Their story is a tragic one. They had been brought up by their uncle, the Rev. Ralph Wilde, a man who was as spruce and tidy in his habits as 'unwashed Willie' was dirty. At the time of their death they were twenty-one and twenty-two years of age, respectively. They were very popular in the district, and went to many parties in the neighbourhood, where their charm captivated both old and young. They were talented as well as charming, and numbered amongst their gifts the capacity for writing verse. They wrote an epitaph for Ireland's famous and beloved greyhound, Master McGrath, which begins:

> 'Master McGrath has passed away,
> He breathed his last on Christmas Day.'

Perhaps not very good poetry, but we need not be too critical.

Among the Christmas festivities of this particular winter was a dance given by the local bank-manager. It was a gay affair in a country mansion, and it is said that drink flowed freely. The party went merrily on until the small hours. When the guests were beginning to go home, and the ballroom began to empty, the host asked one of the girls for a dance. As they whirled past the open fireplace her crinoline swung out and took fire. It was ablaze in an instant; her terrified sister rushed to help her; and soon her dress also was alight. Their host took off his coat and wrapped it round his partner, whom he carried outside and rolled in the snow which lay upon the ground. Her sister, panic-stricken, rushed around in screaming terror until she collapsed, exhausted.

'They were lovely and pleasant in their lives, and in their death they were not divided.' Their father, a lonely, bent figure, saw them laid to rest in the bleak graveyard where they still lie, and where it is hoped this narrative will not be the means of disturbing their repose. He visited them occasionally in the few years that remained to him. For many more years another mourner came, they say from Scotland. Then her visits also ceased.

II

The photograph of Wilde taken about this time showed a depressing change from what had been. He looks old and

emaciated, curmudgeonly and dispirited, with none of the old-time fire. His hair is still long and luxuriant, although grey, and his features do not seem unduly lined. The noble forehead and eyes are still apparent, the betraying mouth is now more deeply concealed. But his whole attitude is brooding and dejected, unlike the Wilde we know. It is that of a man who has tasted the forbidden fruit, and found it bitter.

This, unfortunately, is the only portrait of Wilde which is at all well known. It is reproduced in most of the biographies of Oscar, and it fits in only too well with the William Wilde of tradition, the Minotaur to whom maidens were sacrificed, the cantankerous old crust at whom the children jeered when they saw him coming, his white locks flowing in the breeze. It is a pity that this portrait exists, for it has confirmed posterity in its bad opinion of him. After all, Wilde had only two faults: his bad temper and his mistresses. In extenuation of these we may plead his many good points and remember that he lived in an immoral age; for all the Victorians were not good by any means.

He lived another five years, and on this period he has been judged by the majority. So far only archaeologists have recognized the value of his work, if we except a few medical men. In medicine we kick aside the steps by which we rise as soon as we have ascended them, but the foundations of archaeology are more important, and there are very few modern works on Irish archaeology which do not acknowledge their indebtedness to Wilde's observations. To the general public, however, he is still an old eccentric oddity about whom many stories are told.

Many of these are puns on his name. One concerns a journey to London, in the company of Stokes. They wished to keep the carriage to themselves. At Holyhead some strangers tried to enter, but Stokes took them aside:—'Do you see that man in there? He's *Wilde*!" The startled strangers, thinking he was mad and Stokes his attendant, took themselves off.

This is not a very good one. Another, almost equally feeble, concerns the meeting of the British Association at Belfast in 1874, when Wilde was President of the Anthropological Section, in circumstances for him sadly changed since the Dublin meeting of 1859. On this occasion, his Presidential address over, he entered another section meeting and sat down beside a somnolent fellow-member. He made some remark as he sat down, to which the other made no reply. 'Don't you know me?' he said fiercely. 'I'm Wilde.' 'By God, you look it!" said his neighbour in alarm.

An old apple-woman called on him while he was at his dinner. Wilde came down to see her. 'Sir William, I can't see a stim, but they tould me you could give me back me eyesight.'

'Damn it, woman,' said Wilde, as he bared her pupil. 'What age are ye?"

'Sir William, I won't tell ye a lie. Come next Michaelmas I'll be ninety-foive.'

'Good God, woman! Go down on your marrow bones and

thank the Lord you're alive at all.   Who wants to see anything
at ninety-five?'

Which, paradoxically, goes to show that if Wilde had lost
interest in ophthalmology, he was still kind to the poor.

III

It was unfortunate that Wilde's energies were waning, for a
new school of eye surgeons was arising in Dublin, led by
the brilliant and lovable Charlie Fitzgerald.   It was a rival
school, which owed its success partly to the fact that, after
his trial, Wilde was never wholly reinstated in favour by
the more respectable section of Irish society.   This school had
its headquarters in the National Eye and Ear Infirmary, which
was now in Molesworth Street.   In consequence, St. Mark's no
longer held a monopoly of the work, and badly required Wilde's
assistance.   This was not forthcoming, and Wilson and his
assistant, Rainsford, had to do most of the work.

Henry Wilson was becoming more like his father in appearance
with every year that passed.   His resemblance to Oscar and
Willie is even more striking, and suggests that Speranza's share
in her two sons' heredity is not as great as has been supposed.   I f
not brilliant, Wilson was a sound oculist, whose book on the
ophthalmoscope was the first written in the English language.
He was devoted to his father, who dominated his every thought.
He might perhaps have done better when the older man's shadow
was removed, but, unfortunately, he only survived him by
a year.

Neither Wilson nor Fitzgerald and his followers were greatly
interested in the ear, as Wilde had been.   Perhaps the discovery
of cocaine, which revolutionized ophthalmology in 1884, turned
their attention away from it.   Whatever the cause, aural surgery
declined for many a day, and it is still perhaps the Cinderella
of the recognized specialties in Dublin.   It was not until otology
divorced ophthalmology and found a new spouse in diseases
of the nose and throat that she began to recover, only to find
her new partner unacceptable at her old home; for St. Mark's
in the meanwhile had amalgamated with the National Eye and
Ear Infirmary to form the Royal Victoria Eye and Ear Hospital,
to which for some time throat and nose patients were not
admitted.

The new hospital has never had quite the success which attended St. Mark's in Wilde's palmy days, when American post-graduates before coming to Europe were told not to miss Wilde in Dublin, and Bowman and Nettleship in London. This is an argument in favour of one-man control, for although nobody can deny the brilliance of the Eye and Ear Hospital staff, the Rotunda is now the Mecca of the majority of post-graduates who come to Dublin.

IV

Although he produced no more medical writings, Wilde still worked away at archaeology. The fourth part of the *Catalogue* was now completed, together with an index of all four parts. The final part was an extensive treatise on the silver, iron and ecclesiastical remains in the Academy. Unfortunately for us, it was never printed, and is now lost. Why it suffered this fate we do not know, but the fact that it remained unpublished was a bitter disappointment to Wilde. In the Academy House itself the growing library encroached more and more upon the space allotted to the museum, which after his death was transferred to the National Museum. He started three other manuscripts which he never finished. The principal was *A History of Irish Medicine*. Another was *Irish Fairy Lore*, for which he collected a vast quantity of information from all parts of the country, fairy tales and strange wild stories of banshees and leprechauns. Neither of these was ever completed, although it is probable that Speranza's two books on Irish folk-lore are mainly drawn from the material provided by the latter.

The third was the *Memoir of Gabriel Beranger*, which was published in several parts in the Journal of the Royal Archaeolo-gial Association of Ireland, between 1871 and 1873. The Census return for 1871, which fully taxed Wilde's waning powers, then intervened. Speranza wrote the final part of the *Memoir* for the same journal in the autumn of 1876, and the whole was published as a single volume in 1880.

As a contribution to the history of Irish Art the *Memoir* has a special interest, for no other biography on Beranger is in existence. He was born in Rotterdam in 1729 of mixed Dutch and French parentage, and came to Dublin in 1750. An artist by profession, he kept a print shop in South Great George's

Street. The occupation of a minor artist in those days seems to have been as precarious as it still is, and he was soon glad to exchange it for that of a clerk. Through the patronage of the celebrated General Vallancy and of Colonel Burton Conyngham he became Assistant Ledger Keeper in the Exchequer Office, and he later inherited a considerable fortune which his brother-in-law, Colonel Mestayer, had amassed in India in 'the good old times'.

While at the Exchequer Office General Vallancy, a noted but fanciful antiquarian, encouraged him to use his artistic talent in sketching the ruins and relics of the countryside. He made many expeditions to do so, filling many note-books with sketches and notes of his tours.

Wilde became interested in Beranger about 1860, and from that date onward became an ardent collector of his works.

He eventually obtained a large bound manuscript volume, beautifully written in a clear hand, containing records of Beranger's journeys from 1773 to 1781. He also found two large volumes of water-colour sketches, and three smaller ones. Recently another large volume has been discovered which is now in the National Library in Dublin. These sketches are of considerable value now, as they show the architectural features of Ireland nearly two hundred years ago. Since then, many of the finest castles and abbeys have completely disappeared through vandalism and neglect. The round tower of St. Michael Le Pole in Ship Street, Dublin, and the tower of Trinity Church, Glendalough, for instance, had completely disappeared by Wilde's time. Trinity Church itself became completely ruined after Wilde described it in the *Memoir*, but it has been possible to restore it completely from the original stones, putting each stone into its original place, from the drawing Wilde had made of it— an excellent example of the value of permanent records in archaeology.

Beranger's art was not of a high order, and does not approach that of Petrie, with whom he has been compared. His works are mostly in outline and coloured wash, an excellent medium indeed, and according to our eyes much preferable to the over-worked full-tone Victorian water-colours, but one which requires good draughtsmanship. Unfortunately, Beranger's line is dull and his colour harsh. He drew faithfully, and his buildings are conscientiously to scale, but his landscape work is poor, his trees badly conventionalized, his fields a flat wash of green. He had Petrie's trick of introducing a small note of red, usually himself in his scarlet frock-coat, but sometimes a Western peasant woman in the red skirt which seems to have disappeared almost completely in the last ten years. Occasionally, other dramatic accessories are introduced—ladies in trailing gowns and large feather hats, or sometimes dogs and horses. Most of his animal drawing is poor, but one beast he drew to the life—the good old Irish pig—lengthy, leggy, hog-backed, long-necked, four-eared, with a bushy-ended tail with a twist-and-a-half in it, and a knowing, half-shut eye—an animal whom its more respectable descendants would not care to recogize.

Beranger must have cut a curious figure on his excursions. He was of middle size, spare, with clear quick brown eyes, a well-cut, playful, humorous mouth, his hair well powdered and gathered in a queue. When out sketching he wore his red coat, yellow breeches, and top-boots, a three-cocked hat, and carried in his hand a tall staff and a measuring tape. He was a keen observer of nature, men and manners, and liked a bit of fun when it came his way. His chief companion was an Italian, Signor Bigari, whose work may be seen in the decorative panels of the Lord Mayor's ceremonial state-coach, and in some of the illustrations to Grose's *Antiquities*. Bigari was the better artist and could dance the minuet very nicely, but he was apparently no horseman, to judge by Beranger's comments!

These two made many pleasant journeys through the country,

and to Beranger's journal we are indebted for many happy glimpses of Irish life in the eighteenth century. To Beranger's rosy mind everything was bright, gay and luxurious. Everywhere noblemen and gentlemen received them with great kindness. Distinguished guests were asked to meet them, and no wonder, for they were something the like of which the squires had never seen before. Sometimes it seems, their hosts had the gout, but even then they fed them and put horses, carriages, and boats at their disposal, or put them up while they 'inked their drawings'. Lord Altamont had a cromlech opened for them, at Florence Court they were entertained by Lord Enniskillen, in Roscommon by the Frenches and O'Connors, in Sligo by the Irwins and Ormsbys, and at the Neale by Sir John Browne, and elsewhere by many others.

They worked hard at their records, but it was not all work: 'Saw distinctly the mountain of Croagh Patrick, in the county of Mayo, distance sixty miles. Went in every house, but could not converse with the females, as they only speak Irish: remembered the Irish phrase I formerly learned of "Torum poque Calinogue", which I repeated to every girl, who immediately came to kiss me! How unfortunate it was I could ask no more!'

They visited the great caves at Rathcrogan, a place of great antiquity which Wilde had visited many times in his youth, to see the black cattle driven into the great Fort on May morning to be bled for the benefit of their health, while crowds of country people sat round turf-fires and cooked the blood mixed with oatmeal and onions. Rathcrogan is a ruined city of raths, tumuli, caves and pillar stones, the capital of Queen Maeve. It was the scene of the Tain-Bo-Cuailgne, the great cattle raid into Louth, and the exploits of its Connaught Heroine are celebrated in Irish romance and legend. Here, in his declining years, Wilde often came with Oscar and Willie to re-enact in imagination the scenes of bygone years, when many a king was crowned there, his face to the north, his feet on the sacred stone, as amidst the shouts of thousands he was handed the white wand of sovereignty. Here stands the 'long stone of the Carn', of which Willie made a drawing, and which Wilde identified as the *Lia Fail*, the stone of destiny. It, therefore, disputes this title with the pillar stone at Tara, and the stone at Westminster. Wilde had evidently changed his views since he wrote the *Boyne and Blackwater*, when he suggested that the cross of St. Adamnan might be the real *Lia Fail*.

Wilde's comments are interesting enough, but it might have been better had he published Beranger's journals completely and consecutively, instead of giving extracts with comments. He did intend to publish the drawings later. Perhaps it is left for some future publisher to give us the manuscript and drawings as a whole.

I

IN THE autumn of 1871 Oscar left Portora to enter Trinity. Towards the end of his school career he had distinguished himself, particularly in classics, in which he had won the Gold Medal, and he had gained an exhibition into Trinity. The honours he had won at school were, as was customary, inscribed in gold letters on a board. Many years later, after his disgrace, his name was removed, leaving a blank space for the boys to comment upon, but already, as is well known, a mysterious but ominous crack had appeared across his name. What is not so well known is that some years ago the name was replaced, so that it now

> 'Like bright metal on a sullen ground
> Shows more goodly, and attracts more eyes
> Than that which hath no foil to set it off.'

One could easily moralize upon this board, whose changes bear such an exact relationship to Oscar's reputation. Had he lived fifty years later, would he have been punished so severely? Or would he, in his arrogance, still have drawn his fate upon himself?

On entering Trinity he was only sixteen years of age, still overgrown and awkward. He developed rapidly, and soon became known as a brilliant classical scholar. Shortly after entering he gained a junior exhibition and a month later became a Queen's Scholar. His year in classics was particularly brilliant, and although Oscar did well, he was by no means at the top of his class after the first year. Edward Carson was an exact contemporary, and also gained a junior exhibition in Michaelmas 1871. Although contemporaries, it does not appear that they were ever friends; indeed, their characters were so different that it is hard to understand how they could be. Oscar was already a *poseur*, like his mother, and had a magnetic charm, an infectious gaiety, which could transform his heavy, putty-coloured features. He and Willie, who had preceded him to Trinity, mixed freely with Dublin society, or rather that part of it which was still open to the Wildes. George Bernard Shaw was then a boy in Dublin, and, although he and the Wildes had no social relations in those days, he surmises that his sister, a young and attractive girl who sang beautifully, made an innocent conquest of Willie and Oscar. When the boys got tired of College life they could bring their friends to Merrion Square, where their parents kept more or less open house. 'Come home with me,' Oscar said to a friend; 'my mother and I have formed a society for the suppression of virtue.' Curiously enough, he seldom admitted his friends to his rooms in Botany Bay, which were kept in the state of squalor one might expect. When he did so, the story goes that an unfinished landscape in oils was always prominently exhibited on an easel. He claimed this as his own work, saying with reference to Whistler's famous signature, that he 'had just put in the butterfly'. So that Oscar at this stage apparently had artistic aspirations. He had some slight executive gift in that direction, and had he lived fifty years later, he might have found a niche as a 'modernist'.

Carson, in contrast to Oscar, was still developing, awkward and retiring, a slow, plodding student who lagged behind, both in class and in public. He took honours and worked for scholarship, but failed by a mark and a half. Wilde was successful in his second year, although placed only fifth. They were indeed very diverse characters, these two men, whose lives, at first parallel, were to diverge, only to cross again later with such sinister and dramatic force. Perhaps the only place where Carson showed signs of his coming greatness was in the College Historical Society, the forcing ground of Wolfe Tone and Thomas Davis. He was a constant speaker in debate, and he held high office in the Society. Both Oscar and Willie Wilde preferred the University Philosophical Society, in which Willie was fairly prominent, but where Oscar never shone. On one occasion, at the Philosophical Society, Sir William presided as guest chairman; the debate was on the subject of social evils, and Willie made an impassioned speech in defence of prostitutes. The impression that this was a subject on which both father and son were well qualified to speak was left on the mind of at least one listener.

Trinity College enjoys the distinction of being an ancient University set in the midst of a capital city. As a consequence, its fellows and professors are men of the world; they hold an assured position and mix with all sections of society, and do not become cloistered in the academic life, as in the sister universities. 'Perhaps,' says Marjoribanks, 'this is why Trinity throws such a rare distinction around its alumni'. An up-and-coming young undergraduate with a good conceit of himself, such as Oscar was, is readily admitted to their society, doubtless with good results for both parties.

Amongst the Junior Fellows in Wilde's time was John Pentland Mahaffy, later Provost and now a legend. He dominated the social life of Dublin almost as much as the new gasometer does its streets. Tyrrell was another Fellow. Of him Oscar said later—'I got my love of the Greek ideal and my intimate knowledge of the language at Trinity from Mahaffy and Tyrrell; they were Trinity to me; Mahaffy was especially valuable to me at that time. Though not so good a scholar as Tyrrell, he had been in Greece, had lived there and saturated himself with Greek thought and Greek feeling. Besides, he took deliberately the artistic standpoint towards everything, which was coming more and more to be my standpoint. He was a delightful talker, too, a really good talker in a certain way—an artist in vivid words and eloquent pauses. Tyrrell, too, was very kind to me—intensely sympathetic and crammed with knowledge. If he had known less he would have been a poet.'

And yet it was Tyrrell who wrote: 'Sir William Wilde was a pithecoid person of extraordinary sensuality and cowardice (funking the witness-box left him without a defender!) and his wife was a highfalutin' pretentious creature whose pride was as extravagant as her reputation founded on second-rate verse-making.'

Sir William watched the progress of his two sons with great pride. 'We are asking a few old friends upon Moytura cheer on Thursday, and also to cheer dear old Oscar on having obtained the Berkeley Gold Medal last week with great honour. You were always a great favourite of his, and he hopes you will come.' This was in 1874. Oscar had won the medal in an examination on the Greek comic poets. It had been founded by Bishop Berkeley, a remarkable prelate of the Irish Church. Oscar prized the medal, and preserved it to the end, for after his death Robert Ross found a pawn-ticket for it amongst his belongings.

Wilde saw a great future for his boys. Willie was soon called to the Bar, but before leaving Trinity he also had received a medal, in his case from the University Philosophical Society.

A third medal, and one with which we are more concerned, had been awarded to Wilde himself the year before. This was the Cunningham Gold Medal, the highest award the Royal Irish Academy could bestow. It came as a belated recognition of Wilde's work in connection with the Catalogue. It was presented on St. Patrick's Day, 1873, by the Rev. Professor Jellett, President of the Academy. Dr. Jellett said many complimentary things, and Wilde appreciated the honour done him. It was indeed a notable distinction, for the Academy was chary of awarding the Cunningham Medal, whose previous recipients included Petrie. A greater honour would have been to make him President, but this was not to be.

II

The Wildes still went into society and entertained a great deal. George Bernard Shaw writes: 'I was a boy at a concert in the Antient Concert Rooms in Brunswick Street in Dublin. Everybody was in evening dress; and—unless I am mixing up this concert with another (in which case I doubt if the Wildes would have been present)—the Lord Lieutenant was there with his blue-waistcoated courtiers. Wilde was dressed in snuffy brown; and as he had the sort of skin that never looks clean, he produced a dramatic effect beside Lady Wilde (in full fig) of being, like Frederick the Great, beyond soap and water, as his Nietzschean son was beyond good and evil. He was currently reported to have a family in every farmhouse; and the wonder was that Lady Wilde didn't mind—evidently a tradition from the Travers case, which I did not know about until I read your account, as I was only eight in 1864.'

This was the only occasion on which Shaw saw Sir William Wilde, who was pointed out to him as the man who had operated on his father for squint. 'He overdid the correction so much that my father squinted the other way all the rest of his life. To this day I never notice a squint; it is as normal to me as a nose or a tall hat.' Harry Furniss says: 'Lady Wilde, had she been cleaned up and plainly and rationally dressed, would have made a remarkably fine model of the *grande dame*, but with all her paint and tinsel and tawdry tragedy-queen get-up she was a walking burlesque of motherhood. Her husband resembled a monkey, a miserable-looking little creature, who, apparently unshorn and unkempt, looked as if he had been rolling in the dust. Monkeys were in those days dressed up and accompanied organ-grinders of the oily type. A Dublin woman, soliciting alms, was sharply rebuked by Sir William in Merrion Square: "Go away, go away, you beggars are a perfect nuisance." "Beggar indade!" squealed the woman. "Beggar! an' what are y'self thin when out with your I-talian masther wid a chain on ye."

'Opposite to their pretentious dwelling in Dublin were the Turkish Baths, but to all appearance neither Sir William nor his lady walked across the street. At all the public functions these two peculiar objects appeared in their dust and eccentricity. Living caricatures, in evidence that neither Hogarth nor Dickens in their respective periods had the need to invent characters.'

The Wildes were indeed often pointed out in public, for they were now famous—or perhaps notorious—people. Stories continued to circulate about them both. The credulous poorer classes related how some men from the country came to consult Wilde as an oculist; how he had taken out their eyes and placed them upon a plate, intending to replace them in a moment; and how before he could do so they were eaten by a cat. Of Lady Wilde it was told that she rebuked a servant, saying: 'Why do you put the plates on the coal scuttle? What are the chairs meant for?' Speranza's parties continued to be crowded by all sorts of people; mainly the literary and artistic. All the native and visiting celebrities were to be found there, and not a few nonentities. Like her kinsman, Maturin, she received her guests in shuttered rooms, even in the daytime. Henrietta Corkran has left a vivid account of Speranza's appearance at one of these functions: 'I called at Merrion Square late in the afternoon, for Lady Wilde never received any one till 5 p.m., as she hated what she called "the brutality of strong lights"; the shutters were closed and the lamps had pink shades, though it was full daylight. A very tall woman—she looked over six feet high—she wore that day a long crimson silk gown which swept the floor. The skirt was voluminous, underneath there must have been two crinolines, for when she walked there was a peculiar swaying, swelling movement, like that of a vessel at sea, the sails full with wind.   Over the crimson silk were flounces of Limerick lace, and round what had been a waist, an Oriental scarf, embroidered with gold, was twisted.   Her long, massive, handsome face was plastered with white powder. Over her blue-black glossy hair was a gilt crown of laurels. Her throat was bare, so were her arms, but they were covered with quaint jewellery.   On her broad chest was fastened a series of large miniature brooches, evidently family portraits . . . this gave her the appearance of a walking mausoleum.   She wore white kid gloves, held a scent bottle, a lace handkerchief and a fan.   Lady Wilde reminded me of a tragedy queen at a suburban theatre."

'The Wilde family,' said W. B. Yeats, 'was clearly of the sort that fed the imagination of Charles Lever, dirty, untidy, daring, and what Charles Lever, who loved more normal activities, might not have valued so highly, very imaginative and learned.'   But Lever has not told us how the Wildes struck him in their later life together; perhaps he remembered their youth too well.   He also was old and failing—older indeed than Wilde.   He came to consult his friend about his eyes, for he

saw spots floating before them, and their once bright lustre was
dimmed. He got little consolation, but some good advice about
over-eating and too late suppers.

III

Wilde was still active in antiquarian matters; in particular he
conceived the idea of erecting a monument to the memory of
the Four Masters. He did everything in his power to further
this project. The memorial was eventually erected in the north
side of Dublin, opposite the Mater Hospital, but not until after
he died.

His last antiquarian journey was to Glendalough, 'the glen of
the two lakes'. It is one of the most beautiful places in Ireland,
both in the romantic cliff-bound upper lake and in the gentle
valley below it. Here a splendid round tower now looks over
a valley of ruins, where it once dominated a great monastic
settlement. In this peaceful glen high among the Wicklow
Mountains St. Kevin lived thirteen hundred years ago, and
saints and scholars followed him in thousands. It is not hard
to feel the past in this lonely place, particularly on a summery
evening in spring time before the trippers come.

The seven churches contain many interesting carvings, and
are now carefully preserved. In Wilde's time this was not so.
Active mining for copper was then in progress at the head of
the upper lake, and the Irish Mining Company took some interest
in the remains, but on the whole they were in a state of rapidly
increasing dilapidation. The remaining walls of Trinity church
were in imminent danger of collapsing through the dislocating
action of tree roots, and as we have seen, they did actually fall.
Fortunately this calamity did not occur until after Wakeman
had made a drawing of the church for Wilde, from which it
has since been restored.

Reafert Church, the burial place of seven kings, was also
threatened. When Wilde saw this, he set about its restoration,
and was able to prevent it from suffering a similar fate to Trinity
Church. He was able to persuade the miners from the top
of the lake to help him in this task after their day's work, without
payment—a feat nobody but Wilde could have accomplished.
Together they cut down the trees and cleared out the chancel
and nave.

One of the most interesting features of Glendalough is St. Kevin's bed, which is a square chamber cut in the rocky face of the cliff which bounds the southern side of the upper lake. Here legend says St. Kevin retired occasionally from the world, and from here it is said that he heartlessly threw the beautiful Kathleen into the lake when she tried to seduce him from his solitude. This is the story the guides tell, but the ancient Codex of Kilkenny says otherwise, for it states that the temptation took place when St. Kevin was a student at Glencree; and it further adds that the lady was cured of her infatuation by a good whipping with nettles, and that she afterwards devoted her life to good works. Poor Kathleen seems to have had the worst of it in either case. St. Kevin's bed is certainly a curious place, and well worth the hazards of a visit. It is best reached by boat, after which a fairly difficult climb is necessary. It probably existed long before St. Kevin's time, and is most likely a rock tomb of early Bronze Age date and Mediterranean origin. If it is, it did not remind Wilde of the similar burial chambers he had seen thirty-five years before in the Near East.

IV

In his sixtieth year Wilde's health began to decline. He wrote to his faithful friend, Gilbert: 'I have been very unwell. You might give me a call, as you know I can always see you in my buff, or get you up to my den. I am not up to dining at the Club. Procure me an early copy of the Address, and come and tell me about it. Dr. Petrie ought to have been President, if Todd, Graves, Jellett, and others had not to be first provided for. Whose fault was all that? You know, and will, I hope, tell it some day before we meet in Paradise.'

The habit of work was ingrained upon him, and in spite of illness he managed to complete the Report on the 1871 Census which was published in 1874. The following year a poem, *Chorus of Cloud Maidens*, appeared in the *Dublin University Magazine*. It came from Oscar, who was now at Oxford, and it was his first published literary effort.

It is hard to say exactly from what disease Wilde was suffering; all we know is that his weakness and lassitude increased slowly but unremittingly until the end. There are indications that his chest was affected, and so it may be that he had heart-failure, resulting from his asthma, or perhaps senile consumption.

His terminal illness began in April, 1876, and lasted some two or three weeks. He lay in an upper room in Merrion Square making plans for the coming summer, a summer which in his heart he knew he would never see. At times he thought of his own spring-time and early flowering; of his early days in Steevens', and the travels of his youth; of hard work which was not work because he loved it, and the widespread fame which came to him so early in his career. . . . His thoughts turned to his family life, and to his feminine conquests; an dinevitably to the searing, scorching ordeal of the trial. And just as on that degrading day and in all the troubles of his life he had found shelter in the visionary ages of antiquity, so now

he found solace, not in the future, but in the past. But the earthly future, at least, of William Wilde was safe, for his achievement had made it quite secure. Pharisees might consign his memory to oblivion, but it would inevitably be redeemed by Time.

His slowing mind sank into a deeper reverie. Speranza was constantly by his side, but it is said that his end was hastened by the heartless conduct of his two sons who came in late and filled the house with their friends. As they tramped noisily up the stairs, their father lay in bed, groaning: 'Oh, those boys, those boys!'

He had expressed a wish that he should be buried at Moytura, if possible, and that his funeral should be small and private, but this was not allowed. A great concourse followed the cortège to the family vault at Mount Jerome, including the President and Council of the Royal Irish Academy, accompanied by the mace dressed in crape. Amongst the distinguished people present were Isaac Butt and Arthur Jacob.

And so he was laid to rest, in the soil he had served so well.

DEAR
WILDE

AN ELEGY, 1876

Dear Wilde, the deeps close o'er thee; and no more
Greet we or mingle on the hither shore,
Where other footsteps now must print the sand,
And other waiters by the margin stand.
Gone; and alas! too late it wrings my breast,
The word unspoken, and the hand unpressed;
Yet will affection follow, and believe
The sentient spirit may the thought receive,
Though neither eye to eye the soul impart,
Nor answering hand confess the unburthened heart.
Gone; and alone rests for me that I strive
In song sincere to keep thy name alive,
Though nothing needing of the aids of rhyme,
While they who knew thee tread the ways of time,
And cherish, ere their race be also run,
Their memories of many a kindness done—
Of the quick look that caught the unspoken need,
And back returned the hand's benignant deed
In help or healing, or with ardour high
Infused the might of patriot-sympathy.
And when we all have followed, and the last
Who loved thee living shall have also passed,
This crumbling castle, from its basement swerved,
Thy pious under-pinning skill preserved;
That carven porch from ruined heaps anew
Dug out and dedicate by thee to view
Of wond'ring modern men who stand amazed
To think their Irish fathers ever raised
Works worthy such a care; this sculptured cross
Thou gatheredst piecemeal, every knop and boss
And dragon-twisted symbol, side by side
Laid, and to holy teachings reapplied;

Those noble jewels of the days gone by
With rarest products of progressive man
Since civil life in Erin first began:

.   .   .   .

These all will speak thee; and, dear Wilde, when these,
In course of time, by swift or slow degrees,
Are also perished from the world, and gone,
The green grass of Roscommon will grow on;
And, though our several works of hand and pen,
Our names and memories, be forgotten then,
Oft as the cattle in the dewy day
Of tender morn, by Tulsk or Castlerea,
Crop the sweet herbage, or adown the vale
The ruddy milkmaid bears her evening pail;
Oft as the youth to meet his fair one flies
At labour's close, where sheltering hawthorns rise
By Suck's smooth margin; or the merry round
Of dancers foot it to the planxty's sound,
And some warm heart, matched with a mind serene,
Shall drink its full refreshment from the scene,
With thanks to God whose bounty brings to pass
That maids their sweethearts, and that kine their grass,
Find by His care provided, and there rise
Soft and sweet thoughts for all beneath the skies;—
Then, though unknown, thy spirit shall partake
Refreshment, too, for old communion's sake.

SAMUEL FERGUSON.

POSTSCRIPT ON SPERANZA

She lived in storm and strife,
Her soul had such desire
For what proud death may bring
That it could not endure
The common good of life,
But lived as 'twere a king
That paced his marriage day
With banneret and pennon
Trumpet and kettledrum,
And the outrageous cannon,
To bundle time away
That the night come.

W. B. YEATS.

I

'She was a wonderful woman,' he said, 'and such a feeling as vulgar jealousy could take no hold on her. She was well aware of my father's constant infidelities, but simply ignored them. Before my father died, in 1876, he lay ill in bed for many days. And every morning a woman dressed in black and closely veiled used to come to our house in Merrion Square, and unhindered either by my mother, or any one else, used to walk straight upstairs to Sir William's bedroom and sit down at the head of his bed and so sit there all day, without ever speaking a word or once raising her veil. She took no notice of anybody in the room, and nobody paid any attention to her. Not one woman in a thousand would have tolerated her presence, but my mother allowed it, because she knew that my father loved this woman and felt that it must be a joy and a comfort to have her there by his dying bed. And I am sure that she did right not to grudge that last happiness to a man who was about to die, and I am sure that my father understood her apparent indifference, understood that it was not because she did not love him that she permitted her rival's presence, but because she loved him very much, and died with his heart full of gratitude and affection for her.'

The speaker is Oscar. The reader may place what credence he likes upon the story. There is truth at least in the first sentence, for Speranza undoubtedly *was* a wonderful woman.

Wilde left her most of his estate, but it did not amount to much. His practice had been failing for more than ten years before his death. His family had become increasingly expensive, and the two establishments had run away with money. When it was all added up the estate amounted to £7,000 and some house property—just enough in those days to keep Speranza in genteel poverty. Illaunroe was left to Oscar and Henry Wilson in common.

For a year or so Speranza continued to live at Merrion Square. Her first interest was to complete the life of Beranger, which she did very well, although she made one grievous error, which has since been attributed to her husband, when she referred to the rock formations on the summit of the Three Rock Mountains as a Druid monument. In her preface she paid her late husband a handsome and sincere, if ponderous, tribute. He was no visionary theorist, she said, no mere compiler from the works of other men. His penetrating intellect tested scrupulously the value of everything which came before him, his corrections were the result of rational investigation, and facts formed the basis of his teachings. In the misty cloudland of Irish antiquities he could, therefore, be looked upon as a safe and steadfast guide. But it was not alone in the matter of Irish antiquities that his energy was exerted. Whatever his hand found to do, he did it with all his might, and this energy was the secret of his success in all he undertook.

Willie was now a more or less briefless barrister, practising on the north-east circuit, 'tall, with long black hair and a *dégagé* manner,' probably more interested in music and literature than in his work. When Wilson died of pneumonia in June, 1877, Willie was his chief executor. By the terms of the will all the money, some four or five thousand pounds, was left eventually to St. Mark's Hospital. In 1878 Stokes died. He had succeeded Jellett as President of the Royal Irish Academy, but was not to enjoy the honour for long, for he was obviously in failing health, in the words of his son, 'a deep sleep apparently falling upon him, from which for long he strove to arouse himself.'

Oscar was still at Oxford, and doing well. Speranza never had any doubts about him. Long before she had told George Henry Moore that Willie was clever enough, but 'Oscar was going to be something wonderful'. She never lost her faith in him, any more than she did in his father. She was well content to pay for him at Oxford, and he himself eked out his allowance with scholarships and prizes. In the spring of '77, the great Mahaffy invited him to accompany him to Greece, and Oscar naturally jumped at the opportunity. They were well suited to each other, for both were brilliant, both were snobs. Oscar could not have had a better guide, for Mahaffy's knowledge of Greece was inexhaustible. He probably knew the country better than any man before or since, and, in the words of Brasol, he was a connoisseur of Greek literature, and endowed with a delicate instinct for the genius of classicism. With his old tutor as his guide Oscar worked hard in Greece, examining sites, visiting museums, and discussing Ionic art and Hellenic mythology. Unfortunately, he did not take a lesson from Æschylus and Sophocles—that the arrogance of man will provoke the anger of the gods, and that man who aspires to godhood will be destroyed through the medium of his own achievement. This was the fate of Oedipus, of Agamemnon, of Theseus—but literature held only an æsthetic, and no moral, theme for Oscar. It was on his return to Oxford that he won the Newdigate Prize, to his mother's great delight. But it is no part of my task to describe Oscar's career, and we must return to Speranza.

II

She, poor woman, had begun to find widowed life in Dublin somewhat irksome. When Willie decided to throw up his career at the Irish Bar, and seek success in London as a journalist, she gladly went with him. The house in Merrion Square was sold to 'Silky' Hughes, who had been an exact contemporary of Wilde's at Steevens'. Wilde's famous collection of skulls was given to the Medical Museum of Trinity College. It is still there, but unfortunately the catalogue detailing the provenance of the skulls was lost, and the collection is consequently valueluess. His MS. of Irish folk tales and fairy lore accompanied Speranza and no doubt formed the nucleus of her two books on Irish folk-lore, which are still of interest, and one of which recently saw a new edition.

For a time she lived with Willie in Park Street, Mayfair. Willie secured a position as reporter to the *World*, and later to the *Daily Telegraph*. He was then 'a tall, well-made fellow of thirty or thereabouts, with an expressive, taking face, lit up by a pair of laughing blue eyes', vivacious, good-humoured, but incorrigibly lazy. Here is an impression of him by the late Arthur M. Binstead ("Pitcher" of the *Pink 'Un*): 'The best wit needs lamplight, and no gentler humorist or more polished gentleman ever entertained night after night than Willie Wilde. The personification of good nature and irresponsibility, Willie with ten thousand a year would have been magnificent; without other income, however, than that which his too indolent pen afforded, the poor fellow was frequently in straits which must have proved highly repugnant to his really frank and sunny disposition. No doubt his artistic inactivity was to some extent inherited . . . yet Willie loved to talk of his work and would charm the ears of the uninitiated with such soft south wind as: "The journalistic life irksome? Dear me, not at all. Take my daily life as an example. I report at the office, let us say at twelve o'clock. To the Editor I say: 'Good morning, my dear Le Sage,' and he replies: 'Good morning, my dear Wilde, have you an idea to-day?' 'Oh yes, sir, indeed I have,' I respond. 'It is the anniversary of the penny postage stamp.' 'That is a delightful subject for a leader,' cries my editor, beaming on me, 'and would you be good enough, my dear Wilde, to write us a leader, then, on the anniversary of the penny postage stamp?' 'Indeed I will that with pleasure,' is my answer. 'Ah! thank you, my dear boy,' cried my editor, 'and be sure to have your copy in early—the earlier the better.' That is the final injunction, and I bow myself out. I may then eat a few oysters and drink half a bottle of Chablis at Sweeting's, or alternatively partake of a light lunch at this admirable club, for as rare Ben Jonson says: 'The first speech in my Cataline, spoken by Sylla's ghost, was writ after I had parted friends at the Devil Tavern. I drank well and had brave notions.' I then stroll towards the Park. I bow to the fashionables, I am seen along incomparable

Piccadilly. It is grand. But meantime, I am thinking only of
that penny postage stamp. I try to recall all that I ever heard
about penny postage stamps. Let me see? There is Mr.
So-and-so the inventor, there is the early opposition, the first
postal legislation, then the way stamps are made, putting the
holes in the paper; the gum on the back; the printing—all these
details come back to me, then a paragraph or two about present
postal laws; a few examples of the crude drolleries of the official
postal guides perhaps as a conclusion, something about the crying
need for cheaper postal rates. I think of all the circumstances
as I stroll back along Pall Mall. I might go to the British
Museum and grub up a lot of musty facts, but that would be
unworthy of a great leader writer, you may well understand
that. And then comes the writing. Ah! here is where I earn
my money. I repair to the club. I order out my ink and paper.
I go to my room. I close the door. I am undisturbed for an
hour. My pen moves. Ideas flow. The leader on the penny
postage stamp is being evolved. Three great meaty, solid
paragraphs each one-third of a column—that is the consummation
to be wished. My ideas flow fast and free. Suddenly some one
knocks at the door. Two hours have fled. How times goes!
It is an old friend. We are to eat a little dinner at the Café Royal
and drop into the Alhambra for the new ballet. I touch the
button, my messenger appears. The leader is despatched to 141,
Fleet Street, in the parish of St. Bride, and off we go arm-in-arm.
After the shower the sunshine. Now for the enjoyment of that
paradise of cigar ashes, bottles, corks, ballet, and those countless
circumstances of gaiety and relaxation known only to those
who are in-dwellers in the magic circles of London's Literary
Bohemia. Is it not delightful, boys?" . . .'

III

Oscar had rooms near his mother's house which he occupied
in the intervals of his visits to America and Paris. Speranza
continued to write. She published a travel book, *Driftwood from
Scandinavia*, which had some success, and helped to establish her
reputation amongst the circle of literary and political celebrities
and mediocrities who surrounded her. She entertained on
Saturday afternoons, and many descriptions of her assemblies
have been written. Here is Frank Harris' description of one

of her early parties at Park Street. 'The room and its occupants made an indelible, grotesque impression on me. It seemed smaller than it was because overcrowded with a score of women and half a dozen men. It was very dark and there were empty tea-cups and cigarette ends everywhere. Lady Wilde sat enthroned behind the tea-table looking like a sort of female Buddha swathed in wraps—a large woman with a heavy face and prominent nose; very like Oscar indeed, with the same sallow skin which always looked dirty; her eyes too were her redeeming feature—vivacious and quick-glancing as a girl's. She "made up" like an actress and naturally preferred shadowed gloom to sunlight. Her idealism came to show as soon as she spoke. It was a necessity of her nature to be enthusiastic; unfriendly critics said hysterical, but I should prefer to say high-falutin' about everything she enjoyed or admired. She was at her best in misfortune; her great vanity gave her a certain proud stoicism which was admirable.

'The Land League was under discussion as we entered, and Parnell's attitude to it. Lady Wilde regarded him as the predestined saviour of her country. "Parnell," she said with a strong accent on the first syllable, "is the man of destiny; he will strike off the fetters and free Ireland, and throne her as Queen among the nations."

'A murmur of applause came from a thin bird-like woman standing opposite, who floated towards us clad in a sage-green gown, which sheathed her like an umbrella case; had she had any figure the dress would have been indecent.

'"How like 'Speranza'!" she cooed, "dear Lady Wilde!" I noticed that her glance went towards Willie, who was standing on the other side of his mother, talking to a tall, handsome girl. Willie's friend seemed amused at the lyrical outburst of the green spinster, for smiling a little she questioned him:

'"'Speranza' is Lady Wilde?" she asked with a slight American accent.

'Lady Wilde informed the company with all the impressiveness she had at command that she did not expect Oscar that afternoon; "he is so busy with his new poems, you know; they say there has been no such sensation since Byron." She added: "Already every one is talking of them."

'"Indeed, yes," sighed the green lily, "do you remember, dear Speranza, what he said about *The Sphinx*, that he read to us.

He told us the written verse was quite different from what the printed poem would be just as the sculptor's clay model differs from the marble. Subtle, wasn't it?"

'"Perfectly true, too!" cried a man with a falsetto voice, moving into the circle; "Leonardo himself might have said that."

'The whole scene seemed to me affected and middle-class, untidy, too, with an un-English note about it of shiftlessness; the æsthetic dresses were extravagant, the enthusiasms pumped up and exaggerated. I was glad to leave quietly.'

In 1886 Speranza moved to Oakley Street, Chelsea, no doubt in order to live near Oscar, who had brought his beautiful Irish bride to Tite Street a couple of years before. This ménage was as peculiar as the last, as dirty, dusty and untidy. Speranza was as improvident and impecunious as ever, and Oscar, to his credit, often paid the more pressing bills. The Irish poet, T. D. O'Sullivan, had presented Speranza with a rare and valuable first edition suitably inscribed, some time back in the '50's. Years later he came upon the self-same copy at a second-hand bookstall in London. He bought it back, wrote his name once more upon the fly-sheet, and the new date. Then he brought it to Lady Wilde at Oakley Street, and gave it to her a second time. 'Ah, well,' said she, quite at ease, 'it proved a very useful book, for like Cæsar's dust, it filled a hole—in my purse!'

So many famous people came to Speranza's receptions at Oakley Street that eventually she was compelled to entertain on Wednesdays as well as on Saturdays. The Comtesse de Brémont has described these functions in full—the long line of hansoms and broughams outside the door, the jostling crowds in Rembrandtesque twilight in the first-floor rooms, and finally Speranza herself: 'In the semi-darkness she looked up, a majestic figure, her head-dress with its long white streamers and glittering jewels giving her quite a queenly air.' It was, undoubtedly, Oscar who drew the crowd in the first instance—an Oscar whose dandified splendour was far removed from the grubby boy of Portora and Trinity, Merrion Square and Moytura. Poets, politicians, and artists came in throngs to meet the strange Wildes—Oliver Wendell Holmes, Ouida, Browning, and many others. Three young Irishmen, whose work surpasses Oscar's, often came—George Moore, W. B. Yeats—'my man of genius,'

said Speranza—and George Bernard Shaw. They were all
sympathetic to her. 'I want to live in some high place, because
I was an eagle in my youth,' she told Yeats, and he did not
mock her for it, nor because she received him with blinds
drawn and shutters closed that he might not see her withered
face.

IV

Shaw also is kind to Speranza, but he makes a very acute
observation about her. 'You know that there is a disease called
gigantism, caused by "a certain morbid process in the sphenoid
bone of the skull—viz., an excessive development of the anterior
lobe of the pituitary body" (this is from the nearest
encyclopædia). "When this condition does not become active
until after the age of twenty-five, by which time the long bones
are consolidated, the result is acromegaly, which chiefly mani-
fests itself in an enlargement of the hands and feet." I never
saw Lady Wilde's feet; but her hands were enormous, and never
went straight to their aim when they grasped anything, but
minced about, feeling for it. And the gigantic splaying of her
palm was reproduced in her lumbar region.

'Now Oscar was an overgrown man, with something not
quite normal about his bigness—something that made Lady Colin
Campbell, who hated him, describe him as "that great white
caterpillar." You yourself describe the disagreeable impression
he made on you physically, in spite of his fine eyes and style.
Well, I have always maintained that Oscar was a giant in the
pathological sense, and that this explains a good deal of his
weakness.'

This observation of Shaw's raises a very interesting question;
the same question which we have already met in discussing his
father's premature decline. It is, unfortunately, a subject on
which no finality can be reached in the present state of our
knowledge. Shaw's observation has the elements of truth,
although in the interests of scientific accuracy we must correct
his encyclopaedia, which calls gigantism 'a morbid process in
the sphenoid bone of the skull'. It would be more accurate
to say: 'In a gland which is partially encased by the sphenoid
bone of the skull.' This gland is the pituitary, and one of the
results of its abnormal activity is the condition of gigantism, or

when the disease begins after adult life is reached, acromegaly. But neither Speranza nor Oscar were acromegalics, although they might be described as pituitary types.

Since Shaw wrote, our knowledge of the pituitary and its functions have greatly increased, and it is now placed amongst —possibly at the head of—the group of structures in our body known as the ductless glands. The principal of these are the thyroid, the adrenals, which lie above the kidneys, the 'interstitial cells' of the sex glands or gonads, and the thymus. Each of these glands has its separate use. Some of them are complex structures with a bewildering variety of functions, but they all work in the same way, by discharging a chemical activating agent into the blood stream which bathes them. Hence they are called ductless glands, to distinguish them from glands such as the salivary and sweat glands which discharge their secretion externally through a tube or duct.

It is on the delicate and harmonious co-operation of these glands that our 'behaviourism' depends. With so many powerful forces at action it is very probable that one or other of these glands will predominate over the others, and on this the 'personality' of the individual depends. Thus one person will be highly sexed, like Sir William Wilde, from hyperactivity of the gonads, another will be of the thyroid type, highly strung and nervous. The thymic person will be slow and sluggish, for there is some evidence to show that the thymus slows growth and sexual activity. The pituitary type will be tall and heavy, and so forth. But the subject is not so simple, so cut and dried as this, for each gland normally acts and counteracts upon the others in a bewildering way, and sometimes two or more combine to predominate. Once the bounds of normality are passed, when one particular gland goes berserk, gross pathological abnormalities develop—gigantism in the case of the pituitary, premature sexual development in the case of the adrenals, and so on.

This brings us to a very interesting point. The adrenal glands are composed of two parts—the central portion or medulla, and the outer 'cortex'. When the cortex becomes over-active in adult women, the affected person undergoes a subtle change, which is both physical and mental. She grows coarser, develops a masculine growth of hair on the face and body, and with this she becomes strongly homosexual. If the adrenal gland on either side is removed these characteristics disappear. The hair begins to fall out, and a normal sex appetite develops. Both glands cannot be removed, for the adrenal is necessary to life.

Homosexuality in women, therefore, can be of purely physical origin. It is not improbable that some other but similar cause may produce femininity in men as that which can cause virilism in women. If we accept this explanation it gives us some sympathy for those unfortunate beings, like Oscar, whose perverted impulses twist and destroy their lives. In Oscar's life other factors may enter—heredity is, of course, one of them, for he was very much his mother's son. We may discount some of the many tales of his earlier environment. We are told Speranza dressed him as a girl until he was ten, because she so longed for a daughter. But we know that Speranza's wish was granted. Isola was four years younger than Oscar, according to Brasol, and lived until he was twelve, or more. There is a photograph of Oscar in his infancy, dressed as a girl, but many Victorian mothers did this. To this day little boys are dressed as girls in Connemara lest the fairies should steal them, for, of course, the fairies are only interested in little boys.

Another element which may have influenced Oscar's case is infection, for he is said to have contracted syphilis while at Oxford. He undoubtedly led a sexually dissolute life. Many people blame him utterly, reading his career as one which went through the whole gamut of sensation until he came to those unnatural practices which normal men abhor. Let us be a little more charitable to him. There must have been a physical basis of disease or disordered structure which made him the plaything of Fate. At the same time, we need not pity him too much, for time has brought compensations in his case. Able, and in ways, original as he was, he would not excite such tragic interest to-day had he not suffered so terribly for his sins.

Speranza, some say, was a suppressed homosexualist. If this is true, all the more credit to her, for unlike her son she had the pluck to suppress it. But it is unlikely that she was, for when Oscar was tumbled off his pinnacle to plumb the depths of infamy, she simply could not believe his guilt. If she had ever had similar impulses one would imagine that realization would have been all too easy.

The end of her life reads like a Greek tragedy. On her death-bed she hoped that Oscar might be allowed out of jail to visit her.   When told that this could not be she simply said: 'I hope prison will do him good,' and turned her face to the wall.

In a few more years Oscar, his lovely, broken wife, and Willie, all had gone.

> *But ask not bodies doomed to die*
> *To what abode they go;*
> *Since Knowledge is but Sorrow's spy*
> *It is not safe to know.*

BIBLIOGRAPHY

ACLAND, H. William Stokes. Pamphlet published by The New Sydenham Society, London. 1882.

BAILEY, James Blake. *Diary of a Resurrectionist.* London: Swan Sonnenschein & Co., Ltd. 1896.

BERMAN, Louis. *The Glands Regulating Personality.* New York: The McMillan Co.

BOULTON, W. H. *Palestine.* London: Samson Low, Marston & Co., Ltd.

BOULTON, W. H. *Egypt.* London: Samson Low, Marston & Co., Ltd.

BRASOL, Boris. *Oscar Wilde.* London: Williams & Norgate, Ltd. 1938.

BRÉMONT, Anna, Comtesse de. *Oscar Wilde.* London: Everett & Co., Ltd. 1914.

BROSTER, ALLEN, VINES, PATTERSON, GREENWOOD, MARRIAN, BUTLER. *The Adrenal Cortex and Intersexuality.* London: Chapman & Hall. 1938.

CHANCELLOR, E. Beresford. *Life in Regency and Early Victorian Times.* London: B. T. Batsford, Ltd. 1926.

CHANNON, Henry. *The Ludwigs of Bavaria.* London: Methuen & Co. 1934.

COBB, Svo Geike. *The Glands of Destiny.* London: William Heinemann. 1936.

COLLINS, E. Treacher. *The History and Traditions of the Moorfields Eye Hospital.* London: H. K. Lewis & Co., Ltd. 1929.

DARWIN, Bernard. *The Dickens Advertiser.* London: Elkin Matthews & Marriott. 1930.

DILLON, William. *Life of John Mitchel.* Vols. I & II. London: Kegan Paul Trench & Co. 1888.

DOWNEY, Edmund. *Charles Lever.* 2 vols. Edinburgh & London: William Blackwood & Sons.

DUFFY, Sir Charles Gavan. *Young Ireland.* Vol. I. London: T. Fisher Unwin. 1896.

DUFFY, Sir Charles Gavan. *Four Years of Irish History, 1845–1849.* Cassell, Potter, Galpin & Co., London, Paris and New York. 1883.

DUFFY, Sir Charles Gavan. *Thomas Davis.* London: Kegan Paul Trench, Trübner & Co., Ltd. 1890.

ELLIS, Stewart M. *Mainly Victorian.* London: Hutchinson & Co. 1924.

FERGUSON, Lady. *Sir Samuel Ferguson.* London & Edinburgh: William Blackwood & Sons. 2 vols.

FITZPATRICK, W. J. *Life of Charles Lever.* London: Chapman & Hall. 1879.

FURNISS, HARRY. *Some Victorian Women.* London: John Lane, The Bodley Head Limited. 1923.

GLOVER, James M. *Jimmy Glover, His Book.* London: Methuen & Co.

GOLDZIEHER, Max A. *Practical Endocrinology.* New York and London: D. Appleton-Century Co. Inc.

GRAHAM, Harvey. *Surgeons All.* London: Rich & Cowan, Ltd. 1939.

GRAVES, Robert J. *Life of Sir William Rowan Hamilton.* 3 vols. Hodges, Figgis & Co., Dublin. 1882, 1885, 1889.

GUTHRIE, Douglas. *The Renaissance of Otology: Joseph Toynbee and his Contemporaries. The Journal of Laryngology and Otology,* March, 1937. London: Headley Bros.

HARRIS, Frank. *Oscar Wilde.* London: Constable & Co., Ltd. 1938.

HONE, Joseph. *The Life of George Moore.* London: Victor Gollancz, Ltd. 1936.

KIRKPATRICK, T. P. C. *The Dublin Medical Journals. The Irish Journal of Medical Science,* June, 1932. Cahill & Co., Ltd., Dublin.

KIRKPATRICK, T. P. C. *History of the Medical School in Trinity College, Dublin.* Dublin: Hanna & Neale. 1912.

KIRKPATRICK, T. P. C. *The History of Dr. Steevens' Hospital.* Dublin: Printed at the University Press by Ponsonby & Gibbs. 1924.

LAMBERT, Margaret. *When Victoria Began to Reign.* Faber. 1937.

LAVER, James. *English Costume of the Nineteenth Century.* London: A. & C. Black, Ltd. 1929.

LAVER, James. *Taste and Fashion.* London, Toronto, Bombay and Sydney: George G. Harrap & Co.

LEE, Sidney. *Queen Victoria.* London: Smith, Elder & Co. 1902.

LLOYD, Wyndham E. B. *A Hundred Years of Medicine.* London: Duckworth.

MACALISTER, R. A. S. *Ancient Ireland.* London: Methuen & Co., Ltd. 1935.

MACALISTER, R. A. S. *Archæology of Ireland.* London: Methuen & Co., Ltd. 1928.

MACCALL, Seamus. *Irish Mitchel.* London: Nelson. 1938.

McCALLAN, A. F. *Trachoma.* London: Butterworth & Co., Ltd. 1936.

McDERMOTT, Martin. *Songs and Ballads of Young Ireland.* London: Downey & Co., Ltd. 1896.

McDONNELL, Robert. *The Works of Abraham Colles.* London: The New Sydenham Society. 1881.

MAXWELL, Constantia. *Dublin Under the Georges.* London: George G. Harrap & Co., Ltd. 1936.

Mitchel, John. *Jail Journal.* Dublin: M. H. Gill & Sons, Ltd.; London: T. Fisher Unwin. 1913.

Moore, Colonel M. G. *An Irish Gentleman: George Henry Moore.* London: T. Werner Laurie, Ltd.

O'Brien, W. P. *The Great Famine in Ireland.* London: Downey & Co., Ltd. 1896.

O'Faolain, Sean. *King of the Beggars.* London: Thos. Nelson & Sons, Ltd. 1938.

Ormsby, Lambert Hepenstall. *History of the Meath Hospital.* Dublin: Fannin & Co.; London: Bailliere, Tyndall & Cox. 1888.

Perugini, Mark Edward. *Victorian Days and Ways.* London: Hutchinson & Co., Ltd.

Quennell, Peter. *Victorian Panorama.* London: B. T. Batsford, Ltd. 1937.

Robinson, Victor. *The Story of Medicine.* New York: Tudor Publishing Co. 1931.

Rossi, Mario M. and Hone, Joseph M. *Swift.* London: Victor Gollancz, Ltd. 1934.

Rowlette, Robert J. *The Medical Press and Circular, 1839–1939.* London: 1939.

Sheridan, John Desmond. *James Clarence Mangan.* Dublin: The Talbot Press, Ltd.; London: Gerald Duckworth & Co., Ltd. 1937.

Sherrard, R. H. *The Real Oscar Wilde.* T. Werner Laurie, Ltd.

Sprigge, S. Squire. *The Life and Times of Thomas Wakley.* London, New York and Bombay: Longmans, Green & Co. 1905.

Stevenson, Lionel. *Dr. Quicksilver: The Life of Charles Lever.* London: Chapman & Hall, Ltd. 1939.

Stokes, William. *The Life of George Petrie.* London: Longmans, Green & Co. 1868.

Stokes, Sir William. *William Stokes.* London: T. Fisher Unwin.

Story, J. B. *Sir W. R. Wilde.* The British Journal of Ophthalmology, February, 1918.

Strachey, Lytton. *Queen Victoria.* London: Chatto & Windus. 1921.

Sullivan, A. M. *New Ireland.* London: Samson Low, Marston & Co., Ltd. 1877.

Toynbee, Joseph. *Diseases of the Ear.* London: H. K. Lewis.

Wilson, T. G. *Swift's Deafness and His Last Illness.* Irish Journal of Medical Science, June, 1939. Dublin: Cahill & Co., Ltd.

Winwar, Frances. *Oscar Wilde and the Yellow Nineties.* New York and London: Harper & Bros. 1940.

Wyndham, Horace. *Victorian Sensations.* London: Jarrolds, Publishers.

Yeats, W. B. *The Trembling of the Veil.* London: T. Werner Laurie, Ltd. 1922.

The following publications and periodicals were also consulted:—

The Transactions of the Royal Irish Academy.

The Archives of Otolaryngology.

The Minute Book of the Medico-Philosophical Society.

The Dictionary of National Biography.

The Annual Reports of St. Mark's Hospital, 1851–1876.

Dublin University Magazine, 1833–1876.

Saunders' Newsletter, The Nation, and other contemporary periodicals.

Also most of Sir William Wilde's writings, and some of those of Speranza.

INDEX

Printed in Great Britain by
Wyman & Sons, Ltd., London, Reading and Fakenham.